Work Smarter with

Manage Tasks, Teams, and Time with Ease

Kiet Huynh

Table of Contents

Introduction

What is ClickUp?

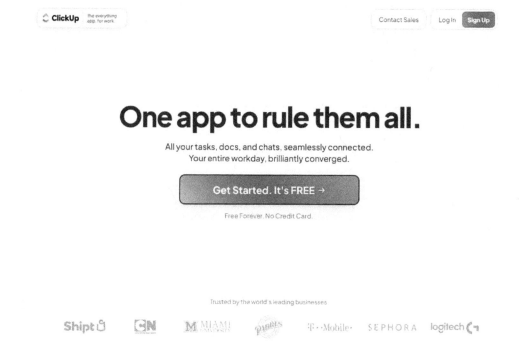

In today's fast-paced, digitally driven world, the way we work has fundamentally transformed. Remote collaboration, agile workflows, and task automation are no longer "nice-to-haves"—they're essential to maintaining productivity, clarity, and control in both personal and professional projects. This is where ClickUp enters the scene as a game-changer.

An All-in-One Productivity Platform

ClickUp is a powerful, cloud-based productivity platform designed to centralize work, streamline processes, and empower individuals and teams to manage everything—from simple to-do lists to complex projects—within a single interface.

Its primary goal is bold but clear: **"One app to replace them all."** ClickUp aims to reduce the chaos of switching between tools like Trello, Asana, Monday.com, Google Docs, Jira, and Slack. Instead, it offers a flexible, modular workspace where users can organize tasks, communicate with their teams, track goals, automate repetitive processes, and gain full visibility into project timelines—all in one place.

Whether you're a freelancer juggling client work, a startup building new products, a marketing team launching campaigns, or a large enterprise running cross-departmental projects, ClickUp provides the infrastructure to keep everything aligned and moving forward.

A Brief History of ClickUp

ClickUp was founded in 2017 by Zeb Evans with a mission to create a more productive world through better technology. Frustrated by the fragmented nature of work tools, Zeb envisioned a solution where teams wouldn't have to sacrifice efficiency for flexibility.

Since its launch, ClickUp has grown rapidly, attracting millions of users across the globe. With frequent updates, a dedicated user community, and a relentless focus on customization and scalability, ClickUp has become one of the most dynamic platforms in the productivity and project management space.

Core Features at a Glance

To understand what makes ClickUp such a powerful tool, let's explore its key features:

1. Task Management

At its heart, ClickUp is a task management platform. Users can create tasks and subtasks, assign them to team members, add priorities, deadlines, and custom statuses, all while linking them to broader goals and initiatives. Task templates, recurring tasks, and checklists enhance consistency and efficiency.

2. Multiple Views

ClickUp supports a variety of ways to visualize your work, including:

- **List View** – A structured, linear view perfect for managing detailed tasks.

- **Board View** – Kanban-style interface ideal for agile workflows.

- **Calendar View** – Great for scheduling and timeline awareness.

- **Gantt View** – For detailed project planning and dependency management.

- **Timeline View** – For high-level strategic planning.

- **Mind Map & Whiteboards** – To brainstorm and organize ideas visually.

3. Docs and Knowledge Management

ClickUp Docs allow teams to collaborate on documentation, meeting notes, wikis, and SOPs directly inside the platform. These docs are linkable to tasks, searchable, and can be structured into knowledge bases.

4. Goals and Objectives

With ClickUp Goals, users can set targets, track progress, and align tasks with company objectives. Each goal can contain measurable targets linked to real-time task data, making it easier to monitor performance and accountability.

5. Time Tracking

Integrated time tracking lets users log work hours, estimate effort, and analyze productivity. Whether using ClickUp's built-in time tracker or third-party integrations, this feature is crucial for freelancers, agencies, and time-based billing.

6. Automations

ClickUp's Automations help eliminate repetitive tasks. For example, when a task's status changes to "Done," ClickUp can automatically assign it to another user or move it to a different list. With dozens of triggers and actions, workflows can be optimized with minimal manual input.

7. Custom Fields and ClickApps

Custom Fields allow for tailored task attributes (e.g., budget, file links, location). ClickApps are modular features you can toggle on or off—like time tracking, dependencies, or custom widgets—to tailor the platform to your specific use case.

8. Collaboration and Communication

Real-time editing, comments, mentions, assigned comments, and even in-app chat foster collaboration without needing to leave the workspace. Everything is recorded and centralized.

9. Dashboards and Reporting

Dashboards offer a visual overview of workloads, performance metrics, sprints, and more. Widgets can display burndown charts, time tracking logs, task progress, goal completion, and even OKRs—perfect for project managers and team leads.

10. Integrations

ClickUp plays well with others. It offers integrations with Slack, Google Drive, Dropbox, Zoom, GitHub, Outlook, Calendars, and hundreds more via native options or tools like Zapier, Make (Integromat), and API access.

Why ClickUp Matters in the Modern Workflow

Modern work is increasingly digital, distributed, and complex. Teams are often remote, deadlines are tighter, and there's a constant pressure to "do more with less." This creates several challenges:

- **Too many tools:** Task management, communication, file sharing, documentation, and reporting often live in separate platforms.

- **Lack of transparency:** Managers struggle to get a real-time picture of team progress.

- **Siloed collaboration:** Information and discussions are scattered across emails, chats, and spreadsheets.

- **Inefficient workflows:** Manual, repetitive work slows down progress and introduces errors.

ClickUp is designed to address all of the above by providing a **centralized**, **highly customizable**, and **scalable** workspace that adjusts to the way you work—not the other way around.

Who Uses ClickUp?

ClickUp isn't limited to tech companies or agile teams. Its flexibility makes it suitable for:

- **Freelancers** – Managing clients, invoices, and deliverables.
- **Marketing Teams** – Campaign planning, content calendars, and creative review workflows.
- **Sales Teams** – Managing pipelines, deals, and customer follow-ups.
- **Agencies** – Handling client projects, timelines, and cross-functional teams.
- **Startups** – Organizing product development, team operations, and investor updates.
- **Enterprise Teams** – Scaling project management across departments with security and compliance.

With templates for industries like design, education, real estate, legal, HR, and IT, ClickUp's utility stretches across nearly every sector.

ClickUp's Philosophy: Customization is King

One of the platform's biggest strengths is how customizable it is. Instead of forcing users into a rigid workflow, ClickUp offers:

- Custom fields
- Custom task statuses
- Unique views per user or team
- Personalized dashboards
- Modular features via ClickApps

This adaptability means a content writer, an agile developer, and a CEO can each view and interact with ClickUp in the way that suits them best.

ClickUp in Numbers

As of recent metrics:

- Over 8 million users globally

- Trusted by companies like Google, Airbnb, Uber, and Netflix

- Available in 10+ languages

- Frequent updates with input from its vibrant user community

The active roadmap and dedicated support make it not just a tool, but a growing ecosystem that evolves with user needs.

A Living Tool for Living Work

ClickUp is more than a task list—it's a dynamic system for aligning your work with your goals. From creating a morning routine checklist to launching a product with a global team, ClickUp scales to meet your needs.

But with power comes complexity. That's where this book comes in—to demystify ClickUp, give you hands-on strategies, and show you how to tailor it to your workflow. Whether you're starting with a clean slate or migrating from another platform, we'll walk through each feature, decision point, and hidden gem to help you *work smarter*.

Final Thoughts on What ClickUp Is

ClickUp is not a single-use tool. It's an evolving digital workspace that combines the structure of a project manager, the insight of an analyst, the communication power of a collaboration suite, and the flexibility of a notebook—into one cohesive experience.

If you've ever said:

- "I wish I could do everything in one place."

- "I hate switching between ten tabs to finish one task."

- "There has to be a better way to manage my team's work."

...then ClickUp was made for you.

Let's dive in and see just how much you can achieve when your tasks, teams, and time live in perfect harmony.

Why ClickUp Over Other Tools?

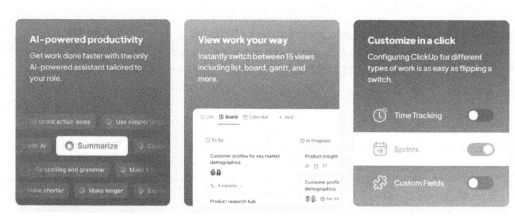

In the ever-expanding universe of productivity and project management tools, choosing the right platform can be overwhelming. With a crowded landscape that includes giants like Asana, Trello, Monday.com, Notion, Jira, and Microsoft Teams, one might ask: **Why ClickUp?** What makes ClickUp different? What gives it a competitive edge, especially for teams striving to **work smarter—not harder**?

The answer lies in ClickUp's **all-in-one approach**, flexibility, deep customization, and user-focused design. Unlike many tools that specialize in one area—task management, document collaboration, or time tracking—ClickUp brings it all under one roof. In this chapter, we'll explore the specific features, philosophies, and innovations that make ClickUp the go-to choice for thousands of companies, entrepreneurs, and professionals worldwide.

1. A True All-in-One Workspace

ClickUp markets itself with the slogan, *"One app to replace them all."* That's not just a clever tagline—it's a reflection of their vision.

Where many productivity tools cover only one or two aspects of work management (e.g., task tracking or team messaging), ClickUp provides an integrated experience that includes:

- Tasks & Project Management
- Docs & Wikis
- Goals & OKRs
- Time Tracking
- Dashboards & Reporting
- Chat & Collaboration
- Whiteboards
- Mind Maps
- Integrations & Automations

Rather than bouncing between multiple apps and losing focus, ClickUp allows individuals and teams to centralize their work—saving time, improving visibility, and creating a more cohesive digital workspace.

2. Extreme Customizability

ClickUp's strength lies in its flexibility. Whether you're a freelancer managing personal projects or a multinational company coordinating global operations, you can shape ClickUp to fit your needs.

Key areas of customization include:

- **Task statuses**: Replace default "To Do / In Progress / Done" with statuses that reflect your actual workflow.
- **Custom fields**: Track anything from budgets to client names to feature requests.

- **Views**: Choose from over a dozen ways to visualize your work—List, Board, Calendar, Timeline, Gantt, Mind Map, and more.

- **ClickApps**: Activate or deactivate features depending on what matters most to your team.

Unlike other tools that force you into their systems, ClickUp molds itself to yours.

3. Scalability for Teams of All Sizes

ClickUp is designed to grow with you. Solo users can start with a free plan that offers surprising depth, while organizations can scale into robust features like:

- Advanced permissions and role-based access

- Workload and resource management

- Time tracking and billable hours

- Enterprise-level security and support

Whereas many tools feel great at first but buckle under the weight of large projects or complex org charts, ClickUp maintains performance, clarity, and control—even at scale.

4. Unified Workflows Across Departments

In a modern organization, siloed tools often lead to fragmented communication and inefficiency. Marketing uses Trello, Engineering uses Jira, HR uses spreadsheets… and suddenly, no one's on the same page.

ClickUp solves this by enabling **cross-functional workflows** within the same workspace:

- **Marketing** can plan campaigns, manage content calendars, and collaborate with design.

- **Sales** can track prospects, manage pipelines, and align with Customer Success.

- **Engineering** can manage sprints, bugs, and product releases with development-focused tools like GitHub integrations and agile templates.

Everyone works differently—but ClickUp brings them together, keeping context and collaboration centralized.

5. Feature-Rich Without Being Overwhelming

One challenge with all-in-one platforms is that they can become bloated or hard to use. ClickUp addresses this with a thoughtful interface and a modular system.

With **ClickApps**, you control which features are active. Want a minimalist task board? Disable unnecessary features. Need detailed time tracking and sprint points? Turn them on.

ClickUp lets you start simple and add complexity as your needs evolve.

6. Competitive Pricing and Value

ClickUp is one of the most affordable tools in its class—especially considering how much it replaces.

- **Free Forever Plan** includes unlimited tasks, members, and projects.
- **Paid Plans** unlock deeper features like automations, custom permissions, advanced dashboards, and integrations.
- **Enterprise Plans** include Single Sign-On (SSO), HIPAA compliance, and priority support.

When compared feature-for-feature with platforms like Monday.com, Asana, or Jira, ClickUp often comes out ahead both in capability and cost.

7. Continual Development and User-Driven Roadmap

ClickUp is known for **rapid development and frequent updates**. The company maintains a **public roadmap** and actively involves its community in suggesting and voting on features.

New features and improvements are released frequently, based on:

- User requests
- Emerging workflow trends
- Feedback loops from real teams

This means you're investing in a platform that listens, adapts, and grows with you—not one that stagnates over time.

8. Integration-Friendly

Despite offering so much out of the box, ClickUp understands that no tool can do everything alone. That's why it integrates with hundreds of popular apps:

- **Communication**: Slack, Microsoft Teams
- **Storage**: Google Drive, Dropbox, OneDrive
- **Development**: GitHub, GitLab, Bitbucket
- **Calendar & Email**: Google Calendar, Outlook
- **Automation Tools**: Zapier, Make (Integromat), Webhooks

ClickUp acts as a central nervous system, connecting all your tools and syncing your information.

9. Smart Automations to Save Time

ClickUp's **built-in automation engine** allows you to reduce repetitive work and increase efficiency.

Examples include:

- When a task is marked complete → notify a manager
- When a due date is missed → change task status to "Overdue"
- When a form is submitted → auto-generate a task with all form details

Other platforms often require third-party tools like Zapier to achieve similar functionality, but ClickUp builds automation directly into your workspace.

10. Strong Community, Support, and Learning Resources

ClickUp offers a thriving ecosystem of:

- **Community forums**

- **Live webinars and workshops**

- **Detailed documentation and video tutorials**

- **ClickUp University**: a free resource center with structured learning paths

Whether you're self-learning or training a team, ClickUp provides ample guidance and support to ensure success.

11. A Tool That Inspires Better Work Habits

Beyond features and integrations, one of ClickUp's greatest strengths is how it encourages better work habits:

- **Clear priorities** through statuses and goals

- **Improved time management** with time estimates and tracking

- **Better accountability** through assigned comments and due dates

- **Greater visibility** across projects and workloads

ClickUp doesn't just digitize your workflow—it enhances it. Many users report being more productive, organized, and efficient after adopting ClickUp, not just because of what it does, but because of **how it helps you think** about your work.

Final Thoughts: Why ClickUp Makes Sense

To sum it up, here are the key reasons why ClickUp stands out:

Feature	Benefit
All-in-one platform	Replace multiple tools
Customizable	Tailored to your team and workflow
Scalable	Suitable for individuals to enterprises
Collaboration-friendly	Unified experience across departments

Feature	Benefit
Smart design	Power without complexity
Affordable pricing	High value at low cost
Fast updates	Constant innovation
Built-in automation	Save time and effort
Extensive integrations	Connect your favorite tools
Robust support	Learn and grow with the platform

Choosing a productivity tool is an important decision—it's where your team spends hours each day. **ClickUp earns its place not by being the loudest, but by being the most capable and thoughtful tool in the space.**

As we dive deeper into this book, you'll see not only **how to use ClickUp**—but how to **unlock its full potential** to manage your tasks, teams, and time with confidence and ease.

Who This Book is For

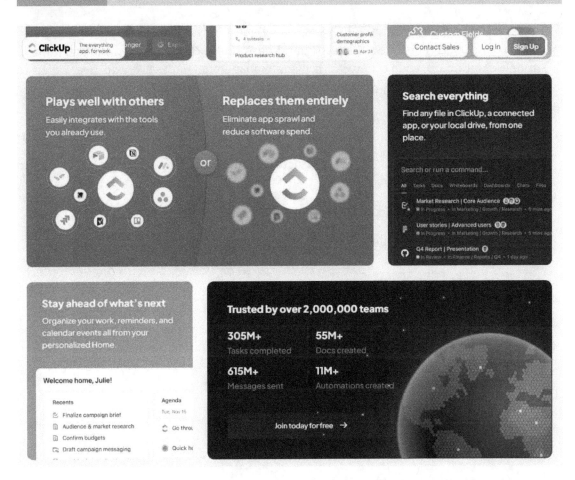

In today's fast-paced, digitally connected world, time, clarity, and collaboration have become the currencies of productivity. Whether you're a team leader managing multiple projects, a freelancer juggling client work, or an entrepreneur scaling your startup, one truth remains the same: you need a system that works for you—not the other way around. That's where ClickUp comes in, and that's where this book becomes your roadmap.

This guide was created with a wide audience in mind, but it speaks most directly to those who seek to work smarter, not just harder. If you've ever felt overwhelmed by task lists, missed deadlines, or uncoordinated teamwork, this book is for you.

1. Professionals New to Project Management Tools

Perhaps you're coming from spreadsheets, sticky notes, or basic to-do apps. You've heard of tools like Asana, Trello, or Monday.com, and now you're exploring ClickUp as a unified, all-in-one solution. If you're new to project management software and are eager to understand how ClickUp can organize your work life, this book will guide you from the ground up.

You will benefit from:

- Clear walkthroughs of ClickUp's structure: Workspaces, Spaces, Folders, Lists, and Tasks.

- Beginner-friendly guidance to set up your first projects.

- Practical examples tailored to solo professionals or small teams.

2. Experienced Users Looking to Go Deeper

Maybe you've dabbled in ClickUp already. You've created some tasks, maybe tried the Kanban view or added a few teammates. But you suspect you're only scratching the surface of what's possible—and you're right.

This book is also for **intermediate users** who are ready to level up:

- You want to automate repetitive actions.

- You want better visibility into your team's workload.

- You want custom dashboards that give you real-time insights.

- You want to stop reacting and start managing proactively.

This book will help you:

- Use ClickUp's automation engine to save hours each week.

- Create templates that standardize and speed up your recurring workflows.

- Integrate ClickUp with your existing tech stack for seamless operation.

3. Team Leaders, Managers, and Department Heads

Managing people is a balancing act of vision, delegation, and accountability. If you're leading a team—whether it's three people or thirty—ClickUp can become the operational backbone of your entire department.

As a manager, you're not just interested in "tasks." You're interested in:

- Visibility: Who's doing what, and when?

- Efficiency: Are we repeating manual processes?

- Alignment: Are we working toward the right goals?

This book teaches you how to:

- Set up Spaces that reflect your department's structure and priorities.

- Implement SOPs using Docs, templates, and recurring checklists.

- Track performance through custom dashboards, Goals, and time-tracking.

You'll gain tools to foster a culture of transparency and execution—without micromanaging.

4. Remote and Hybrid Teams

ClickUp has become a favorite in remote-first companies for good reason. It offers a centralized place for tasks, docs, communication, and collaboration. If you're part of a remote or hybrid team, you know the pain of tool overload, siloed conversations, and dropped balls.

This book helps you unify your team, no matter where they're working from:

- Learn how to use comments, mentions, and ClickUp Chat for asynchronous collaboration.

- Explore integrations with Slack, Zoom, and Google Calendar.

- Build workflows that support accountability without constant check-ins.

Whether your team is in four cities or four time zones, this book shows how to bring them together inside ClickUp.

5. Freelancers, Consultants, and Solo Entrepreneurs

Not every user is part of a large organization—and ClickUp is just as powerful for solo operators. If you're wearing multiple hats, managing multiple clients, or simply running your business alone, ClickUp can serve as your virtual assistant.

This book will help you:

- Set up templates for client onboarding, project delivery, and invoicing.

- Track billable hours with the built-in time tracker.

- Manage sales pipelines, creative workflows, and support tasks—all in one place.

You'll discover how to use ClickUp as your **CRM, calendar, file system, and to-do list**, replacing the mess of apps you might currently be juggling.

6. Students, Educators, and Academic Teams

ClickUp isn't just for corporations—it's a phenomenal tool for managing coursework, lesson planning, group assignments, and research.

This book includes strategies for:

- Students managing class schedules, exams, and group projects.

- Teachers organizing lesson plans, grading, and student communication.

- Academic teams collaborating on research or administrative workflows.

Whether you're planning a semester or organizing a thesis, ClickUp provides structure and clarity.

7. Creative Teams and Agencies

Designers, marketers, and content creators live in a world of deadlines, client feedback, and asset coordination. If you're part of a creative team, you need more than just a to-do list— you need a **collaborative platform**.

This book will show you how to:

- Build content calendars using List, Board, and Calendar views.

- Collect feedback directly on tasks using comments and attachments.

- Automate repetitive content production tasks.

- Keep your brand assets and campaign documents stored in an organized way.

With the right setup, your team will spend less time managing the workflow—and more time doing the work that matters.

8. Operations, HR, and Administrative Roles

ClickUp isn't just for projects—it's also a powerful engine for **process management**. If you work in HR, finance, administration, or ops, this book shows you how to turn ClickUp into a **process library and control center**.

Examples include:

- Employee onboarding checklists

- Vendor management workflows

- Standard operating procedure documentation

- Approval workflows with dependencies and assigned comments

You'll learn how to maintain consistency, eliminate bottlenecks, and keep key operations running smoothly.

9. Anyone Who Wants to Build Better Work Habits

Lastly, this book is for you if you're looking to take control of your time and develop better work habits. You don't need to manage a team or own a business to benefit from ClickUp.

Whether you're trying to:

- Organize your week

- Track personal goals

- Build a habit tracker

- Journal your daily progress

...ClickUp gives you the flexibility to **design a system that works for your life**. And this book will show you how.

Is This Book for You? Let's Find Out

This book is probably a good fit for you if: ☑ You've heard of ClickUp and want to see what the hype is about
☑ You're overwhelmed by scattered tools or messy workflows
☑ You manage projects, people, or processes
☑ You're looking for clarity, consistency, and control
☑ You want a tool that grows with you and adapts to your needs

Whether you're a **beginner just getting started** or an **experienced user looking for advanced tips**, you'll find practical, real-world guidance in the pages ahead.

We'll take you step-by-step through ClickUp's core features, from task creation and view customization to time tracking, automations, and team collaboration. And by the time you finish this book, you'll have the knowledge—and confidence—to build your ideal workflow inside ClickUp.

How to Use This Guide

Welcome to ***Work Smarter with ClickUp: Manage Tasks, Teams, and Time with Ease***, a practical and user-friendly guide designed to help you unlock the full potential of one of the most powerful productivity platforms available today: ClickUp. Whether you're completely new to project management tools or transitioning from other platforms like Trello, Asana, or Monday.com, this guide was created with you in mind.

This book isn't just a reference manual—it's a **step-by-step journey** through ClickUp's features, use cases, best practices, and hidden gems. Its purpose is to teach you how to use ClickUp **efficiently and effectively**, making your work life more organized, collaborative, and productive.

1. Who This Book Is For

Before diving into how to use this guide, it's important to understand who it's intended to serve:

- **Beginners** who have never used ClickUp before and want a structured way to learn from scratch.

- **Managers and team leaders** who want to adopt a tool that supports collaboration, task delegation, and performance tracking.

- **Freelancers** and **solopreneurs** looking for a way to centralize their tasks, goals, and documentation in one system.

- **Business owners** implementing ClickUp as part of their digital transformation strategy.

- **Power users** from other platforms looking for a deeper understanding of ClickUp's advanced capabilities and workflow automation.

This guide is for **anyone who wants to work smarter**, not harder.

2. The Structure of the Book

To make your learning journey as smooth and intuitive as possible, the book is organized in a **progressive format**, from basic setup to advanced features. Each chapter builds on the knowledge from previous ones.

Here's how it's laid out:

- **Introduction**: Sets the context and explains the purpose of the book.

- **Chapter 1: Getting Started with ClickUp** – Helps you set up your account and get comfortable with the interface and structure.

- **Chapter 2: Mastering Task Management** – Teaches how to create and manage tasks, use different views, and organize work.

- **Chapter 3: Collaborating with Your Team** – Focuses on team roles, permissions, communication, and notifications.

- **Chapter 4** and onward (in upcoming sections) will tackle automation, reporting, integrations, and more.

Each chapter contains **three levels of structure**:

- **Sections (e.g., 1.1, 1.2)** that introduce the major topic.

- **Subsections (e.g., 1.1.1, 1.2.2)** for specific how-tos and best practices.

- **Examples and tips** within each subsection for real-world application.

---

3. How to Read This Book

This guide is designed to be **flexible**, depending on your learning style and current familiarity with ClickUp. You can read it:

- **Cover to cover**: Ideal for beginners or new users setting up ClickUp for the first time.

- **Jumping between chapters**: Great for experienced users who need help with specific features, like automations or time tracking.

- **As a reference**: Use the detailed table of contents to locate instructions on particular tools or challenges.

To make this easier:

- **Clear headings and subheadings** will help you scan quickly.

- **Visual cues and formatting** (like bullet points, code blocks, and callouts) help you identify key points.

- **Examples and use cases** demonstrate how each feature is applied in real-life scenarios.

4. What You'll Need Before You Start

While this book will walk you through everything step by step, having a few things in place will make your learning experience smoother:

- **A ClickUp account** (free or paid).

- **A real project or use case** to apply what you're learning—personal or professional.

- **Access to a team**, if you're planning to collaborate (optional but recommended).

- **A laptop or desktop**, though many features work on mobile, too.

You'll get the most from this book if you **practice as you read**. Don't just skim—try things out in ClickUp as you go. The interface is intuitive, and experimenting is part of the learning process.

5. Learning Principles Behind This Guide

This guide follows a few core principles to help ensure what you learn **sticks** and is **usable** in your daily workflow:

Learn by Doing

Each feature introduced in this book comes with practical examples or exercises. For example, when we discuss task creation, we'll walk you through creating a real task in your own ClickUp environment.

Contextual Learning

Instead of listing functions in isolation, we teach ClickUp through **scenarios**: managing a content calendar, planning a product launch, setting team goals, etc. This helps you see how features connect in real work.

Best Practices + Pitfalls

For each major function, we include **best practices**, **common mistakes**, and **pro tips** from seasoned ClickUp users. You'll learn not just *how* to use a feature, but *why* and *when* it makes the most sense.

6. Icons and Visual Aids

Throughout the guide, we'll use special icons and callouts to draw your attention to useful information:

- 📌 **Tip** – Helpful shortcuts or insights.

- ⚠ **Watch Out** – Common mistakes or limitations to avoid.

- ☑ **Best Practice** – Recommended workflows and habits.

- 🔧 **Try It Yourself** – Actionable exercises you can do immediately.

These make it easier to scan and return to important content later.

7. ClickUp Updates and Versioning

ClickUp is a **constantly evolving platform**, with frequent updates, new features, and UI redesigns. This book was written using ClickUp's interface and functionality as of **[Month Year]**, but we've included **timeless workflows** that adapt across versions.

To stay updated:

- Bookmark ClickUp's release notes

- Join the ClickUp Community

- Follow ClickUp's YouTube channel or blog

As much as possible, we use **descriptive terms** instead of relying only on where buttons are located. That way, even if the UI changes slightly, you'll still understand what to look for.

8. What This Book Won't Cover in Depth

While this book is extensive, there are a few things we **intentionally do not cover in full depth**, including:

- ClickUp API development

- Enterprise security policies

- Custom-built integrations or code-based automations

These are more advanced topics better suited to technical documentation or ClickUp's developer hub. That said, we will point you in the right direction if you want to go deeper later.

9. Ready to ClickUp Your Workflow?

Whether you're a team leader tired of juggling tasks across spreadsheets, a remote team trying to stay aligned, or a solopreneur managing dozens of client projects—ClickUp can change how you work.

And this book is here to help you make that shift.

Let's begin. In the next chapter, you'll set up your ClickUp account and learn the foundational structure that powers everything: **the ClickUp hierarchy.**

CHAPTER I
Getting Started with ClickUp

1.1 Creating Your ClickUp Account

1.1.1 Signing Up

Starting your journey with ClickUp begins with one simple but essential step: signing up for an account. ClickUp is a cloud-based productivity and project management platform, which means that everything begins online. Whether you're a solo entrepreneur, a small business owner, a team leader, or part of a global enterprise, the signup process is designed to be accessible and quick. In this section, we'll walk you through everything you need to know about creating your ClickUp account, step-by-step.

Why Signing Up Properly Matters

Before diving into the actual steps, it's worth understanding **why this phase is important**. ClickUp is a highly customizable tool. The way you sign up—what information you provide, how you set up your workspace, and what choices you make at the start—can affect how effectively you're able to use the platform in the future. Many users make the mistake of skipping setup options without realizing how powerful those initial configurations can be.

By signing up with intention, you lay the groundwork for smoother onboarding, better team collaboration, and faster task execution later on.

Step-by-Step Guide to Signing Up

Let's break the process down into manageable steps.

Step 1: Navigate to the ClickUp Website

To start, open your preferred browser and go to:

👉 https://clickup.com

ClickUp's homepage typically features a **"Get Started"** or **"Sign Up"** button in the top right-hand corner and in the center of the page. Clicking this will take you to the signup form.

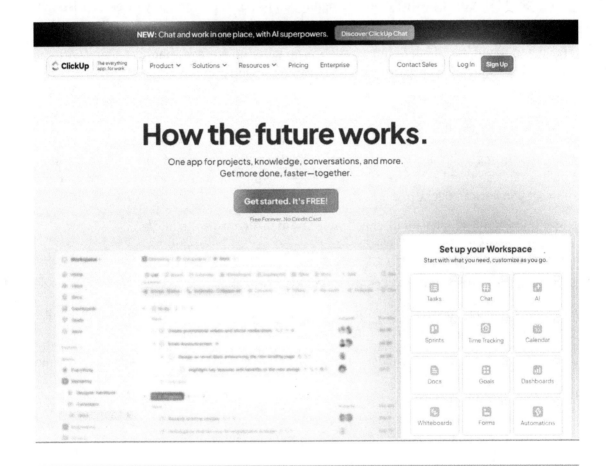

Step 2: Choose a Signup Method

ClickUp allows several methods of signing up:

- **Email and Password**: This is the most common method. You simply enter your email address and create a secure password.

- **Google Account**: For faster signup and integration with Google Workspace tools, use your Google account.

- **Microsoft Account**: If your team uses Office 365, this is a great option for direct integration.

- **SSO (Single Sign-On)** If you're signing up as part of a company or enterprise that uses SSO, you can use your organization's credentials.

Tip: If you're unsure which option to choose, go with the method that best aligns with the tools your organization already uses (Google or Microsoft).

Step 3: Verify Your Email Address

After submitting your signup information, ClickUp will prompt you to verify your email. You'll receive an email with a verification link—clicking this will confirm your account and redirect you back to ClickUp.

Note: If you don't see the email, check your **Spam** or **Promotions** folder.

Step 4: Enter Your Name and Create a Workspace

Once verified, you'll be asked to enter your **name** and create your **Workspace**. Think of a Workspace as the main container for all your projects, teams, and tasks.

- **Workspace Name:** Choose something meaningful. If you're a freelancer, it could be your name or brand. If you're signing up for a company, use the team or organization's name.

Example:

- "Design Projects"

- "Acme Corp"

- "Jessica's Freelance Studio"

Tip: You can always change your workspace name later, so don't stress too much over this.

Step 5: Invite Your Team (Optional)

ClickUp will prompt you to invite teammates. If you're not ready, you can **skip this step** and come back later. However, if you already know who will be using ClickUp with you, inviting them now can help you hit the ground running.

Reminder: You can control roles and permissions later, so don't worry about giving people access at this stage.

Step 6: Answer Setup Questions (Optional Onboarding Preferences)

ClickUp offers a **short onboarding wizard** to tailor your experience. It may ask questions like:

- "What kind of work do you do?"

- "What will you use ClickUp for?"

- "How familiar are you with productivity tools?"

Your answers help ClickUp provide relevant suggestions, templates, and default settings. These can be changed later, but taking the time to fill them out can make the learning curve smoother.

Choosing the Right Interface (Home vs. Everything View)

After signing up, you'll land in the ClickUp interface. By default, it may direct you to the **Home view**, which highlights your Inbox, tasks, and upcoming items.

You may also explore:

- **"Everything View"** – lets you see all tasks and projects across your workspace.

- **"Spaces" and "Projects"** – where you can start organizing your work.

ClickUp's layout might feel overwhelming at first—but don't worry, we'll cover how to navigate everything in detail in the next sections.

Common Signup Issues and Troubleshooting

Here are a few common roadblocks and how to solve them:

- **Didn't Receive Verification Email?**
  - Check all email folders
  - Add no-reply@clickup.com to your safe list
  - Try resending the verification link

- **Browser Compatibility Issues**
  - Make sure your browser is updated
  - Use Chrome, Firefox, Safari, or Edge
  - Disable browser extensions that might block forms

- **Already Have an Account?**
  - Try logging in at https://app.clickup.com
  - Use "Forgot Password" if needed

Security Tips for New Accounts

Security should always be a priority—especially if you'll be managing sensitive client data or internal operations. Here are some quick recommendations for your ClickUp account:

- **Use a strong password:** Include uppercase, lowercase, numbers, and symbols

- **Enable Two-Factor Authentication (2FA):** ClickUp supports this feature and we'll explore it further in section 1.1.3

- **Don't share your login credentials:** Invite team members individually with appropriate permissions

Signing Up on Mobile

ClickUp also offers a fully functional mobile app. You can sign up via:

- **iOS App Store**

- **Google Play Store**

The steps are similar to the web-based process, and your data will sync across platforms. Signing up on mobile is great for on-the-go professionals who want to test the app while commuting or away from a computer.

What Comes Next?

Congratulations—you now have a ClickUp account! 🎉

You've taken the first step toward organizing your work life. Next, we'll walk through **choosing the right plan**, understanding what's included in the free tier versus paid options, and how to upgrade if needed. That's all in the upcoming section **1.1.2 Choosing the Right Plan**.

But for now, take a moment to explore your new workspace. Try creating a dummy task or exploring the layout. Don't worry about making mistakes—ClickUp is highly forgiving, and everything can be edited, deleted, or reorganized later.

1.1.2 Choosing the Right Plan

Choosing the right ClickUp plan is a foundational decision that can shape how you and your team work together. ClickUp is designed to be scalable and flexible, accommodating individual freelancers, small teams, growing startups, and large enterprises alike. Each plan offers a distinct set of features and capabilities, making it crucial to select a plan that aligns with your goals, team size, budget, and workflow needs.

In this section, we'll walk you through:

- An overview of all available plans

- A comparison of core features

- Recommendations for different user types

- Pricing and cost considerations

- How to upgrade, downgrade, or switch plans

- FAQs about billing and trial periods

Overview of ClickUp's Pricing Tiers

As of this writing, ClickUp offers five main tiers:

1. Free Forever
2. Unlimited
3. Business
4. Business Plus
5. Enterprise

Each of these tiers is designed to serve different types of users, from solo workers to enterprise-level organizations. Let's explore them in detail.

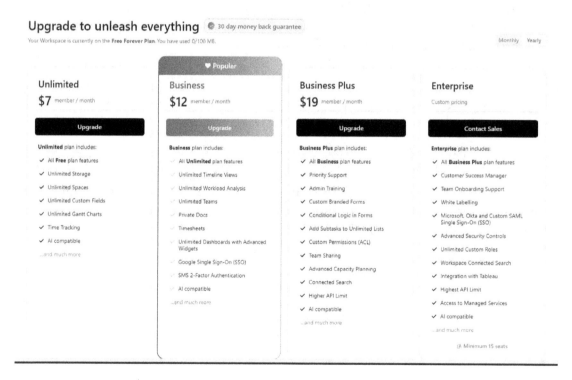

Which Plan Is Right for You?

Here's a quick breakdown by user type:

- **Freelancer or Solo Entrepreneur:** Free or Unlimited

- **Startup Team (2–10 users):** Unlimited or Business

- **Small Business (10–50 users):** Business

- **Large Business (50–200 users):** Business Plus

- **Enterprise (200+ users):** Enterprise

Pricing Considerations

- **Annual Billing Discount:** ClickUp offers a significant discount (up to 45%) if you pay annually instead of monthly.

- **Nonprofit Discounts:** Eligible nonprofits can apply for special pricing—check ClickUp's Help Center or contact support.

- **Trial Periods:** Most paid plans come with a 14-day trial with no credit card required. Use this time to explore premium features and see what suits your workflow.

- **Per-User Model:** Plans are priced per active member. You can add/remove users as needed, and you're billed accordingly.

How to Upgrade or Downgrade Your Plan

1. **Click your profile avatar > Billing.**

2. View your current plan, usage, and billing cycle.

3. Select "Upgrade" or "Change Plan."

4. Choose between annual or monthly billing.

5. Confirm and authorize payment details.

Your workspace will update immediately with the new features or limitations.

Note: Downgrading a plan may remove features like dashboards, automations, or custom fields. Make sure to back up important configurations before changing plans.

Billing & Payment FAQs

- **Can I cancel anytime?** Yes, you can cancel your subscription at any time from the billing section.

- **Do you offer refunds?** Generally, ClickUp does not provide refunds, especially for monthly plans. Annual plans may be evaluated on a case-by-case basis.

- **Can I add more users later?** Absolutely. You can add new members at any time, and billing will adjust accordingly.

- **Can I pay via invoice?** Invoice billing is usually available only on Enterprise plans. Contact sales for more information.

Tips Before You Choose

- Make use of the **Free Forever plan** to test drive the interface and core features.

- Take full advantage of the **trial period** for Unlimited or Business to explore what's possible.

- If unsure, start with **Unlimited**, then scale up as your needs evolve.

- Consider **team feedback** when selecting a plan—ensure it aligns with everyone's workflows and collaboration habits.

- If you're growing quickly, opt for a plan that supports future scalability rather than immediate cost-cutting.

Choosing the right plan sets the tone for how well your team adapts to and benefits from ClickUp. While every plan offers valuable features, the real power of ClickUp lies in how you use it. So take time to match your choice with your long-term goals and day-to-day needs.

1.1.3 Setting Up Two-Factor Authentication

In today's digital world, securing your personal and professional data is more important than ever. When managing tasks, projects, and sensitive team information in ClickUp, ensuring your account is properly secured should be a top priority. That's where **Two-Factor Authentication (2FA)** comes in. This section walks you through everything you need to know about setting up and using 2FA within ClickUp to enhance your account security.

What is Two-Factor Authentication (2FA)?

Two-Factor Authentication is a security mechanism that adds a second layer of protection beyond your password. Instead of only needing a password to log in, you're also required to provide a **second piece of information** — typically a code sent to your phone or generated by an authenticator app.

Think of 2FA like a lock and key system, where your password is the key and the authentication code is the deadbolt. Even if someone guesses or steals your password, they would still need access to your mobile device or authentication app to log into your ClickUp account.

Why 2FA is Essential for ClickUp Users

Here are a few reasons why you should activate Two-Factor Authentication for your ClickUp account as soon as possible:

- 🔐 **Enhanced Security**: Protects your data from unauthorized access.

- 🔏 **Sensitive Information**: ClickUp may contain client data, project timelines, business strategies, and more.

- 🌐 **Team Environments**: In collaborative setups, a single compromised account can affect the entire workspace.

- ☑️ **Best Practice**: Many security standards and compliance policies require or recommend 2FA.

Before You Start: What You'll Need

To enable 2FA in ClickUp, you'll need:

- A ClickUp account (already created)

- A smartphone or device with an **authenticator app** such as:

    o Google Authenticator

    o Authy

    o Microsoft Authenticator

    o Duo Mobile

- Access to your email (used as a backup recovery method)

Step-by-Step: Enabling 2FA in ClickUp

Follow these steps to set up Two-Factor Authentication:

Step 1: Access Your ClickUp Settings

1. Log in to your ClickUp account.

2. Click your **profile avatar** in the bottom-left corner.

3. Select **"My Settings"** from the dropdown menu.

Step 2: Navigate to the Security Section

1. In the **Settings** panel, look for the **"Security & Permissions"** tab (sometimes just labeled "Security").

2. Click it to access your security preferences.

Step 3: Begin the 2FA Setup

1. Scroll down to the **Two-Factor Authentication** section.

2. Click **"Enable Two-Factor Authentication."**

Step 4: Scan the QR Code

1. Open your **authenticator app** on your phone.

2. Select **"Add Account"** (usually a plus icon).

3. Choose **"Scan a QR Code"**.

4. Scan the QR code displayed on ClickUp's setup screen.

Alternatively, you can use the **manual setup key** if scanning the QR code isn't possible.

Step 5: Enter the Authentication Code

1. Once you scan the QR code, the authenticator app will generate a **6-digit code**.

2. Enter that code into the prompt in ClickUp.

3. Click **Verify** or **Enable**.

Step 6: Save Backup Codes

ClickUp will now show you **backup codes**. These are essential if you ever lose access to your phone or authenticator app. Be sure to:

- Download the codes

- Save them in a secure place (e.g., a password manager or encrypted file)

- Avoid storing them in plain text or your email inbox

Logging In With 2FA Enabled

Once 2FA is enabled, each time you log into ClickUp, you'll need to:

1. Enter your email and password as usual.

2. Enter the **6-digit code** generated by your authenticator app.

3. Optionally, check **"Remember this device for 30 days"** if you're on a personal, trusted device.

If you enter the wrong code or your code expires (they refresh every 30 seconds), you'll need to re-enter a valid code.

Recovering Access If You Lose Your Device

Losing access to your authentication device can be stressful, but ClickUp offers recovery options:

Option 1: Use Your Backup Codes

When you set up 2FA, you were provided with one-time-use backup codes. Enter one of those in place of the 6-digit code.

Option 2: Contact ClickUp Support

If you don't have access to your backup codes:

- Visit ClickUp's Help Center or support page.

- Submit a request to **disable 2FA** on your account.

- Be prepared to verify your identity (email, billing details, recent activity).

ClickUp typically responds within 24–48 hours.

Tips for Managing Your 2FA Setup

- **Label Your Account in the Authenticator App**: This makes it easier to find the right code if you use the app for multiple services.

- **Use a Password Manager**: Many password managers like 1Password and Bitwarden also support 2FA code generation.

- **Backup Your Authenticator App**: Some apps like **Authy** allow you to sync across multiple devices for recovery.

- **Reconfigure if Changing Phones**: If you switch devices, remember to reconfigure 2FA before wiping or discarding the old one.

Team-Level 2FA Enforcement (for Admins)

If you're an **admin** of a ClickUp workspace and want to **enforce 2FA for all members**, you can do so via:

1. Workspace Settings → Security

2. Enforce 2FA for all members

3. Notify users that they'll be required to enable it upon next login

This is highly recommended for teams dealing with sensitive data or who are subject to regulatory compliance.

Common Questions & Troubleshooting

Q: Can I use SMS instead of an authenticator app?
A: As of now, ClickUp only supports authenticator apps, not SMS-based 2FA.

Q: Why is my code being rejected?
A: Ensure your phone's clock is synchronized. Even a few seconds of time difference can cause issues.

Q: Can I disable 2FA later?
A: Yes, but it is not recommended. To disable, go to your Security settings and click "Disable Two-Factor Authentication."

Q: What happens if I try to log in too many times with the wrong code?
A: Your account may be temporarily locked. You'll need to wait a few minutes before retrying or contact support.

Conclusion: A Small Step for a Big Impact

Enabling Two-Factor Authentication may seem like a small, quick setup task, but the **impact on your account security is enormous**. Whether you're a solo freelancer, a project manager, or part of a large enterprise team, taking this proactive step helps ensure that your data — and your team's — stays safe.

Once you've set up 2FA, you can proceed confidently knowing that you've added a vital layer of protection to your ClickUp workspace. Now that your account is secure, let's dive deeper into understanding how ClickUp is structured — up next: **1.2 Understanding the ClickUp Hierarchy**.

1.2 Understanding the ClickUp Hierarchy

1.2.1 Workspaces, Spaces, Folders, Lists

ClickUp is a highly flexible and powerful project management platform. To fully harness its capabilities, it's crucial to understand its organizational hierarchy. At the heart of ClickUp's efficiency lies its structural architecture—a hierarchy designed to scale with teams of any size, from freelancers to large enterprises. This section breaks down the hierarchy so you can confidently structure your workspace for maximum clarity, collaboration, and productivity.

What Is the ClickUp Hierarchy and Why Does It Matter?

The ClickUp hierarchy is the organizational framework that lets you manage everything from top-level strategy to the smallest task detail. It allows you to break your work down into manageable layers, providing structure while maintaining flexibility. Whether you're managing a company-wide strategy or a simple to-do list, the hierarchy ensures your information stays well-organized.

ClickUp's core hierarchy levels are as follows:

1. **Workspace**
2. **Spaces**
3. **Folders**
4. **Lists**
5. **Tasks and Subtasks**

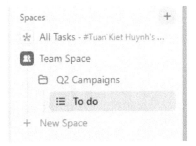

Let's explore each of these components in detail, focusing on how they work together and how you can use them to design your ideal productivity system.

Workspace: Your Organization's Headquarters

A **Workspace** is the highest level of organization in ClickUp. It functions as your company or team's virtual headquarters. When you first create your ClickUp account, you'll be prompted to create a Workspace—this is where all your projects and collaboration will happen.

Key Characteristics of Workspaces:

- Each user can be part of multiple Workspaces (useful for freelancers or consultants working with different clients).

- Billing, integrations, and user management are handled at the Workspace level.

- Think of it as the roof under which all your departments or business units exist.

Best Practices for Setting Up a Workspace:

- Use your company or team name as the Workspace name.

- Invite team members only after you've structured the core Spaces and folders to avoid confusion.

- If you work across several businesses or brands, consider creating separate Workspaces for each.

Spaces: Departments or Major Divisions

Within your Workspace, you create **Spaces**, which are the next layer of organization. Spaces are commonly used to represent **departments, teams, product lines**, or major projects.

For example, a marketing agency might have Spaces like:

- Digital Marketing

- Graphic Design

- Client Accounts

- Admin

Space-Level Features:

- Customizable statuses (e.g., "To Do," "In Progress," "Review")

- Space-specific ClickApps (features like Time Tracking or Dependencies)

- Permissions and visibility controls

- Docs and views associated with that Space

Naming Tip:

Use clear, intuitive names for your Spaces so your team can easily understand their purpose. Avoid abbreviations unless everyone on the team understands them.

Folders: Organize Projects or Campaigns

Inside each Space, you can create **Folders** to group related Lists together. Folders are optional, but they are especially useful for organizing multiple projects within the same department or function.

Think of **Folders** as containers for projects, client accounts, or campaigns. For example, in the "Marketing" Space, you might create folders like:

- Q2 Campaigns

- Social Media Strategy

- Client X Deliverables

Folder Benefits:

- Allows you to group Lists (which contain tasks) under a single project heading.

- Folders can have their own statuses, which can override or differ from the Space-level statuses.

- Folders can be archived or hidden when no longer needed.

Folder Use Cases:

- In a software development Space, use folders for "Frontend," "Backend," and "Testing."

- In a content production team, use folders for "Blog," "Video," and "Podcast."

Folders make it easy to track progress at the project level while still maintaining access to task-level details.

Lists: Task Containers

Lists live inside Folders (or directly inside a Space if no Folder is used). They contain **Tasks**, which are the actionable items that your team will be working on. You can think of Lists as project phases, categories, or specific work streams.

For instance, in a Folder called "Website Redesign," you might have Lists such as:

- Research & Discovery

- Wireframes

- Development

- QA & Testing

What Makes Lists Powerful:

- Lists are highly customizable with views (List View, Board View, Calendar View, etc.).

- You can apply statuses at the List level if desired.

- Each List can have its own unique name, view configuration, and even automation rules.

Tips for Creating Effective Lists:

- Keep Lists focused and action-oriented (e.g., "Weekly Content Planning" instead of just "Content").

- Avoid creating too many Lists with overlapping tasks—clarity is key.

- Leverage Custom Fields to make Lists even more dynamic.

Putting It All Together: An Example Hierarchy

Let's walk through an example to visualize how these layers interact in a real-world scenario.

Scenario: A Startup Building a Mobile App

- **Workspace**: SmartApp Technologies
  - **Space**: Product Development
    - **Folder**: Mobile App v2.0
      - **List**: UX Research
      - **List**: Feature Development
      - **List**: Beta Testing

In this hierarchy:

- The **Workspace** houses all company operations.
- The **Product Development** Space contains all software-related projects.
- The **Mobile App v2.0** Folder is dedicated to the newest app iteration.
- The **Lists** break the project into clear phases, each with its own set of tasks.

This structure gives clarity to the team, ensures separation between projects, and makes it easier to manage permissions, statuses, and timelines.

Flat vs. Nested Structure: Which Should You Choose?

While ClickUp supports deep hierarchies, it also excels at letting users build **flat structures**. Depending on your team's size and complexity, you might not need Folders and can work directly in Lists within a Space.

Use a Nested Structure When:

- You manage multiple distinct projects in the same department.
- You need different sets of statuses for each Folder.
- Your team has multiple stakeholders and workflows.

Use a Flat Structure When:

- You're a solo user or very small team.

- You want a minimal setup with fewer clicks.

- Your workstreams don't need extensive separation.

Tips for Managing the Hierarchy Effectively

1. **Plan Before You Build:** Don't start creating Spaces and Folders without a rough outline of your team's needs. Poor planning can lead to messy structures that confuse users.

2. **Name with Purpose:** Use names that describe the function or goal of each level in the hierarchy.

3. **Use Templates:** Save time by creating Space, Folder, or List templates that follow a proven structure.

4. **Review Regularly:** Projects change. Conduct monthly or quarterly reviews to archive outdated Folders and reorganize active ones.

Conclusion: Mastering the ClickUp Framework

Understanding and utilizing ClickUp's hierarchy is the first major step toward mastering the platform. When used properly, the hierarchy transforms chaotic task lists into a well-oiled productivity machine. Whether you're a solo entrepreneur, a department manager, or a project leader, the way you design your Workspace, Spaces, Folders, and Lists will directly impact your efficiency and your team's collaboration.

In the next section, we'll dive into the ClickUp interface—because once you know where everything belongs, the next step is learning how to navigate your tools like a pro.

1.2.2 Tasks and Subtasks

In ClickUp, tasks are the backbone of your productivity. They represent everything from the smallest to-do to the largest, most complex project deliverables. Understanding how to effectively use **tasks and subtasks** is essential to mastering your ClickUp workspace and keeping your workflow streamlined, transparent, and scalable.

This section will dive deep into the structure, functionality, and best practices around **tasks and subtasks** in ClickUp — helping you understand when to use them, how to set them up, and how to take advantage of their full range of features to supercharge your productivity.

What is a Task in ClickUp?

At its core, a **task** in ClickUp is a single unit of work. It could be as small as "Send a client follow-up email" or as significant as "Prepare Q2 marketing report." Tasks hold essential information and act as the primary place where action happens.

Each task contains many attributes that make it a powerful project management tool:

- **Title**: A clear, descriptive name
- **Description**: Supporting information, details, or context
- **Assignees**: Who is responsible
- **Due Dates**: When the task should be completed
- **Status**: Workflow stage (e.g., "To Do," "In Progress," "Complete")
- **Custom Fields**: Additional data like budget, effort estimation, client name
- **Priority**: Indicator of importance (e.g., Low, Normal, High, Urgent)
- **Attachments**: Files, screenshots, or documents
- **Time Tracking**: Amount of time spent on the task
- **Dependencies**: Relationships with other tasks
- **Comments**: Communication hub for collaboration

ClickUp tasks can be incredibly simple or richly detailed based on your needs. The platform allows for flexibility, whether you're managing a personal to-do list or coordinating a large cross-functional team.

What are Subtasks?

Subtasks are smaller, dependent items that break down a larger task into manageable pieces. They follow the same format as tasks and can include their own:

- Assignees

- Due dates

- Statuses

- Priorities

- Checklists

- Comments

This allows teams to **delegate responsibilities**, **track individual components**, and **monitor progress more accurately** within a single task's context.

Tasks vs. Subtasks: When to Use Each

One of the most common questions for new users is: *When should I use a task, and when should I use a subtask?*

Here are some general guidelines:

Use Case	Create a Task	Create a Subtask
Independent piece of work	✓	✗
Part of a larger deliverable	✗	✓
Needs to be tracked separately across lists	✓	✗
Needs own assignee, time estimate, and deadline	✓	✓
Belongs entirely under another task	✗	✓
A checklist of steps within a single task or Use a checklist	✗	✓

Think of subtasks as **actionable components** that need to be completed to finish the parent task. If a subtask starts to feel too big or requires collaboration across teams or lists, it might be worth turning it into a **standalone task** instead.

How to Create Tasks and Subtasks in ClickUp

Creating a Task

You can create a new task from nearly anywhere in ClickUp:

- **From the "+ Task" button** in your List or Board view

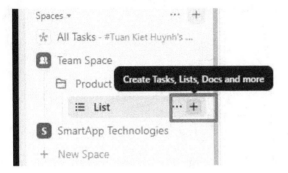

- **From the Quick Create menu** (lightning bolt icon)

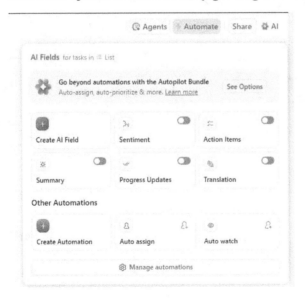

- **Using a slash command** like /task in Docs

- **Via templates** or imported data

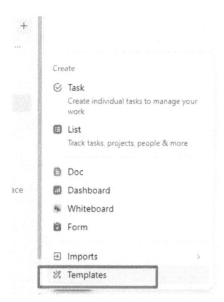

You'll then be prompted to fill out the task fields, assign users, set deadlines, and more. Don't worry if you miss anything—you can always edit it later.

Creating a Subtask

To add subtasks:

1. Open a task.

2. Scroll down to the **Subtasks** section.

3. Click **+ Add subtask**.

4. Give it a name and hit Enter.

5. You can assign the subtask, add a due date, and customize just like a normal task.

Each subtask is nested under the main task but still allows robust functionality, including:

- Own time tracking
- Own attachments
- Own comments and discussion thread
- Completion tracking separate from the parent

Nesting Subtasks (Multiple Levels)

ClickUp allows **nested subtasks** (subtasks within subtasks) up to 7 levels deep. While this gives you detailed flexibility, **it's important not to over-nest**, as too much hierarchy can lead to confusion and difficulty in tracking progress across your project.

Best Practice: Use no more than 2-3 levels of subtasks. If you find yourself going deeper, consider using a checklist, separate tasks, or a different organizational structure (e.g., a Folder or List).

Visualizing Tasks and Subtasks

Depending on the **View** you're using in ClickUp, subtasks may appear differently:

- **List View**: Subtasks can be expanded under parent tasks.
- **Board View**: Subtasks appear as cards and can be filtered or grouped separately.
- **Gantt View**: Subtasks show as connected items under the parent, ideal for project timelines.
- **Calendar View**: Subtasks appear individually if they have due dates.
- **Table View**: Offers granular data across all tasks and subtasks with filtering options.

You can **choose to hide or show subtasks**, and even customize how they are displayed in filters, grouping, and sorting criteria.

Task Relationships and Dependencies

You can enhance the power of tasks and subtasks by using **relationships**:

- **Dependencies**: Mark tasks as "Blocking" or "Waiting On" other tasks.

- **Linked Tasks**: Add connections between tasks or subtasks that are related but not dependent.

- **Milestones**: Turn any task into a milestone for project tracking.

Subtasks can also have dependencies — this allows you to create **task chains**, where one must be completed before another begins.

Using Templates for Reusable Task Structures

ClickUp supports **Task Templates** and **Subtask Templates**. If you frequently use the same task + subtask structure (e.g., a content publishing process, onboarding checklist, or sprint planning), save time by:

1. Setting up the task with all necessary subtasks.

2. Clicking the ellipsis menu (...) > **Save as Template**

3. Naming and customizing the template settings.

Later, you can apply this template with a click and customize it as needed.

Automation with Tasks and Subtasks

ClickUp's **Automation** tools can help reduce repetitive work:

- Automatically create subtasks when a new task is added to a specific list.

- Change the status of a parent task when all subtasks are completed.

- Send notifications when a subtask is overdue.

- Auto-assign users when tasks are created in a workflow.

These automations are especially useful when scaling project management with multiple contributors and timelines.

Best Practices for Using Tasks and Subtasks

1. **Name Tasks Clearly**: Use action verbs and specific language (e.g., "Write Blog Post for July" instead of "Blog").

2. **Limit Subtasks**: Avoid over-complicating. Too many subtasks can become overwhelming.

3. **Define Responsibility**: Always assign someone to both tasks and subtasks.

4. **Use Checklists When Appropriate**: If you don't need full subtask features, a checklist might suffice.

5. **Review Subtasks Regularly**: Make sure none are stuck or forgotten. Use Dashboards or filtered Views.

6. **Use Dependencies Thoughtfully**: Don't overuse them, but they're powerful for critical paths.

7. **Apply Templates Strategically**: Save time on recurring task structures.

Common Mistakes to Avoid

- **Creating subtasks for everything**: Overuse leads to messy hierarchies.

- **Leaving subtasks unassigned**: This creates confusion over ownership.

- **Not aligning due dates**: Subtasks shouldn't be due *after* the parent task.

- **Forgetting to track progress**: Subtask completion doesn't always mean the parent is done—monitor both.

- **Ignoring task relationships**: Missed dependencies can derail timelines.

Final Thoughts

Understanding and leveraging **tasks and subtasks** is one of the most important skills in mastering ClickUp. When used wisely, they create clarity, reduce chaos, and ensure that no step in your process gets missed. Whether you're working solo or with a large team, investing the time to structure your work with tasks and subtasks thoughtfully will result in higher productivity, stronger accountability, and smoother execution of projects from start to finish.

1.2.3 Views and Levels of Organization

One of the core features that makes ClickUp a powerful and versatile productivity tool is its **views**—ways of visualizing your data—and the **levels of organization** that help you manage work efficiently. Understanding how these two aspects interact is crucial to building a system that works for your team, no matter how small or complex.

This section will walk you through:

- The role of views in ClickUp

- The different types of views available

- Best practices for organizing your tasks and projects using levels of hierarchy

- Real-world scenarios of when to use which view

- Customizing and saving views for teams and individuals

The Purpose of Views in ClickUp

In ClickUp, *views* allow users to see their tasks and projects in the format that best suits the way they work. Think of them as lenses—you can look at the same data in a variety of ways depending on what you need to accomplish. Whether you prefer a list, a Kanban-style board, a calendar, or a timeline, ClickUp adapts to your workflow, not the other way around.

Views do not change the content of your tasks—they only affect how that content is displayed. This flexibility makes ClickUp useful for everyone, from individual contributors to team leads and executive decision-makers.

ClickUp's Hierarchical Structure Recap

Before diving into views, let's quickly recall the hierarchy in ClickUp:

1. **Workspace** – The top-level structure representing your entire organization.

2. **Spaces** – Broad categories or departments within your Workspace.

3. **Folders** – Subdivisions within Spaces that group similar projects or task types.

4. **Lists** – Individual task groups within folders.

5. **Tasks** – Actionable items.

6. **Subtasks** – Smaller, break-down components of tasks.

Each level can have its own views, allowing you to drill down or zoom out, depending on your needs.

Types of Views in ClickUp

ClickUp offers a rich variety of views that cater to diverse workflows. Here are the most widely used ones:

1. List View

- The most traditional and commonly used view.
- Displays tasks in a vertical list, grouped by status or other custom fields.
- Ideal for detail-oriented workflows and step-by-step task management.

Key Benefits:

- Easy sorting and filtering.
- Great for data-heavy projects.
- Can show columns like assignee, due date, priority, and more.

Use Case Example: A content team tracking blog posts through drafting, editing, and publishing.

2. Board View (Kanban)

- Tasks are displayed as cards in columns, usually grouped by status.

- Supports drag-and-drop functionality to move tasks through workflows.

Key Benefits:

- Visual and intuitive for process flows.

- Excellent for agile teams and sprint planning.

Use Case Example: A development team managing software features across sprints using "To Do," "In Progress," "Code Review," and "Done" statuses.

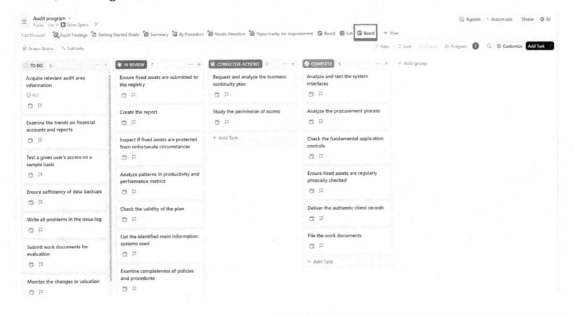

3. Calendar View

- A time-based layout that displays tasks by due date.

- Great for planning and scheduling tasks, especially in deadline-driven environments.

Key Benefits:

- Drag-and-drop tasks to reschedule.

- Weekly, monthly, and daily views available.

Use Case Example: An event planning team laying out milestones for an upcoming product launch.

4. Gantt View

- A timeline-based view that allows you to plan and manage project timelines.
- Tasks are represented as bars across a calendar with dependencies.

Key Benefits:

- Visualizes the big picture.
- Great for spotting overlaps and bottlenecks.
- Task dependencies are clearly shown.

Use Case Example: A project manager overseeing the launch of a new website, tracking stages from wireframe to development to QA.

5. Timeline View

- Similar to Gantt but better for ongoing workflows and less complex planning.

- A simpler, linear view of tasks over time.

Key Benefits:

- Helps teams balance workloads.

- Easier to use than Gantt for smaller teams.

Use Case Example: A social media team scheduling content creation across weeks.

6. Box View

- A high-level overview grouped by assignee.

- Great for managers to see workloads across the team.

Key Benefits:

- Helps monitor resource allocation.

- See who is overloaded or underutilized.

Use Case Example: A team lead reviewing weekly assignments to ensure no one is overwhelmed.

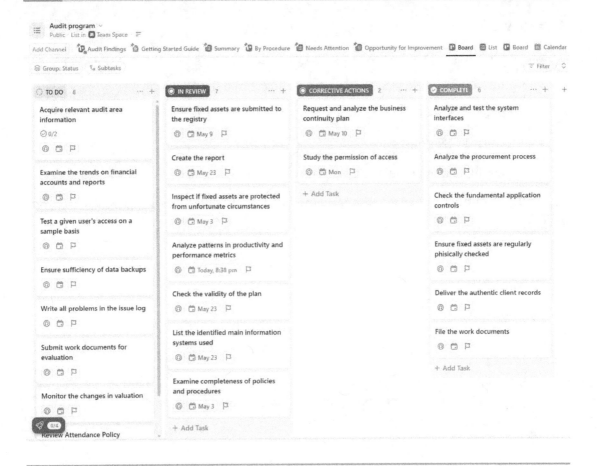

7. Mind Map View

- Allows you to build a visual map of tasks and their relationships.

- Great for brainstorming and planning workflows.

Key Benefits:

- Idea-centric layout.

- Helps in outlining projects or breaking down complex goals.

Use Case Example: A marketing team outlining the steps of a new campaign before creating tasks.

8. Table View

- Spreadsheet-like interface for users who love working in rows and columns.

- Allows inline editing, column sorting, and custom field control.

Key Benefits:

- Familiar to Excel users.

- Powerful data manipulation for project tracking.

Use Case Example: A finance team tracking budget tasks with cost, approval status, and deadlines.

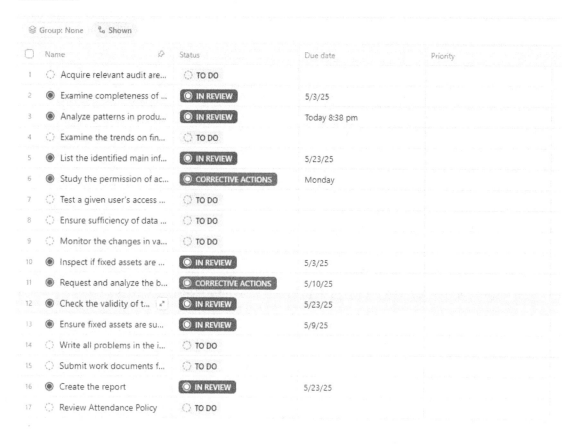

Levels of View Application

Views can be applied at different levels of the ClickUp hierarchy:

- **Workspace View:** Gives a cross-functional look across all teams and tasks.

- **Space View:** Helps focus on departments like Marketing, Development, or HR.

- **Folder View:** Focused on a specific project or initiative.

- **List View:** The most granular level, great for task-specific views.

Each level can have **default views**, and you can also set **personal views** (visible only to you) or **shared views** (visible to the team).

Customizing Views for Workflow Optimization

Once you've selected a view, ClickUp allows you to customize it with filters, sorting, grouping, and more:

- **Filtering:** Show only tasks that meet specific criteria (e.g., overdue tasks).

- **Sorting:** Organize tasks by priority, due date, assignee, etc.

- **Grouping:** Group tasks by status, assignee, tags, or custom fields.

- **Columns:** Choose which fields are visible (due date, priority, time tracked, etc.)

You can then **save this view** for future use and **pin it** for easy access.

Best Practices for Using Views

- **Standardize across teams:** Agree on default views so everyone starts on the same page.

- **Create team dashboards:** Use Gantt or Calendar views for managers and stakeholders.

- **Make use of templates:** Save your view setup and reuse it across projects.

- **Don't overcomplicate:** Keep views simple and relevant to your workflow.

Real-World Scenarios: When to Use What

Scenario	Recommended View
Managing tasks by priority	List View
Scrum board for agile teams	Board View
Planning marketing calendar	Calendar View
Resource management	Box View
Strategic project planning	Gantt or Timeline
Brainstorming project flow	Mind Map
Budget and cost tracking	Table View

Conclusion: The Right View for the Right Job

Views in ClickUp are not just cosmetic—they're critical to making your workflows more intuitive, effective, and tailored to how you and your team work. Whether you're a visual learner, a numbers person, or a strategic planner, ClickUp's variety of views ensures there's something that matches your mindset and task flow.

As you grow more comfortable in ClickUp, experimenting with views becomes second nature. The more intentional you are with customizing and organizing your workspaces, the more time you save and the clearer your work becomes.

In the next section, we'll explore **navigating the interface**, so you'll know exactly where everything is and how to get the most out of your ClickUp experience—no matter what view you choose.

1.3 Navigating the Interface

1.3.1 The Sidebar and Menu

When you first log in to ClickUp, the interface can feel both sleek and expansive. One of the most essential elements you'll interact with constantly is the **Sidebar**—a central navigation panel that guides you through every part of the platform. Mastering the Sidebar and Menu system is your first step to confidently using ClickUp for everyday productivity and team collaboration.

In this section, we'll walk you through:

- The layout of the Sidebar

- The purpose of each main element

- How to customize the Sidebar to fit your workflow

- Best practices to keep your navigation clean and intuitive

Understanding the ClickUp Sidebar Layout

The Sidebar in ClickUp sits on the left-hand side of your screen. Think of it as your control panel—it gives you instant access to your spaces, views, dashboards, notifications, and more.

The Sidebar includes several major areas:

- **Spaces and Workspaces**

- **Favorites**

- **Everything View**

- **Inbox**

- **Dashboards**

- **Docs**

- **Goals**

- **Home**
- **Notifications**
- **Settings**

Let's explore these in detail.

Spaces and Workspaces: Your ClickUp Structure

At the top section of the Sidebar, you'll see the **Workspace name**, followed by a list of **Spaces**. A **Workspace** in ClickUp is the highest level of your organization's hierarchy—this might be your company, your department, or a client account if you're a freelancer or agency.

Under the Workspace are **Spaces**, which act like departments or broad categories of work. For example, your Workspace might be "Acme Corp," and your Spaces might include:

- Marketing
- Development
- Operations
- HR

Each Space can contain **Folders**, **Lists**, and **Tasks**, giving you the structure to manage projects granularly. Clicking on a Space will expand it to show its internal structure, which you can collapse or expand based on your needs.

Favorites: Quick Access to Important Views

You can mark any view—whether it's a List, Folder, Doc, or Dashboard—as a **Favorite**, and it will appear near the top of your Sidebar. This is extremely helpful if you work with multiple teams or projects but want to keep daily go-to views accessible without deep navigation.

To favorite something:

- Hover over a view and click the **star icon**.

- Once favorited, it'll show up under the "Favorites" section at the top of your Sidebar.

Organize favorites strategically to reduce navigation fatigue.

Everything View: See All Your Work in One Place

The **Everything** view is a powerful feature that lets you see all tasks across your Workspace. Whether you're a manager or an individual contributor, this is where you can:

- Search and filter tasks

- View workload across projects

- Find overdue tasks and bottlenecks

Clicking on **Everything** brings up a global view where you can customize filters by assignee, due date, tag, or priority. It's ideal for getting a high-level overview.

Inbox: Your Personal To-Do Center

The **Inbox** is a personalized, chronological list of tasks, reminders, and mentions relevant to you. Think of it as your daily planner inside ClickUp.

It's divided into:

- **Today**

- **Overdue**

- **Next**

- **Unscheduled**

This makes it easier to focus on what matters now and plan what's coming next. You can drag and drop tasks to adjust dates or open them directly from the Inbox to work on details.

Dashboards: Data-Driven Control Panels

The **Dashboards** tab in the Sidebar takes you to a customizable visual workspace where you can track:

- Team performance
- Project progress
- Time tracking
- Goal completion
- Workload

Dashboards are made up of widgets like bar charts, pie graphs, task lists, and more. You can create multiple dashboards for different purposes (e.g., client reporting, internal KPIs).

Docs: ClickUp's Built-In Documentation Hub

ClickUp includes a robust Docs feature that allows you to create internal wikis, SOPs, meeting notes, and brainstorming documents. Docs can be nested within Spaces, Folders, or linked to tasks.

In the Sidebar, the **Docs** section shows all documents shared across the Workspace. You can also pin important Docs to your Sidebar for even faster access.

Goals: Align Projects with Measurable Outcomes

The **Goals** area lets you track long-term and short-term objectives. You can break goals down into:

- **Targets** (measurable milestones)
- **Tasks** (execution items)
- **Numerical values** (e.g., revenue, hours)

Goals can be linked to tasks and auto-updated as progress is made. For team leads or project managers, this is an excellent way to align daily work with broader initiatives.

Home: A Central Hub for Your Day

The **Home** screen provides a personalized view of:

- Assigned tasks

- Upcoming reminders

- Calendar

- Trending documents or projects

This is your dashboard for the day, consolidating what you need to do and where your attention should go.

Pro tip: Make checking your Home screen a daily ritual.

Notifications: Stay Informed Without Overwhelm

The **bell icon** on the Sidebar opens up your Notifications center, where you'll receive updates about:

- Task mentions

- Status changes

- Assignments

- Comments

You can configure notification preferences in **Settings** to avoid overload. Choose to be notified in-app, via email, or on mobile.

Settings: Customize Your Experience

The gear icon at the bottom of the Sidebar opens up **Settings**, where you can manage:

- Account info

- Workspace settings

- Integrations

- Security preferences

It's also where you can activate **ClickApps**, the modular features in ClickUp that allow you to tailor the platform for your specific workflow (we'll go deeper into ClickApps in Chapter 6).

Customizing the Sidebar

ClickUp gives you full control over how your Sidebar appears. You can:

- **Collapse** the Sidebar to give yourself more screen space.

- **Pin or unpin** elements for convenience.

- **Reorder Spaces and favorites** via drag-and-drop.

- **Hide inactive Spaces or Lists** to keep things clean.

To customize:

1. Click on the three-dot menu in the Sidebar.

2. Choose "Manage Sidebar."

3. Drag and drop elements or click the eye icon to show/hide.

This flexibility is a huge productivity booster, especially for power users.

Best Practices for Sidebar Navigation

1. **Limit Favorites** to 5–7 items you use daily. More than that, and you may lose the benefit of quick access.

2. **Collapse inactive Spaces** to reduce visual clutter.

3. **Name Spaces and Folders clearly** so you don't waste time guessing.

4. **Use emojis or icons** in Space names to visually differentiate them.

5. **Set a weekly Sidebar review** to archive or remove unused views.

Troubleshooting and Tips

- If your Sidebar looks too busy, check for **legacy or test Spaces** and archive or remove them.

- Use the **Search bar (Cmd/Ctrl + K)** to jump to tasks or views instantly.

- Try the **Compact Sidebar mode** if you're working on a smaller screen.

Final Thoughts

The Sidebar is your command center in ClickUp. When used intentionally, it saves time, reduces mental overhead, and helps you stay organized across even the most complex project environments. Whether you're managing a solo freelance gig or a cross-functional enterprise team, learning to navigate this panel efficiently will pay off immediately.

In the next section, we'll explore another key part of the ClickUp interface: the **Search and Command Center**—a hidden gem for power users.

1.3.2 Search and Command Center

Navigating any productivity tool efficiently requires mastering its shortcuts and built-in tools to access what you need, fast. In ClickUp, the **Search** and **Command Center** serve as the heart of navigation and quick action, helping you move through workspaces, access tasks, execute commands, and take action without wasting time clicking through layers of menus.

In this section, we'll explore:

- The difference between Search and Command Center

- How to use the Search bar effectively

- Filtering and sorting results

- Using the Command Center to execute tasks faster

- Real-life use cases and best practices

Understanding the Difference: Search vs. Command Center

Though both are accessible via the same hotkey (by default Cmd + K on macOS or Ctrl + K on Windows), **Search** and **Command Center** in ClickUp serve two distinct purposes:

- **Search**: Helps you locate items — tasks, docs, views, lists, spaces, and more — across your entire ClickUp workspace. It's ideal when you're trying to *find* something.

- **Command Center**: Allows you to take *action* — create tasks, navigate to a different workspace or list, assign people, open settings, switch views, and more.

Think of **Search** as a GPS to find your destination, and **Command Center** as a remote control to operate the entire ClickUp system without touching the mouse.

Mastering the Search Bar

The Search bar in ClickUp is simple on the surface but incredibly powerful under the hood.

How to Access the Search Bar

- Click on the **Search icon** (magnifying glass) in the top-right corner.

- Or, use the shortcut:

    o   Cmd + K (macOS)

    o   Ctrl + K (Windows/Linux)

When you open Search, a clean, modal interface appears, ready to help you locate any item.

What You Can Search

- **Tasks** (by name, ID, or contents)

- **Lists and Folders**

- **Spaces and Workspaces**

- **Docs and Comments**

- **People**

- **Views**

- **Goals**

- **Tags**

ClickUp indexes nearly everything, so you're rarely out of luck.

Search Suggestions and Recent Items

As soon as you open the Search window, ClickUp shows:

- Your **recently opened** tasks and docs

- **Frequent locations**

- Smart suggestions based on your activity

This speeds up workflow by predicting where you want to go.

Using Search Operators and Filters

ClickUp supports filters to narrow down your search. Some common filters include:

- **Location**: Limit search to a specific Space, Folder, or List

- **Assignee**: Find tasks assigned to a specific user

- **Due Date**: Locate time-sensitive tasks

- **Tag**: Filter by tag name

- **Status**: Find tasks that are open, done, or in custom states

You can combine filters to create powerful queries, for example:

"Find all overdue tasks assigned to me in the 'Marketing' space with the tag 'urgent'"

Advanced users may also make use of keyboard commands to jump between filters without clicking.

Best Practices for Using Search

- **Use specific keywords**: If you remember even part of the task or doc title, type that in.

- **Filter first**: Start narrowing the scope if you're in a large workspace.

- **Pin frequent items**: If you access certain tasks or docs often, pin them in your sidebar.

- **Clear filters after use**: Filters persist sometimes, which can lead to confusion. Always clear them if your results seem off.

The Power of the Command Center

The **Command Center** acts like a universal action launcher — your personal control panel inside ClickUp. Once activated, you can search *and* take action with just a few keystrokes.

How to Open the Command Center

Same hotkey as Search:

- Cmd + K (macOS)

- Ctrl + K (Windows)

Once opened, it presents a streamlined interface where you can:

- Navigate quickly to a Space, Folder, List, Task, or Doc

- Create a new task or doc instantly

- Switch between views

- Adjust your notification settings

- Change theme or personal settings

- Open your inbox, task tray, or settings

- Search for anything across ClickUp

It's like Spotlight Search (macOS) or Windows Search — but optimized for ClickUp.

Common Actions from the Command Center

Here are some commands you can execute:

- **Create a task**: Start typing create task or just hit t to launch the new task modal

- **Open a doc**: Type docs or part of the doc name

- **Jump to list/folder**: Type go to, then the name of the target location

- **View notifications**: Type notifications

- **Open a specific setting**: Type settings, then the specific option you want

Command Center even allows you to **toggle between dark/light mode**, or open your **Time Tracking dashboard** in seconds.

Customizing the Command Center

ClickUp allows you to fine-tune what shows up in the Command Center and Search via:

- **Favorites**: Pin views, lists, docs, or tasks

- **Recents**: These automatically bubble to the top

- **Keyboard Shortcuts**: You can remap or discover more shortcuts in your ClickUp settings

Real-Life Use Cases

Let's explore a few practical scenarios where Search and Command Center dramatically improve productivity:

Scenario 1: A Manager Checking Project Progress

You're a marketing manager and want to quickly see the latest updates in your "Q2 Campaigns" list. You hit Cmd + K, type "Q2 Campaigns," and jump right into the list. From there, you can instantly filter to see "in-progress" tasks or sort by due date.

Scenario 2: A Developer Creating a Bug Report

A developer receives a Slack message about a new bug. Rather than navigating through the interface:

1. They hit Cmd + K, type Create task.

2. Enter task title: "Bug: Checkout button not working."

3. Assign to QA, set due date, and add a tag, all within seconds.

Scenario 3: A Freelancer Managing Time

You want to log time spent on a client project:

- Use Cmd + K, type "Time tracking," and instantly access the timer interface.

- Choose the relevant task and begin recording time — all without a single click.

Tips for Boosting Efficiency with Search and Command Center

1. **Memorize Common Shortcuts**: The more often you use Cmd/Ctrl + K, the faster it becomes second nature.

2. **Use Natural Language**: ClickUp supports intelligent parsing, so you can type "create task" or just "new task."

3. **Avoid Mouse Overload**: Keep your hands on the keyboard and flow through tasks smoothly.

4. **Teach Your Team**: Encourage your team to use Command Center — it speeds up collaboration when everyone can navigate with ease.

5. **Leverage ClickUp University**: If you're managing a team, enroll in ClickUp's learning platform to dive deeper into these tools.

Troubleshooting Common Issues

Sometimes, Search and Command Center may not work as expected. Here are some things to check:

- **Indexing Delay**: New tasks or docs may take a few seconds to appear.

- **Workspace Permissions**: You won't see items in spaces you don't have access to.

- **Outdated Keyboard Shortcut**: Make sure your app is updated, and keyboard shortcuts are still mapped correctly.

Final Thoughts on Search and Command Center

The **Search and Command Center** are more than just convenience features — they're essential for serious productivity in ClickUp. Whether you're managing a small to-do list or running complex product sprints, mastering these tools will save you hours every week.

By learning how to search smarter and execute actions faster, you turn ClickUp into a true command hub for your work. No more hunting through folders, wasting time scrolling through notifications, or forgetting where that one task went — everything is just a few keystrokes away.

In the next section, we'll explore how to **personalize your experience** by diving into **User Settings and Preferences**, unlocking ways to make ClickUp feel like *your own* tailored workspace.

1.3.3 User Settings and Preferences

When you first start using ClickUp, the interface might feel feature-rich to the point of overwhelming. But once you understand where everything lives—and more importantly, how to customize it to fit your unique needs—you'll unlock a powerful, streamlined productivity experience. One of the most important areas to get familiar with is your **User Settings and Preferences**.

ClickUp is built for personalization. Whether you're a minimalist who prefers clean layouts or a power user who wants everything at your fingertips, ClickUp gives you the tools to make your workspace feel like home. In this section, we'll walk through everything you need to know to tailor ClickUp to suit your personal workflow, communication style, visual preferences, and device usage.

1. Understanding the User Settings Panel

To access your user settings, simply click on your avatar (usually your initials or profile picture) located at the bottom-left corner of the ClickUp sidebar. A menu will appear, where you can select **"Settings"**. This brings you to a dashboard of tabs that control your personal experience with ClickUp—independent from global workspace settings that only admins can adjust.

The user settings menu includes:

- Profile
- Notifications
- Apps
- Import/Export
- My Settings
- Sidebar

- Integrations
- Themes & Appearance
- Security & Privacy

Let's break these down one by one.

2. Customizing Your Profile

Your profile is your identity within ClickUp. This includes:

Display Name and Email

You can change the name that appears in mentions and comments, and update your primary email address. It's important to keep this up to date, especially for team communication and notification management.

Profile Picture

ClickUp allows you to upload a profile photo or use an avatar. A clear and recognizable image can help team members quickly identify who's who in larger organizations.

Time Zone and Language Settings

Make sure your time zone is accurate, especially if you're managing deadlines, automations, or working in distributed teams. You can also choose your preferred language, which is helpful for international users.

3. Notifications Preferences

ClickUp gives you **granular control over notifications**, ensuring you stay informed without getting overwhelmed.

Email Notifications

You can decide whether you want to receive email updates about new tasks, comments, assigned mentions, reminders, and more. You can even set quiet hours to avoid late-night pings.

In-App Notifications

ClickUp's notification center, accessible through the bell icon in the top-right corner, gathers all alerts. You can configure exactly which changes or events you want to be notified about.

Mobile Push Notifications

If you have the mobile app installed, you can enable or disable notifications for specific triggers like task assignments or due date changes.

Assigned Comments & Mentions

You'll be alerted when you're tagged or assigned a comment, but you can fine-tune these settings to reduce noise—especially in active teams.

Pro Tip: If you're receiving too many notifications, consider disabling updates for changes like status updates or comments on tasks you're just watching.

---

4. Visual Preferences and Themes

Customizing the appearance of your workspace can make long work sessions more pleasant and less mentally fatiguing.

Light vs. Dark Mode

ClickUp supports both light and dark modes. Many users prefer dark mode for evening work or to reduce eye strain.

Compact View and Density Settings

Under your **My Settings**, you can choose how dense you want your interface to feel— Compact, Comfortable, or Expanded. This changes padding and spacing across views, which can significantly improve readability.

Sidebar Customization

The sidebar is your navigation control center. ClickUp allows you to:

- Collapse/expand the sidebar
- Pin frequently used Spaces or Folders
- Rearrange items to match your workflow

This is particularly useful when managing multiple clients or projects.

Color Preferences

You can customize workspace colors or label statuses with colors to improve at-a-glance navigation.

---

5. Productivity and UX Enhancements

ClickUp offers smart settings to make task management more intuitive.

Default View Options

Choose which view you want to see by default when entering a Space or Folder—whether it's a Kanban board, a list, or calendar.

Task Creation Settings

ClickUp lets you adjust whether new tasks are added to the top or bottom of the list, and which fields show by default during task creation.

Recently Visited and Favorites

The system keeps track of recent pages, and you can manually pin high-use pages to your favorites bar.

---

6. Device and App Preferences

ClickUp is available on desktop, browser, and mobile—and the user settings allow you to tailor the experience for each platform.

Desktop App Options

From the ClickUp desktop app, you can enable desktop notifications, auto-launch on startup, and ensure smooth syncing with the web version.

Mobile App Settings

Within the mobile app, you can:

- Set default task views

- Enable biometric authentication

- Configure swipe actions (e.g., swipe to complete or delete)

Keyboard Shortcuts

Power users benefit from customizing keyboard shortcuts (to some extent) and learning built-in ones like:

- T to create a new task

- Q to open quick switch

- / to search

7. Privacy, Security, and Account Controls

Security matters, especially in team-based, cloud-hosted software.

Two-Factor Authentication

You can activate 2FA through Google Authenticator, Authy, or SMS for added protection.

Session Management

See all devices logged into your account and remotely log out of inactive or suspicious ones.

Data Export and Backup

Export your tasks and projects for backup or migration. You can also import data from Trello, Asana, or other tools.

8. Workspace Switching and Personal Tasks

ClickUp supports multiple Workspaces (great for freelancers or agencies working across clients).

Switching Workspaces

From your avatar menu, switch between different environments quickly without logging out.

Personal vs. Team Tasks

ClickUp lets you create private tasks or lists that only you can see, perfect for daily to-dos or planning before sharing.

9. Saving and Syncing Preferences

Most changes in user settings are automatically saved, and ClickUp's cloud-first architecture ensures your settings follow you across devices.

Still, it's a good idea to periodically check:

- Whether your app is updated

- If syncing is working correctly

- That you're using the correct workspace

10. Best Practices for Setting Up User Preferences

To close out this section, here are some proven tips for maximizing efficiency through your settings:

- **Start Simple**: Use default settings when you're new, and gradually introduce changes as your needs grow.

- **Review Monthly**: As your team scales or your workflows evolve, update your preferences.

- **Minimize Distraction**: Trim down notifications and visual noise. Only enable what's truly useful.

- **Create a Setup Template**: If you work across teams, document your ideal settings for easy replication.

Conclusion: Own Your Experience

ClickUp is powerful because it adapts to you—not the other way around. By taking the time to fine-tune your user settings and preferences, you're building a workspace that reflects your thinking, your habits, and your goals. This isn't just about toggles and themes; it's about **taking control of your productivity environment**.

Now that you've mastered the user settings, you're ready to dive deeper into building, organizing, and managing tasks like a pro. In the next chapter, we'll explore how to **Master Task Management**—the heart of every ClickUp user's journey.

CHAPTER II
Mastering Task Management

2.1 Creating and Managing Tasks

2.1.1 Task Details and Custom Fields

Effectively managing tasks is the heart of productivity in ClickUp. Whether you're a freelancer juggling multiple clients, a project manager overseeing complex workflows, or a student organizing study routines, understanding the full scope of a task's capabilities is essential. ClickUp's task system is one of the most powerful in the productivity world— packed with rich detail options and an unmatched level of customization. This section focuses on two of its core components: **task details** and **custom fields**.

Understanding Task Details

At the core, every task in ClickUp is more than just a to-do item—it's a complete unit of work. Each task can store a wealth of information, making it a flexible space for planning, tracking, and collaborating.

Let's explore the key elements you'll encounter when creating or editing a task:

1. Task Title

This is the most basic and visible part of a task. It should be clear and concise while conveying the essence of the work. For example:

- ☑ "Design Homepage Banner"

- ☑ "Review Q2 Budget Proposal"

- ✕ "Stuff to do"

Good titles help with quick recognition and make searches more effective.

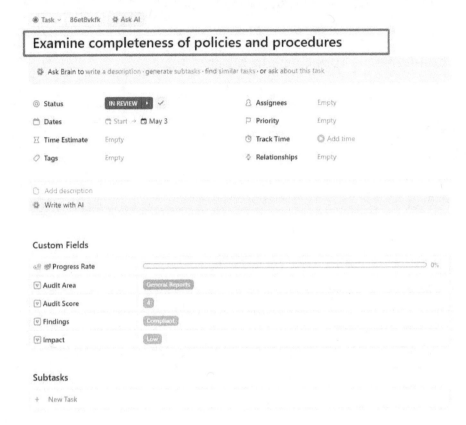

2. Description Field

This rich text editor allows you to provide detailed information about the task. You can:

- Format text (bold, italic, underline, headers)

- Add checklists

- Embed links

- Insert images or videos

- Use bullet points or numbered lists

It's best used to explain context, provide instructions, or outline expectations. Think of it as your mini brief.

Pro Tip: Use the description for step-by-step guides or to link reference materials—especially helpful for onboarding new team members or recurring tasks.

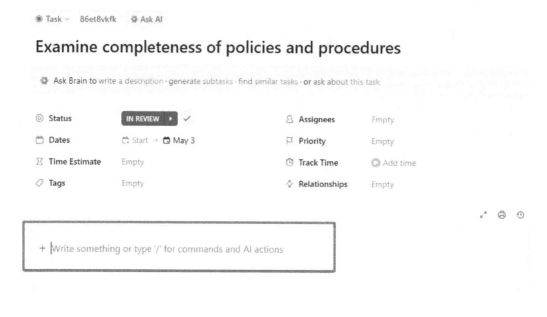

3. Assignees

You can assign the task to one or more people. Unlike many other platforms, ClickUp supports **multiple assignees** per task. This makes it ideal for shared responsibilities, though it's wise to define who is ultimately accountable.

Use roles like:

- **Primary Owner** – The person responsible for completing the task.

- **Collaborators** – Those contributing or reviewing.

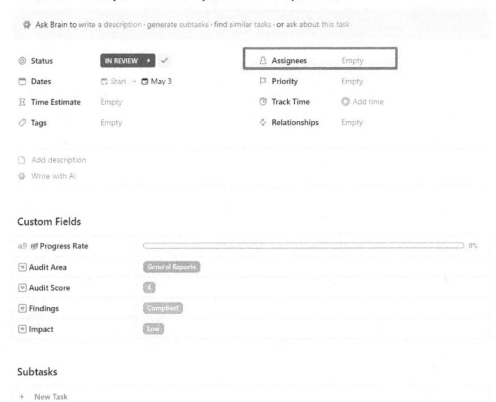

4. Due Dates & Start Dates

These are essential for time management. ClickUp lets you assign:

- A **due date** (deadline)
- A **start date** (when the task should begin)
- **Time ranges**, which are especially useful for scheduling or Gantt charts

You can also:

- Set **recurring tasks**
- Use **reminders**

- Enable **notifications** when tasks are overdue or upcoming

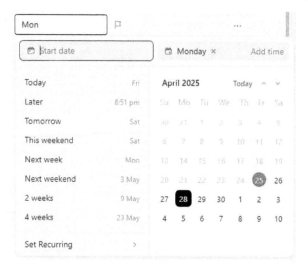

5. Priority Levels

ClickUp offers four levels of priority by default:

- Urgent
- High
- Normal
- Low

Use these to help team members understand what to tackle first, especially in shared spaces.

Use Case: During sprint planning, product managers might mark all bug fixes as "Urgent" and new features as "High."

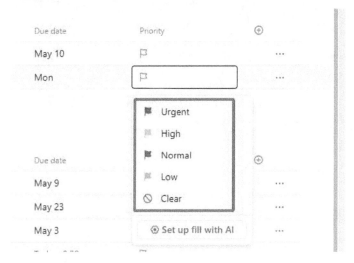

6. Tags

Tags are flexible labels that help categorize tasks. They can denote status, type, phase, or even mood—whatever works for your workflow. Some common tag systems:

- #design, #marketing, #urgent

- #QA, #review-needed, #blocked

Tags also enhance filtering and searching capabilities.

7. Attachments

You can upload files directly into tasks or link to Google Drive, Dropbox, OneDrive, etc. Drag and drop from your desktop or paste URLs. Use attachments for:

- Design mockups

- Briefing documents

- Code snippets

- Feedback forms

◉ **Study the permission of access**

Custom Fields

⊛ 💯 Progress Rate	⟨⎯⎯⎯⎯⎯⎯⎯⎯⎯⎯⎯⎯⎯⎯⎯⎯⎯⎯⎯⟩ 0%
▽ Audit Area	Information Systems
▽ Audit Score	2
⟆ Corrective Actions	Post credentials. Can also be added during the onboarding.
▽ Effort Level	Low
▽ Findings	Minor Noncompliance
▽ Impact	Medium
⟆ Root Cause	Limited access across departments.

Subtasks

+ New Task

Checklists

+ Create Checklist

Attachments   +

Drop your files here to upload

8. Comments

Tasks double as communication hubs. The comment section allows:

- Text responses

- File attachments

- Emojis

- Threaded replies

You can **mention users** (@teammate) or **link to other tasks** (#taskname). Assigned comments are especially powerful—they turn feedback into actionable subtasks.

Custom Fields: Personalizing Your Workflow

ClickUp's **Custom Fields** feature is a game changer. It allows you to add unique data types to tasks, tailored to your team's needs. This flexibility is one of the platform's strongest differentiators.

What Are Custom Fields?

Custom fields are additional columns or inputs that go beyond the standard task options. You define them. You control them. They turn ClickUp into your own project management playground.

Common examples include:

- Budget (currency)
- Estimated time (number)
- Client name (text)
- Campaign phase (dropdown)

- Approval status (checkbox)

Types of Custom Fields

ClickUp offers a wide range of field types, including:

1. **Text** – Short notes or descriptions (e.g., location, platform).

2. **Number** – Quantities, budgets, scores (e.g., "hours worked").

3. **Dropdown** – Predefined categories (e.g., "project phase": Planning, Execution, Review).

4. **Date** – Additional timelines outside of start/due dates.

5. **Checkbox** – Simple yes/no or done/not done toggles.

6. **Label** – Multi-select categories.

7. **Email/Phone/Website** – For CRM-style fields.

8. **Progress Bar** – Visual representation of task completeness.

9. **People** – Assign non-assignees or other responsible parties.

Creating Custom Fields

To add a custom field:

1. Open any task or list.

2. Click **"+ Add Custom Field"**.

3. Choose a field type.

4. Name it and define any options (for dropdowns, labels, etc.).

5. Save and apply to current view or globally across multiple spaces.

Field Management and Templates

You can reuse custom field setups across lists or projects using **Custom Field Manager** or by saving them into **Templates**. This keeps your workspace consistent and efficient.

Use templates for:

- Repetitive project structures

- Recurring client work

- Departmental workflows (HR, Sales, Development)

Practical Examples: Custom Fields in Action

🧠 Marketing Team

- Campaign Name (Text)

- Status (Dropdown: Draft, Scheduled, Live, Archived)

- Platform (Label: Facebook, Google, Email)

- Budget (Currency)

🧱 Construction Project

- Task Location (Text)

- Material Needed (Dropdown)

- Contractor Assigned (People)

- Inspection Date (Date)

- Approved (Checkbox)

👨‍💼 Freelance Business

- Client Name (Text)

- Invoice Sent (Checkbox)

- Hours Worked (Number)

- Payment Status (Dropdown: Unpaid, Paid, Partial)

These fields make it easier to slice and dice your task views into digestible, trackable insights.

Best Practices for Task Details & Custom Fields

☑ Keep It Clean

Don't overload tasks with unnecessary fields—use only what adds value to your process.

☑ Be Consistent

Standardize naming conventions and field types across teams to ensure smooth collaboration.

☑ Use Views to Your Advantage

Custom fields shine in **List View**, where you can sort, group, and filter tasks based on your field data.

☑ Revisit and Revise

As your process evolves, review your custom fields. Are they still useful? Are there redundancies? Don't be afraid to prune.

Conclusion: Building a Task the ClickUp Way

ClickUp empowers you to create rich, fully detailed tasks tailored to your unique workflow. With robust task properties and a dynamic custom field system, you're no longer limited by traditional task structures. Every task can tell a story—where it belongs, who it involves, how urgent it is, when it's due, and what it needs to be completed.

Mastering task details and custom fields doesn't just improve organization—it enhances accountability, transparency, and performance.

In the next section, we'll take these tasks into motion by exploring how **different views** (like Kanban boards and Gantt charts) help visualize your work in powerful, flexible ways.

2.1.2 Priorities, Tags, and Statuses

Managing tasks effectively is at the heart of using ClickUp productively. While creating a task is the first step, the real power of task management lies in how you **organize**, **prioritize**, and **categorize** tasks to ensure your work—and your team's efforts—move forward efficiently. In this section, we'll dive into three powerful features of ClickUp: **Priorities**, **Tags**, and **Statuses**.

Each of these tools plays a specific role:

- **Priorities** help you decide what to focus on next.

- **Tags** make your tasks searchable and context-rich.

- **Statuses** show where each task stands in your workflow.

Let's unpack each of them and see how they can transform your productivity.

Understanding Task Priorities in ClickUp

What Are Priorities?

In ClickUp, **Priorities** are a visual way to indicate how urgent or important a task is. They help your team quickly identify what needs attention first and what can wait. By default, ClickUp offers four priority levels:

- ⚫ **Urgent** – Tasks that are time-sensitive or critical.

- ⚫ **High** – Important tasks that should be completed soon.

- ⚪ **Normal** – Routine or standard tasks.

- ⚫ **Low** – Tasks that are not time-sensitive or can be done later.

These colored flags not only help visually organize your tasks but also aid in filtering and sorting them in different views.

Why Use Priorities?

Imagine managing a list of 50 tasks without knowing which ones need to be done immediately. You'd waste precious time trying to decide what to tackle next. Priorities bring clarity.

Benefits of Prioritizing Tasks:

- **Focus on high-impact work**

- **Avoid decision fatigue**

- **Improve team alignment** on what's truly important

- **Enable better planning** in sprints or work cycles

How to Set Priorities in ClickUp

To set a priority:

1. Open any task.

2. Click on the flag icon (usually located near the top of the task view).

3. Select your desired priority level.

You can also bulk edit task priorities from the List View or Board View.

💡 *Pro Tip:* Use filters to create a view that only shows "Urgent" or "High" priority tasks. This becomes your quick-access work queue.

Best Practices for Using Priorities

- Avoid marking everything as "Urgent"—this defeats the purpose.

- Establish a **team-wide definition** of each priority level.

- Review task priorities at the start of each sprint or work week.

- Use priorities **in combination with due dates** for a more powerful workflow.

Using Tags for Smarter Task Categorization

What Are Tags?

Tags are flexible, **customizable labels** that you can apply to any task. They're not bound to workflow logic like statuses, and they don't have a visual hierarchy like priorities. Instead, tags are used to add context or categorize tasks in creative and dynamic ways.

Examples of Useful Tags:

- #clientA, #marketing, #devops

- #quick-win, #backlog, #research

- #Q2-project, #urgent-legal, #admin

Tags are excellent when you need **cross-cutting filters**—labels that apply across projects, lists, or spaces.

How to Add Tags to Tasks

1. Open a task.

2. Scroll to the **Tag section** on the task sidebar.

3. Click **+ Add tag**, then either select from existing tags or create a new one.

You can also:

- Add tags from **Bulk Actions** in List View.

- Use **automations** to apply tags under specific conditions.

- Filter views by tag combinations.

Managing Tags at Scale

ClickUp allows Workspace Admins to **manage and clean up tags** in the Workspace Settings. This helps maintain consistency and prevents a cluttered tag library.

⚠ *Tip:* Tags are **not case-sensitive**, but you should establish naming conventions. For example, use all lowercase and hyphens (#email-campaign) or underscores (#team_lead).

When to Use Tags vs Custom Fields

Some users confuse tags with custom fields. Here's a quick comparison:

Feature	Tags	Custom Fields
Purpose	Add quick labels	Track structured data
Visibility	Always visible in task	Visible if included in layout
Filtering	Yes	Yes
Flexibility	High	Structured (dropdowns, etc.)
Ideal Use Case	Contextual grouping	Project-specific tracking

Mastering Task Statuses for Workflow Clarity

What Are Task Statuses?

Statuses define the **progression** of a task through your workflow—from idea to completion. They reflect real-time stages and ensure that your whole team understands the current state of work.

In ClickUp, statuses are **customizable per space or folder**, which means you can tailor them to your exact process.

Common Examples of Statuses:

- To Do, In Progress, Review, Completed

- Backlog, Design, Development, QA, Done

- Open, Awaiting Feedback, Blocked, Closed

You can also **group statuses into status categories**:

- Open (e.g., To Do, In Progress)

- Closed (e.g., Done, Completed)

These groupings affect how the task is treated in reports and views like Dashboards or Widgets.

How to Configure Statuses

To customize statuses:

1. Navigate to your **Space** or **Folder** settings.

2. Click on **Statuses**.

3. Add, rename, or rearrange statuses to match your workflow.

4. Assign colors for visual clarity.

You can even **import default workflows** or **save templates** for use across projects.

Statuses vs Checklists vs Subtasks

Let's quickly differentiate:

- **Statuses** reflect **macro-level progress**.

- **Checklists** break down tasks into minor to-dos.

- **Subtasks** are child tasks that can have their own assignees, due dates, and statuses.

Combining all three gives you a layered, flexible system for work management.

Using Statuses Across Views

Every ClickUp view (List, Board, Calendar, Gantt) respects the status configuration.

- **Board View** visualizes tasks by status columns—ideal for agile workflows.

- **Gantt View** tracks tasks and dependencies along a timeline using statuses to color-code progress.

- **List View** gives you quick editing and filtering by status.

Power Tip: Automate Status Changes

ClickUp's **Automations** feature allows you to **change task statuses automatically** based on events like:

- Task created

- Subtask completed

- Due date reached

- Comment added

- Custom field updated

For example: "When all subtasks are complete → change status to 'Ready for Review.'"
Or
"When priority is set to 'Urgent' → assign to project lead."

Putting It All Together

Imagine a marketing team working on multiple campaigns:

- Each task gets a **priority** based on urgency and impact.

- Tags like #social-media, #email, or #design provide thematic categorization.

- Statuses move tasks from Backlog → Planning → In Progress → Done.

Now multiply this by several teams, and you'll see how **a smart use of priorities, tags, and statuses builds the foundation for scalable collaboration** in ClickUp.

Checklist for Best Practices

- ☑ Establish **team conventions** for priority definitions.

- ☑ Use **limited, meaningful tags**—avoid over-tagging.

- ☑ Create **workflow-specific statuses** for each space.

- ☑ Leverage **automations** to reduce manual updates.

- ☑ Combine with **views and filters** for full control.

2.1.3 Due Dates and Recurring Tasks

Introduction

In any task management system, timing is everything. You can have the most detailed tasks, the most intuitive labels, and the most comprehensive notes—but without clear deadlines and recurring functionality, you risk falling behind or missing essential repeat work. ClickUp provides powerful, flexible tools for managing due dates and automating recurring tasks that help individuals and teams stay on track, boost productivity, and reduce the need for manual rescheduling.

This section will walk you through everything you need to know about **setting due dates** and **automating recurring tasks** in ClickUp, from the basics to advanced strategies used by productivity experts and project managers.

Why Due Dates and Recurrence Matter

Deadlines create accountability and structure. When you're managing multiple projects or collaborating with a team, due dates ensure everyone knows what needs to be done—and by when.

Recurring tasks, on the other hand, remove mental clutter. You don't need to remember to re-create the same weekly report task or monthly billing reminder. ClickUp can do it for you, saving time and ensuring nothing slips through the cracks.

1. Setting Due Dates in ClickUp

ClickUp gives you multiple ways to define a task's time frame. Here's how to work with the **Due Date** field effectively:

1.1 Adding a Due Date

To add a due date to any task:

1. Open the task.

2. Locate the calendar icon in the top panel.

3. Click on it to open the date picker.

4. Choose your preferred date.

5. Optionally, set a **start date** if the task spans multiple days.

1.2 Start Date vs. Due Date

-   **Start Date**: When work on the task is expected to begin.

-   **Due Date**: The deadline or final delivery date.

Together, these form a **date range**. This is helpful for time-blocking, resource planning, or when tasks require more than one work session.

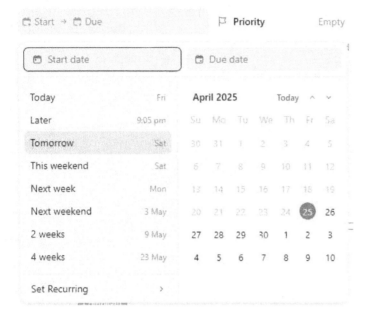

1.3 Adding Times

You can also set specific times for your due dates. ClickUp allows:

- **All-day tasks**, ideal for items without specific timing.

- **Timed tasks**, which allow you to set a specific hour/minute, such as 3:00 PM.

This is especially useful for:

- Meetings

- Appointments

- Deadlines for submissions or client delivery

1.4 Smart Scheduling with ClickUp Views

Once due dates are in place, ClickUp's various views (Calendar, Timeline, Gantt) help you visually plan and adjust. For example:

- **Calendar View** shows your upcoming deadlines across a month or week.

- **Timeline View** lets you see task durations and overlap.

- **Gantt View** is ideal for project planning and understanding dependencies.

---

2. Recurring Tasks in ClickUp

Tasks that happen regularly—daily standups, weekly reports, monthly invoices—should not be manually re-created. Instead, use **recurring task automation** in ClickUp.

2.1 Creating a Recurring Task

To set a task to recur:

1. Open the task.

2. Click the **calendar icon** to open the date picker.

3. Click **Set Recurring** at the bottom of the calendar.

4. Define the recurrence rules:

   o **Repeats**: Daily, weekly, monthly, yearly, or custom.

   o **Starts**: When the task is due, completed, or created.

   o **Ends**: After a number of times, on a certain date, or never.

2.2 Customizing Recurrence

You can tailor the recurrence pattern extensively:

- Repeat **every X days/weeks/months** (e.g., every 2 weeks)

- Choose **specific days** (e.g., Mondays and Thursdays)

- **Only recur after task is completed**—ideal for tasks that shouldn't reappear until done.

- **Reschedule missed tasks**—this ensures nothing gets forgotten even if delayed.

2.3 Recurrence Triggers Explained

ClickUp provides three trigger options:

- **On schedule**: New task is created regardless of whether the previous one was completed.

- **When marked complete**: Next instance appears only after you finish the current one.

- **When created**: A new recurring task is generated after the current task is first created.

Each has its use:

- **Project management** teams often prefer "when marked complete."

- **Calendar-based workflows** might opt for "on schedule."

---

3. Best Practices for Managing Due Dates and Recurring Tasks

Use Start and Due Dates Together

Adding both allows you to:

- Visualize the actual work period

- Improve Gantt and Timeline clarity

- Communicate workload expectations better

Use Time Estimates with Due Dates

Pairing due dates with **time estimates** helps in planning realistic timelines and understanding resource allocation.

Combine with Priorities and Statuses

Due today? High priority? In progress? These attributes together create a complete view of urgency and importance.

Avoid Overusing Recurring Tasks

While recurring tasks are powerful, use them intentionally. Too many recurring tasks can:

- Lead to notification overload

- Create a cluttered task view

- Introduce "task fatigue" if not well-managed

Make sure to regularly **audit and adjust** your recurring task library.

4. Use Cases for Recurring Tasks

To help you visualize, here are real-life examples:

Personal Productivity

- Weekly review (Every Sunday at 6 PM)
- Daily journaling (Every day at 8 AM)
- Monthly goal check-in

Team Management

- Weekly team meetings
- Bi-weekly sprint planning
- Monthly performance reports

Client Work

- Invoicing (1st of every month)
- Project check-ins
- Weekly content publishing reminders

Maintenance and Admin

- Backup database (every Friday)
- Clean up workspace (last Friday of each month)
- Software updates (quarterly)

5. Advanced Tips and Troubleshooting

Using Recurrence with Templates

Combine task templates with recurrence to generate pre-filled tasks each time. This is ideal for:

- SOPs (Standard Operating Procedures)

- Event planning

- Recurring checklists

Automate Workflow Using Automations + Recurrence

You can trigger additional actions when a recurring task is created:

- Assign it to a user

- Add a specific tag

- Move it to a designated list or folder

Dealing with Missed Recurring Tasks

ClickUp gives you options for handling missed recurring tasks:

- **Skip it** (let it go)

- **Recreate it** (add a backdated copy)

- **Push it forward** (reschedule the recurrence)

Choose your strategy based on context. For high-stakes tasks, auto-rescheduling is often best.

6. Conclusion

Due dates and recurring tasks are the heartbeat of effective task management in ClickUp. When used thoughtfully, they transform how you approach time and productivity. From setting precise deadlines to automating repetitive work, ClickUp's features empower you to focus less on remembering and more on doing.

Mastering due dates ensures that your tasks are aligned with priorities and project goals. Leveraging recurring tasks, meanwhile, reduces cognitive load and builds repeatable systems for long-term success.

Whether you're managing a personal to-do list, coordinating a marketing campaign, or leading a remote team, due dates and recurrence can turn chaos into clarity—and turn ClickUp into your ultimate productivity partner.

2.2 Working with Views

2.2.1 List View

The **List View** is the cornerstone of ClickUp task management. It's where many users begin—and for good reason. Structured, organized, and familiar (especially to those coming from spreadsheets or to-do apps), the List View offers a linear, no-frills way to interact with your work that is both powerful and intuitive.

In this section, we'll dive deep into what makes the List View essential, how to customize it to fit your needs, and best practices to help you and your team manage tasks more efficiently.

What Is the List View?

At its core, the **List View** is a vertically structured layout that displays tasks in a checklist or spreadsheet-like format. Tasks are presented in rows, and each row contains data such as:

- Task name
- Status
- Assignee
- Due date
- Priority
- Time tracked
- Custom fields

The List View is ideal for seeing tasks grouped under a specific folder or list and provides a clean, straightforward layout for reviewing and managing your workflow.

Navigating the List View

When you open a list in ClickUp, the List View will likely be the default view unless you've configured it otherwise. It looks much like a project table or a to-do list:

- The **left column** features checkboxes, allowing you to mark tasks complete.

- The **main body** displays task names.

- The **right columns** include metadata—assignees, due dates, priorities, and any custom fields you've added.

You can also **sort**, **filter**, and **group** tasks in this view, giving you maximum flexibility in how your tasks are displayed and interacted with.

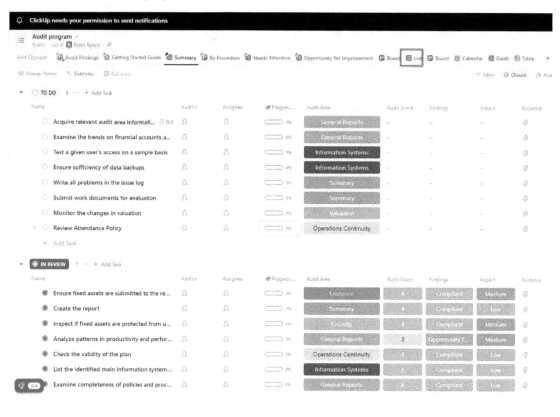

🛠 Customizing Your List View

ClickUp gives you the ability to tailor the List View according to your preferences. Here's what you can customize:

● Columns

You can add or remove columns based on the data points you want to view:

- Click the **"+" button** to add a new column.
- Choose from standard fields (like Priority or Due Date) or **Custom Fields** that you or your team have defined.
- Rearrange columns by dragging the headers.

This makes it easy to create a view tailored for **sales pipelines**, **content calendars**, **bug trackers**, or whatever your workflow needs.

● Grouping

The "Group By" feature allows you to segment tasks by:

- **Status** (e.g., To Do, In Progress, Done)
- **Assignee**
- **Priority**
- **Custom Fields** (e.g., Client, Department, Sprint)

Grouping is especially helpful in team settings—letting you quickly see who's working on what, or where a bottleneck may be occurring.

● Sorting

Click the top of any column to **sort** tasks ascending or descending. You might sort by:

- Due Date (soonest first)
- Priority (high to low)
- Status (alphabetically or by workflow)

Sorting is real-time and specific to your personal view—meaning you won't disrupt what others see unless you're sharing the view intentionally.

● Creating a Custom Saved View

Once you've tailored your List View with the right columns, grouping, sorting, and filters, you can **save it** as a custom view. This is especially useful when:

- You want a "My Tasks" view that only shows tasks assigned to you

- Your manager wants a "Team Overview" grouped by assignee

- You're tracking a client project and want to isolate deliverables

To save your configuration:

1. Click the **View Options** menu (three dots).

2. Choose **Save as New View**.

3. Name the view and decide whether to make it **default**, **shared**, or **private**.

Using Templates for List Views

ClickUp allows you to **save your List View as a template** so it can be reused across other spaces or folders. This is a huge time-saver for recurring processes, such as:

- Onboarding new employees

- Product development sprints

- Weekly content publishing schedules

To save a List View template:

1. Configure your view as desired.

2. Click the three-dot menu > **Save as Template**.

3. Name it and choose where it can be applied.

Collaborating in List View

The List View isn't just for solo work—it's built for team collaboration. Here's how you can collaborate right from the view:

Comments

Each task in List View has a comments section. From here, you can:

- @Mention teammates

- Assign comments (as action items)

- Embed links, files, and rich formatting

📎 Attachments

You can attach files directly to tasks from the List View interface, ensuring all related documentation is centralized.

🚨 Notifications

ClickUp will notify you when:

- A task you're watching is updated

- You're mentioned in a comment

- A due date is approaching

These notifications help you stay in the loop without needing to switch views.

📊 Use Cases for List View

Let's look at some real-world examples of how List View can be used across different industries and roles:

🔬 Project Management

- Group by Status to monitor progress

- Sort by Due Date for timeline accuracy

- Filter by Task Owner to delegate efficiently

✏️ Content Creation

- Use Custom Fields like "Article Type" or "Word Count"

- Group by Status: Idea, Draft, Review, Published

- Add deadlines and assign editors for review

Sales and CRM

- Use List View as a pipeline tracker
- Add Custom Fields like Deal Size, Stage, or Client Name
- Group by Rep or Status for weekly meetings

Marketing Campaigns

- Track deliverables across channels (Email, Ads, Social)
- Assign due dates and group by campaign type
- Tag stakeholders and agencies involved

Integrating Other Features into List View

Even in List View, you're not limited to static data. You can integrate:

- **ClickApps** (like Time Tracking, Tags, Automations)
- **Custom Fields** (rich text, dropdowns, checkboxes)
- **Dependencies** (to map out task sequences)

This transforms the List View from a static checklist into a **dynamic command center**.

Best Practices for Using List View

1. **Keep it Clean** – Avoid overwhelming views by hiding unused columns.
2. **Use Filters Liberally** – Build focused lists for review, meetings, or sprint planning.
3. **Color Code with Tags** – Use tags or priorities to visually organize your list.
4. **Save Views for Reuse** – Standardize views for the whole team.
5. **Combine with Automations** – Trigger updates or status changes directly from the list.

🔍 Troubleshooting List View Issues

If something feels off in your List View, check for:

- **Filters** that might be hiding tasks

- **Sorting or Grouping conflicts** causing strange task order

- **Permissions**—some tasks may not appear due to access limits

- **View Sharing Settings**—you may be seeing a private or outdated view

---

📌 Summary: Why List View Matters

To recap, List View is:

- **Flexible** – Customize to match any workflow

- **Clear** – Organizes data in a readable format

- **Collaborative** – Enables communication, tracking, and task ownership

- **Powerful** – When combined with ClickApps, filters, and templates

Whether you're managing a team, flying solo, or somewhere in between, mastering the List View will elevate your ClickUp experience from basic to brilliant.

2.2.2 Board (Kanban) View

Introduction to the Board (Kanban) View

The **Board View** in ClickUp is a visual, card-based layout that enables users to manage tasks by status, custom field, or other categories using drag-and-drop functionality. It's based on the **Kanban** methodology, which originated in lean manufacturing and later became a staple in Agile software development. Today, it's widely used across industries to manage workflows with clarity and flexibility.

The Kanban-style board view is especially helpful when you want to visualize the flow of tasks from one stage to another — think **"To Do," "In Progress," "Review," "Done"**, or any custom workflow that suits your team. In ClickUp, the Board View transforms static task lists into dynamic workflows that are easy to interact with and customize.

Why Use the Board View?

The Board View is a powerful choice when:

- You want a **visual overview** of task progress

- You need a **clear, drag-and-drop workflow**

- Your team follows **Agile**, **Scrum**, or **Kanban** methodologies

- You're managing multiple tasks with changing **statuses** or **categories**

- You prefer **columns over rows** for cognitive clarity

Whether you're running a content production pipeline, managing client requests, or developing software, the Board View provides a tangible interface for seeing how work is moving forward (or getting stuck).

Getting Started with the Board View

To access the Board View in ClickUp:

1. **Navigate to a Space, Folder, or List**

2. In the top navigation bar, click the **+ View** button

3. Choose **Board View** from the list

4. Name your view and decide whether to **pin it** or make it **default**

5. Click **Add View**

Once created, your Board View is ready to be configured and customized to suit your needs.

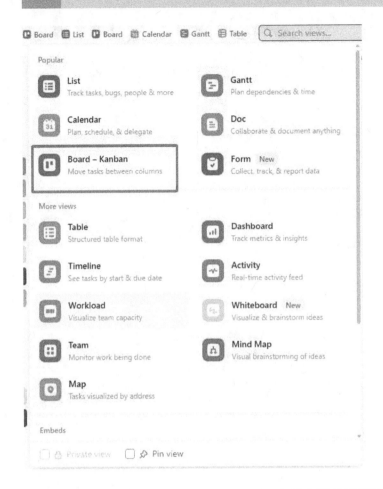

Understanding Columns in Board View

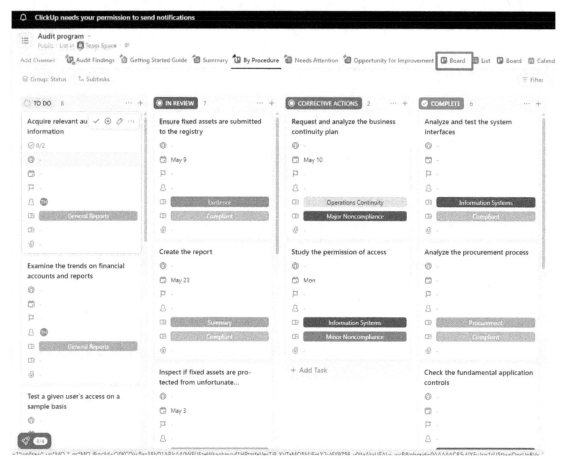

Each **column** in the Board View represents a grouping of tasks. By default, tasks are grouped by **Status**, but you can also group them by:

- **Assignee**

- **Priority**

- **Due Date**

- **Custom Fields**

Grouping by **Status** is the most popular option, as it reflects the stages of task completion. For example:

To Do In Progress Review Done

You can also create **custom statuses** for specialized workflows such as:

| Backlog | Designing | Editing | Publishing | Complete |

Customizing the Board View

ClickUp allows extensive customization of your Board View. Key customization options include:

1. Grouping Options

Choose what you want your columns to represent:

- **Status** – Default, commonly used for task progress
- **Assignee** – Group tasks by who is responsible
- **Priority** – See high, medium, and low-priority tasks
- **Custom Fields** – E.g., project phases, departments, content types

To change the grouping, click the **"Group by"** dropdown menu on the top-right of the Board View.

2. Sorting Options

You can sort the cards in each column by:

- Task name
- Priority
- Due date
- Start date
- Custom fields
- Date created
- Last updated

This helps you bring the most urgent or relevant tasks to the top.

3. Filtering Tasks

Use filters to control what appears in your view. For example:

- Only tasks assigned to me

- Tasks due this week

- Tasks with a specific tag or label

- Tasks within a certain priority level

Filters are **stackable**, meaning you can apply multiple filters to hone in on exactly what you want to see.

Creating and Managing Tasks in Board View

You can **create tasks directly within any column** by clicking the **+ New Task** button at the bottom of a column.

To create a task:

1. Click **+ New Task**

2. Enter a name and hit **Enter**

3. Click on the card to open task details

4. Fill in details like:

    o   Description

    o   Assignee

    o   Priority

    o   Due Date

    o   Subtasks

    o   Comments

Tasks created in Board View will automatically adopt the status (or grouping) of the column they're created in.

Drag-and-Drop Functionality

The **drag-and-drop** nature of the Board View is one of its best features. Simply click and hold on a task card, then move it to another column to:

- Change its status

- Reassign it (if grouped by assignee)

- Update its custom field (if grouped by custom fields)

ClickUp automatically updates the underlying data. For example, if you drag a task from "To Do" to "In Progress," its status changes to "In Progress" immediately — no need to edit the task manually.

Using Board View for Agile Project Management

If you're working in **Agile**, you can use the Board View as your **Scrum board** or **Kanban board**. Here's how:

Set Up:

- **Columns** = Sprint stages (e.g., To Do, In Progress, Review, Done)

- **Cards** = User stories, bugs, or tasks

- Use **tags** or **custom fields** for epics or categories

- Apply **filters** to display current sprint only

Weekly Standups:

- Use Board View during meetings to discuss task movement

- Drag cards across columns as updates are shared

- Quickly identify blockers or bottlenecks

Sprint Reviews:

- Group by **assignee** to see individual contributions

- Group by **priority** to evaluate if goals were aligned

Integrating Board View with Other Features

The beauty of ClickUp lies in how different features work together. Here are a few integrations worth exploring:

- **Automations**: Automatically move a task to "In Progress" when a subtask is completed

- **Custom Statuses**: Tailor stages to your process

- **Dashboards**: Add widgets showing how many tasks are in each column

- **Time Tracking**: View which tasks have time logs directly on the cards

- **Checklists and Subtasks**: Visualize task depth right from the card preview

- **Recurring Tasks**: Set tasks to reset weekly or monthly as needed

Tips for Using Board View Effectively

Here are some best practices to optimize your workflow:

1. **Limit Columns**: Keep your workflow simple and easy to follow. Too many columns lead to visual clutter.

2. **Use Colors**: Tags, priorities, and custom statuses can be color-coded for quick scanning.

3. **Pin Your Board View**: If Board View is your go-to, pin it as the default.

4. **Create Multiple Board Views**: One for each use case — e.g., one grouped by assignee, another by priority.

5. **Maintain Discipline**: Encourage your team to update task statuses consistently.

6. **Review Weekly**: Use your board to conduct weekly reviews and retrospectives.

Common Use Cases for Board View

Here are examples of how different teams can use the Board View:

Team Type	Example Workflow
Marketing	To Do → Draft → Review → Scheduled → Published
Design	Brief Received → Design Started → In Review → Approved
Sales	Lead → Contacted → Demo Scheduled → Proposal Sent → Closed
Product	Idea → Backlog → In Sprint → QA → Released
HR	Job Posted → Applications Received → Interviews → Hired

Troubleshooting and FAQs

Q: My Board View is not showing all tasks. Why?
A: Check your filters and ensure no conditions are hiding tasks. Also, confirm that you're looking in the correct List or Folder.

Q: Can I have more than one Board View?
A: Yes. You can create multiple views with different settings and filters.

Q: Can I view subtasks in Board View?
A: Yes, you can toggle subtasks on or off in the view settings.

Q: Can I drag and drop tasks between groups if grouped by a custom field?
A: Yes, and the field will update automatically when you move the task.

Final Thoughts

The Board (Kanban) View in ClickUp offers an intuitive, flexible, and powerful way to manage tasks visually. Whether you're tracking your daily to-dos or running enterprise-level projects, mastering this view will drastically improve your ability to manage workflows, identify roadblocks, and keep your team aligned.

As you explore more features in ClickUp, you'll find that the Board View often becomes the heart of your daily operations — the place where tasks live, move, and get done.

Up next, we'll dive into the **Calendar, Timeline, and Gantt Views**, so you can continue to visualize and manage your tasks from every angle.

2.2.3 Calendar, Timeline, and Gantt Views

Efficient task management in ClickUp isn't just about creating to-dos and checking boxes—it's about **visualizing your work** in the way that makes the most sense for your goals and workflow. ClickUp provides multiple view options to help you see your tasks from different angles. Among the most powerful of these are the **Calendar**, **Timeline**, and **Gantt** views. These three are essential for managing time-sensitive projects, allocating resources, and keeping teams aligned on deliverables.

This section will walk you through each view in detail, show you how to set them up, and help you determine when and how to use each for maximum productivity.

Calendar View: Managing Deadlines with Clarity

The **Calendar View** is a straightforward yet powerful tool that displays your tasks across days, weeks, or months. It's the perfect option for planning your schedule, tracking deadlines, and managing time-blocked activities.

Key Features of Calendar View

- **Drag-and-Drop Interface:** Easily reschedule tasks by dragging them across dates. This is great for adjusting deadlines on the fly.

- **Multiple Date Support:** If a task has both a start and due date, it will span across multiple days.

- **Recurring Tasks Visibility:** See repeating tasks laid out clearly across your timeline.

- **Filters and Sorting:** You can filter by assignee, task status, priority, tags, or custom fields.

- **Color Coding:** Tasks can be color-coded based on status or priority for quick visual scanning.

Use Cases for Calendar View

- **Freelancers** planning weekly deliverables

- **Marketing teams** organizing a content calendar

- **Product teams** managing sprints and release cycles

- **Customer support** scheduling daily follow-ups and calls

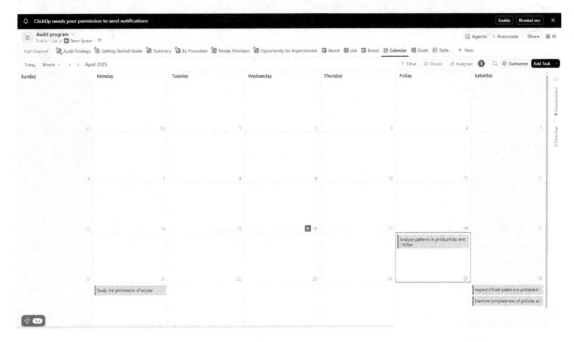

How to Set Up Calendar View in ClickUp

1. Navigate to any list, folder, or space.

2. Click on the "+ View" button.

3. Choose **Calendar** and name the view (optional).

4. Apply filters if necessary (e.g., "Only show tasks assigned to me").

5. Start interacting with your tasks in calendar format.

Tips for Using Calendar View Effectively

*   Use **start and due dates** instead of just due dates to plan workloads more precisely.

*   Combine the calendar view with the **Workload** view to assess team capacity.

*   If you have many tasks, narrow your calendar to **Week** or **Day** mode for clarity.

Timeline View: Seeing the Flow of Work

The **Timeline View** gives you a horizontal, time-based layout similar to a simplified Gantt chart. It's perfect for **planning, sequencing, and tracking workflows**, especially when task duration and overlap are important.

Key Features of Timeline View

- **Stretchable Tasks:** Click and drag either side of a task bar to extend or reduce its duration.

- **Dependencies:** Visual indicators of task relationships (e.g., Task B can't start until Task A is complete).

- **Grouping and Sorting:** Group tasks by assignee, status, or any custom field (like department or category).

- **Zoom Levels:** View tasks by day, week, or month for high-level or granular planning.

- **Milestones:** Mark major checkpoints or deliverables to track project progression.

Use Cases for Timeline View

- **Project managers** mapping out the critical path

- **Event planners** sequencing event logistics and staff duties

- **Design and development teams** balancing overlapping sprints

- **HR departments** visualizing onboarding timelines

How to Create a Timeline View

1. Open a folder or list where the relevant tasks live.

2. Click the **+ View** button and select **Timeline**.

3. Name your view and choose your grouping method.

4. Start dragging tasks to align them along your timeline.

Best Practices for Timeline View

- Set **dependencies** to ensure your workflow logic is solid (e.g., one task waits on another).

- Use **grouping by assignee** to spot resource overloads and adjust workloads.

- Don't forget to update task dates regularly—this view is only as accurate as your data.

Gantt View: Full Project Planning Power

The **Gantt View** is where ClickUp becomes a true powerhouse for **project planning and tracking**. It's the most feature-rich view for complex timelines, giving you the ability to manage dependencies, critical paths, milestones, and team schedules all in one place.

Key Features of Gantt View

- **Task Dependencies and Path Tracking:** Draw arrows between tasks to set relationships; see how changes affect other tasks.

- **Critical Path Identification:** Quickly view the chain of tasks that directly impacts the final deadline.

- **Progress Bar:** Visualize task completion in real time.

- **Milestones:** Set important markers to signal achievements or handoffs.
- **Multiple Project Overlay:** Combine several lists or folders to see cross-project timelines.

Use Cases for Gantt View

- **Agencies** juggling multiple clients and campaigns
- **Product development** from idea to launch
- **Software projects** with complex interdependencies
- **Construction teams** managing site work, equipment, and staffing

How to Create and Use the Gantt View

1. Go to your folder or space.
2. Click **+ View** and choose **Gantt**.
3. Select which tasks to display.
4. Use the timeline to create, extend, or link tasks.
5. Watch ClickUp automatically update task relationships and progress.

Gantt View Functional Highlights

- **Slack Time Calculation:** Shows how much wiggle room you have between tasks.
- **Color Options:** Customize task colors to reflect status, assignee, or type.
- **Zoom In/Out:** Toggle between daily, weekly, and monthly views.
- **Collapse/Expand Hierarchies:** Simplify complex trees of tasks and subtasks.

When to Use Calendar, Timeline, or Gantt

View Type	Best For	Complexity	Team Size
Calendar	Deadline visibility, personal planning	Low	Any
Timeline	Overlapping tasks, team workload	Medium	Small to Medium
Gantt	Full project management, dependencies	High	Medium to Large

Integrating Views with Other ClickUp Features

- **ClickApps:** Use features like **Time Tracking**, **Milestones**, or **Dependencies** to enhance view functionality.

- **Automations:** Trigger actions based on changes in views (e.g., when a due date changes, notify the team).

- **Docs & Comments:** Reference linked Docs or comment threads within a task bar to access context without switching screens.

- **Dashboards:** Create visual dashboards that pull data from these views to track KPIs and progress reports.

Common Mistakes to Avoid

- **Over-relying on a single view:** You may miss key insights by not switching between Calendar, Timeline, and Gantt.

- **Neglecting date updates:** These views are only useful if tasks have correct start and due dates.

- **Not setting dependencies:** Especially in Gantt view, this can lead to broken workflows or unrealistic timelines.

- **Under-communicating changes:** Use comments or ClickUp notifications when rescheduling critical tasks.

Conclusion: Choosing the Right View for the Right Job

Each view in ClickUp serves a unique purpose:

- **Calendar** brings clarity to your schedule.

- **Timeline** shows the flow of your team's work.

- **Gantt** empowers you to manage complex, multi-step projects with confidence.

Learning how and **when** to use each view will give you the edge in managing both small tasks and large initiatives with finesse. As your team grows or projects become more layered, these views evolve with you, ensuring ClickUp remains not just your to-do list—but your **command center**.

2.3 Subtasks, Checklists, and Dependencies

2.3.1 Using Subtasks Effectively

Introduction

Subtasks are an essential building block in ClickUp that empower users to break down large, complex tasks into manageable pieces. They help create structure, improve clarity, delegate work efficiently, and track progress granularly. While tasks represent high-level objectives, **subtasks serve as the actionable steps that drive completion.**

In this section, we'll explore how to use subtasks effectively in ClickUp—from creation and organization to assignment, visualization, and reporting. We'll also discuss common pitfalls and best practices to ensure subtasks contribute meaningfully to productivity, not complexity.

What Are Subtasks in ClickUp?

A **subtask** in ClickUp is a task nested within a parent task. It has all the capabilities of a regular task—such as due dates, assignees, priorities, statuses, and custom fields—but is designed to support the completion of its parent task.

Think of it as a "task within a task." For example, if your main task is **"Launch Website"**, subtasks might include:

- "Write homepage content"
- "Design landing page"
- "Set up hosting and domain"
- "Conduct pre-launch testing"

Each of these subtasks can be tracked independently while still rolling up to the larger goal.

Benefits of Using Subtasks

Using subtasks effectively in ClickUp offers several key benefits:

1. **Better Task Organization:** Break complex projects into digestible components.

2. **Focused Work Allocation:** Assign individual responsibilities to different team members.

3. **Independent Tracking:** Monitor the progress, time, and completion of individual subtasks.

4. **Improved Accountability:** Ensure clarity about who is doing what and by when.

5. **Clear Dependencies:** Sequence work logically and avoid bottlenecks.

How to Create a Subtask in ClickUp

Creating a subtask in ClickUp is easy and intuitive. Here's how to do it:

Option 1: From Within the Parent Task

1. Open the parent task.

2. Click the **"+ Subtask"** button at the bottom of the task window.

3. Enter the subtask name.

4. Click **Enter** to create it.

5. Click on the subtask to open and customize it (add assignee, due date, priority, etc.)

Option 2: Use the Command Center

1. Press **Cmd/Ctrl + K** to open the command center.

2. Type **"Create Subtask"**, and ClickUp will prompt you to choose a parent task.

Option 3: Drag-and-Drop

- In **List View**, drag a task into another task to automatically make it a subtask.

Best Practices for Creating Subtasks

Here are proven strategies to make your subtasks work **for you**, not against you:

1. Keep Subtasks Actionable

Each subtask should represent a clear, actionable step—not a vague concept. Instead of "Marketing," use "Create Instagram Ad Copy" or "Schedule Newsletter Campaign."

2. Limit the Number of Subtasks

Too many subtasks can be overwhelming. Avoid turning a single task into a micro-project unless necessary. If you exceed 7–10 subtasks, consider creating a new task or list altogether.

3. Use Subtasks for Ownership and Delegation

Assign different subtasks to different team members. This helps split workload logically and ensures everyone is aware of their role in the bigger picture.

4. Add Deadlines to Subtasks

Every subtask should have a **start and due date**. This allows ClickUp to properly reflect progress in Gantt charts, calendars, and time reports.

5. Use Priority and Status

Customize the **priority** (Low, Normal, High, Urgent) and set appropriate **statuses** for each subtask. Don't just rely on parent task completion.

Customizing Subtasks for Workflow Efficiency

ClickUp gives you several powerful features to make subtasks more dynamic and personalized:

☑ Custom Fields

You can assign specific custom fields to subtasks just like regular tasks. For example:

- Estimated time

- Cost

- Stage

- Approval status

🔁 Recurring Subtasks

Just like tasks, subtasks can recur. This is useful for repeatable steps like "Run QA Test" or "Weekly Report Review."

📎 Attachments and Comments

You can attach files directly to subtasks, tag team members, and start threaded discussions right within the subtask.

🗓 Start and Due Dates

Always provide a clear timeline. With the **Timeline View**, you can visualize when subtasks need to be done in relation to one another.

Visualizing and Managing Subtasks

ClickUp offers different ways to manage and view your subtasks based on how you like to work:

1. List View

Shows subtasks nested under their parent tasks. Great for seeing all the details in one glance.

2. Board View

Shows subtasks in Kanban-style columns. You can drag them between statuses visually.

3. Gantt View

Allows you to see subtasks over time. Ideal for scheduling and resource planning.

4. Me Mode

Use "Me Mode" to only see tasks and subtasks assigned to you—perfect for daily planning.

Tracking Progress with Subtasks

ClickUp offers smart progress tracking for parent tasks based on subtasks:

- **Progress Bar**: Parent task progress is auto-calculated by how many subtasks are marked complete.

- **Roll-Up Fields**: Fields like time spent, cost, and task count can roll up from subtasks to parent tasks.

- **Dependencies**: You can set subtasks as blocking or waiting on one another.

Subtasks vs. Checklists: When to Use What?

A common question is: *Should I use subtasks or checklists?*

Use Subtasks When...	Use Checklists When...
Tasks require separate assignees	Simple, single-person to-do items
Each step has its own deadline	Tasks are done all at once
You want to track time per step	You don't need time tracking
Subtasks affect project timeline	Checklist is internal to one task

You can also **convert checklist items into subtasks** in ClickUp—making it flexible depending on how your work evolves.

Common Pitfalls (And How to Avoid Them)

1. **Over-Nesting Subtasks**
   - Avoid creating sub-sub-subtasks unless truly needed. Deep nesting can make it hard to track work.

2. **Subtasks with No Assignee or Due Date**
   - These can slip through the cracks. Always assign and date subtasks.

3. **Using Subtasks as Projects**
   - If a subtask feels too big, it probably deserves to be a task, list, or even a folder.

Subtasks in Team Collaboration

When working with teams, subtasks become more than a checklist—they're part of your **communication process**. Here's how to integrate subtasks into your team culture:

- Assign subtasks during meetings for clarity

- Use subtasks as "mini-contracts" of responsibility

- Follow up via task comments and use **assigned comments**

- Link subtasks to related tasks via relationships

Real-World Examples

Example 1: Marketing Campaign Launch

Parent Task: Launch June Email Campaign
Subtasks:

- Write Email Copy (Assigned to Copywriter)

- Design Visual Assets (Assigned to Designer)

- Schedule Campaign in Email Platform (Assigned to Marketing Lead)

- QA and Final Approval (Assigned to Manager)

Example 2: Software Feature Release

Parent Task: Release v2.1.0 Feature Update
Subtasks:

- Finalize Feature List

- Write Release Notes

- Code Freeze

- QA Testing

- Push to Production

Integrating Subtasks into Automations

Subtasks work beautifully with ClickUp Automations. For example:

- **When a parent task is marked complete**, mark all subtasks as complete.

- **When a subtask is overdue**, notify the assignee.

- **When a subtask is created**, assign it to a specific person automatically.

This saves time and ensures consistent workflows.

Final Thoughts

When used correctly, subtasks can become the engine of structured, focused, and efficient work. They allow teams to zoom in and out—from high-level objectives to tiny details—with clarity. However, the key is **intentionality**. Subtasks should never be created just for the sake of it. Instead, they should serve a purpose, align with the overall workflow, and enhance collaboration.

By implementing best practices and leveraging ClickUp's smart features, you can transform subtasks from simple task fragments into powerful productivity tools.

2.3.2 Creating and Managing Checklists

In project management, even the most organized tasks can unravel when small details are missed. That's where **checklists** come in—they offer a structured way to break down a task into actionable, bite-sized steps, ensuring that nothing gets forgotten. In ClickUp, checklists are one of the most powerful, yet often underutilized, features available to help you manage both simple and complex workflows with greater accuracy and clarity.

This section will guide you through the process of **creating, customizing, and managing checklists** within ClickUp, along with real-world use cases, best practices, and productivity tips that will help you and your team work smarter, not harder.

☑ What Is a Checklist in ClickUp?

In ClickUp, a **checklist** is a to-do list embedded within a task. It allows users to divide a single task into smaller steps, making it easier to manage detailed processes. Each checklist item can be marked as complete, assigned to a person, given a due date, or even converted into a standalone task if it becomes more complex.

Unlike **subtasks**, which are more structured and independent (with their own statuses, fields, and workflows), checklists are lightweight, fast to create, and perfect for routine or procedural steps.

📋 When to Use Checklists Instead of Subtasks

It's important to know **when** to use a checklist and when to use subtasks. Here's a quick guideline:

Use Checklists When...	Use Subtasks When...
Steps are small and procedural	Steps are complex and require more structure
Tasks don't require different assignees	Each step needs to be assigned to different people
You don't need separate statuses for steps	You need custom statuses or workflows per step
You want a quick way to break a task into parts	You want to track detailed progress for each part

For example, in a **"Publish Blog Post"** task, a checklist might include:

- Proofread content
- Add images
- Format headings
- Run SEO audit
- Schedule post

Each item doesn't need its own task—just a checkbox to confirm it's been done.

🛠 How to Create a Checklist in ClickUp

Creating a checklist is simple and intuitive. Here's how to do it:

Step 1: Open or Create a Task

You can only create checklists inside a task, so either create a new task or open an existing one.

Step 2: Add a Checklist

- In the task view, scroll to the **Checklist** section.

- Click **"+ Add Checklist"**.

- Name your checklist (e.g., "Launch Steps", "QA Review").

Step 3: Add Items

- Type in each step of your process, pressing **Enter** after each item.

- You can **drag-and-drop** to reorder items.

Step 4: Assign Checklist Items (Optional)

- Hover over an item and click the **assignee icon** to assign it to a team member.

- You can also set **due dates** for individual items by clicking the **calendar icon**.

Step 5: Mark Items Complete

- Click the checkbox next to an item when it's done.

- ClickUp will automatically track completion progress (e.g., 3/5 items completed).

Advanced Checklist Features

ClickUp takes checklists to another level with a suite of smart features:

Nested Checklists

- You can create **checklists within checklists** for multi-layered processes.
- Ideal for complex tasks that still don't need subtasks.

Example:
Checklist: *"Marketing Prep"*

- Write draft
    o Grammar check
    o Style check
- Schedule newsletter

Convert to Task

- If a checklist item becomes too complex, you can **convert it into a full task**.
- Right-click (or click the three dots next to the item), then choose **"Convert to Task"**.

Checklist Templates

- Reuse standard checklists for recurring processes.
- Save any checklist as a **template** by clicking the three-dot menu next to its title.
- Use templates for things like onboarding, QA procedures, or publishing workflows.

Progress Indicators

- ClickUp visually shows your checklist completion progress.
- This is especially useful when multiple people are involved in a single task.

Best Practices for Managing Checklists

To get the most out of ClickUp checklists, follow these tried-and-true tips:

1. Be Specific and Actionable

Write checklist items as **clear action verbs** (e.g., "Send approval email" instead of just "Email").

2. Keep Items Short and Focused

If a step has multiple parts or seems overwhelming, break it into multiple checklist items or consider making it a subtask.

3. Use Checklist Templates for Repeated Work

Templates save time, reduce errors, and ensure consistency across projects.

4. Assign and Schedule When Necessary

If you're collaborating with others, **assign ownership** and set deadlines so nothing falls through the cracks.

5. Integrate with Automations

Use ClickUp Automations to mark tasks complete when all checklist items are finished.

Example: *"When all checklist items are done → mark task as complete"*

Use Cases Across Different Teams

ClickUp checklists are versatile. Here's how different departments can use them:

Marketing

- Campaign launch steps
- Social media scheduling checklist
- Content review process

Product Development

- Sprint planning to-dos
- QA and testing steps

- Feature deployment tasks

HR and Operations

- New hire onboarding

- Employee offboarding process

- Interview checklist

Design and Creative

- Client design approval flow

- Final file packaging

- Asset version review

Checklist vs. Subtask: A Decision Tree

To help you decide whether to use a checklist or a subtask, follow this mini decision tree:

Does the item require its own status, attachments, or due date?
➤ Yes → Use a subtask
➤ No → Use a checklist item

Will multiple people work on different parts?
➤ Yes → Consider subtasks or assigning checklist items
➤ No → A checklist will work fine

Do you need to report on progress at the step level?
➤ Yes → Subtasks provide better tracking
➤ No → Checklists are faster and simpler

Common Questions About ClickUp Checklists

Q: Can I assign multiple people to a checklist item?
A: Currently, you can only assign **one person** per checklist item. For collaborative items, consider breaking the step down or using subtasks.

Q: Do checklist items appear on dashboards or reports?
A: Not directly, but checklist progress contributes to **task completion stats**, which are reflected in dashboards.

Q: Can I reorder entire checklists within a task?
A: Yes! Drag-and-drop the checklist title to rearrange multiple checklists in a task.

Q: Are there keyboard shortcuts for managing checklists?
A: Yes—**Enter** to add a new item, **Shift + Enter** to create a new line in the same item, and **Tab** to indent (create nested items).

🚀 Take Action: Start Using Checklists Today

Here's how to apply what you've learned:

1. Audit your current workflows. Where are you repeating small steps?

2. Replace manual reminders with checklist templates.

3. Assign ownership and track progress.

4. Review and improve your checklists regularly.

Checklists in ClickUp may seem small, but their impact is massive. They're not just to-do items—they're a tool for **consistency, quality, and peace of mind**.

Ready to take your task management to the next level? In the next section, we'll explore **task relationships and dependencies**, so you can build workflows that adapt and respond to real-world complexity.

Let's keep going 🚀

2.3.3 Task Relationships and Dependencies

In any project—whether it's a simple to-do list or a complex product launch—understanding how individual tasks relate to one another is key to success. When working in ClickUp, you can go far beyond just listing what needs to be done. You can **map out task**

relationships and **set dependencies**, giving your project structure, clarity, and flow. In this section, we'll explore exactly how to use these features effectively to manage timelines, team collaboration, and the natural sequence of work.

Understanding Task Relationships

ClickUp provides powerful tools to connect tasks to one another. These relationships are more than just visual links—they define how work should progress, which tasks rely on others, and how you can avoid missed steps or bottlenecks.

There are **four primary types of task relationships** in ClickUp:

1. Dependency ("Blocking" and "Waiting On")

2. Related Tasks

3. Subtasks

4. Linked Tasks (References)

Let's dive into each one.

1. Task Dependencies ("Blocking" and "Waiting On")

Task dependencies allow you to show that one task cannot begin or finish until another task has started or completed. This is often referred to as a **"blocking" relationship**.

☑ **Example:**

- Task A: Finalize design

- Task B: Begin development
  Task B depends on the completion of Task A. If Task A is delayed, Task B cannot start.

In ClickUp, you can define:

- **"Blocking"** – This task is preventing another from starting.

- **"Waiting On"** – This task is waiting on another to be completed.

💡 **Why Use Dependencies?**

- To prevent team members from working on tasks prematurely.

- To reflect a real workflow structure.

- To identify critical paths and delays in project timelines.

🔧 **How to Set Dependencies in ClickUp:**

1. Open a task.

2. Go to the **"Relationships"** section or click the **+ icon** to add a new dependency.

3. Choose **"Blocking"** or **"Waiting On"**.

4. Select the relevant task.

Tasks with dependencies will display a small chain icon, and in views like Gantt or Timeline, these links are visually represented.

⏰ **Smart Scheduling:**

If you're using **Gantt View**, you can enable **"Reschedule Dependencies"**, which will automatically shift dependent tasks if the parent task is delayed. This makes ClickUp act more like advanced project management tools like Microsoft Project, but with a far more intuitive UI.

---

2. Related Tasks

These tasks aren't directly dependent on one another but are contextually linked. Use this to show that two or more tasks are associated in some way—even if there's no strict order between them.

📌 **Use Cases:**

- Tasks belonging to the same initiative but assigned to different departments.

- Brainstorming and execution tasks that share resources or goals.

- Cross-project links that benefit from mutual updates.

📍 **How to Add Related Tasks:**

1. In the task view, click **+ Add Relationship**.

2. Choose **"Related To"**.

3. Search for and select the task(s) you want to relate.

This is great for building a **web of context** around your work without overwhelming the project structure with dependencies.

---

3. Subtasks vs Dependencies: When to Use What

Many users get confused between subtasks and dependencies. Here's a quick breakdown:

Feature	Use Case	Advantages
Subtasks	Small parts of a single task	Keeps everything in one place
Dependencies	Separate tasks that influence one another	Clarifies work sequence across the project
Related Tasks	Informationally connected items	Helps trace connections without sequence limits

✔ **Tip:**

Don't use subtasks when each part requires separate assignees, statuses, or timelines. Instead, use tasks with dependencies.

---

4. Task Linking and References

ClickUp allows you to **link** tasks by referencing them directly in comments, descriptions, or even checklists. This is a softer relationship, designed for visibility and documentation.

📎 **Example:**

In a task description, you might write:

"See related research in Task #456"

This helps users navigate connected work easily and promotes **cross-functional collaboration**.

Managing Dependencies in Different Views

Each of ClickUp's views offers unique insights into task dependencies. Let's explore how they help.

A. List View

Dependencies in List View are shown using icons or columns you can enable via the **column settings**. It's a simple overview but useful for quick checks.

B. Gantt View

This is where ClickUp's dependencies shine. You can:

- See arrows connecting dependent tasks.

- Drag-and-drop dependencies directly.

- Adjust timelines visually.

- Enable **"Reschedule Dependencies"** to cascade changes automatically.

Gantt View gives **project managers** and **team leads** a full picture of how tasks affect one another across timelines.

C. Board View

While Board View doesn't show dependency links visually, it's helpful when combined with the "Dependencies" column or as a drag-and-drop workspace for reviewing work in progress.

D. Timeline View

This view is a hybrid of Calendar and Gantt. It's great for individual or team workloads and makes it easier to **spot overlap and task blocking**.

Using Dependencies for Agile and Waterfall Projects

ClickUp is flexible enough to support both **Agile** and **Waterfall** methodologies.

- In **Agile**, dependencies may be minimal since sprints emphasize flexibility, but they can still be useful for epics and user stories that must follow a logical order.

- In **Waterfall**, dependencies are often essential to sequence phases (design → development → testing → deployment).

Setting dependencies ensures that **no one jumps ahead** or works out of turn, which can compromise quality and timelines.

Best Practices for Managing Task Relationships

Here are some proven strategies to keep your task structure effective:

☑ **Use Dependencies Sparingly**

Too many dependencies can make your project hard to manage. Only use them where **sequential work is essential**.

☑ **Regularly Review the Dependency Map**

ClickUp doesn't yet have a full dependency map, but using Gantt View as your "map" helps you spot bottlenecks and recalibrate.

☑ **Combine with Priorities and Custom Fields**

Dependencies work best when combined with **priority tags**, **custom fields**, or **statuses** to provide a fuller picture of task readiness.

☑ **Communicate Dependencies with Team Members**

Make sure everyone understands what's blocking them and what they're blocking. Use assigned comments to alert people when a dependency has been cleared.

Common Pitfalls to Avoid

- **Over-dependencing**: Not every task needs to be connected. Keep it meaningful.

- **Poor communication**: Setting dependencies without notifying the team leads to confusion.

- **Ignoring automation**: Use ClickUp's automation features to notify assignees when dependencies are cleared.

ClickUp Automations for Dependencies

Take advantage of **ClickUp Automations** to manage task relationships dynamically:

- "When a blocking task is completed → change the status of the dependent task to 'In Progress'"

- "When a dependency is removed → notify the assignee"

- "If due date changes → adjust dependent tasks"

This reduces manual follow-ups and makes your workflows more responsive and intelligent.

Conclusion: Mastering the Art of Task Relationships

Understanding and utilizing task relationships in ClickUp is a **game-changer**. It transforms a list of tasks into a **strategic roadmap**. When you define dependencies, create related tasks, and link them thoughtfully, you build a **structure that scales**, guides, and empowers your team.

Remember:

- Use dependencies to **guide workflow**.

- Use related tasks to **enhance context**.

- Use subtasks when detail matters but hierarchy should stay tight.

ClickUp gives you the tools—but how you use them will define your **project's success**.

CHAPTER III
Collaborating with Your Team

3.1 User Roles and Permissions

3.1.1 Adding and Managing Members

In any productivity or project management tool, collaboration begins with people. In ClickUp, users are the core of your workflows—every task assigned, every comment made, and every deadline tracked is linked to a real human being. This section will guide you step-by-step through the process of adding team members to your ClickUp Workspace, managing their roles, setting permissions, and keeping your team structure clean, functional, and scalable.

Understanding the ClickUp User Structure

Before diving into the how-to, it's helpful to understand how ClickUp structures its users. In ClickUp, users fall into several main categories:

- **Owners**: Full administrative access. Can manage billing, Workspaces, permissions, and more.

- **Admins**: Can manage Spaces and invite members, but have limited billing access.

- **Members**: Collaborators who can create and manage tasks depending on permissions.

- **Guests**: External users with limited access to specific tasks, lists, or folders.

- **View-Only** (Free Plan only): Users who can view content but cannot interact with it.

Each of these roles has a different level of access, which we'll explore further in Section 3.1.2. For now, let's focus on **how to add users to your Workspace** and manage them effectively.

Inviting Members to Your Workspace

ClickUp makes it relatively simple to invite new members. The process differs slightly depending on your role (only Admins and Owners can add members) and the type of user you're inviting.

Step-by-Step: How to Invite a User

1. **Open Workspace Settings**

   o Click your Workspace avatar (usually in the lower-left corner).

   o Select **"People"** or navigate to **Workspace Settings > People**.

2. **Click "+ Invite People"**

   o This button is located at the top-right corner of the "People" page.

3. **Enter Email Addresses**

   o You can invite multiple users at once by separating email addresses with commas.

4. **Choose Role and Access Level**

   o Select whether the user will be a Member or a Guest.

- o   If inviting a Guest, assign specific Lists or Folders to them.

5. **Add Message (Optional)**

- o   You can personalize the invite with a short welcome message.

6. **Click "Send Invitation"**

- o   The users will receive an email with an invitation link.

💡 **Pro Tip**: To streamline onboarding, create a "Welcome List" or "Getting Started Project" and share it with new users. Include introductory tasks like "Set Up Your Profile," "Watch the Team Onboarding Video," and "Join Our Workspace Chat."

Managing Existing Members

After inviting users to your Workspace, it's crucial to manage their roles, adjust their permissions, and ensure your team structure is secure and logical.

Viewing and Editing Member Information

From the **"People"** tab in Workspace settings:

- See all active users and their current roles.

- Use the **ellipsis (⋮)** next to each user to:

  - o   Change their role (Owner/Admin/Member/Guest).

  - o   Remove them from the Workspace.

  - o   View their last login.

  - o   Reset their password (if needed).

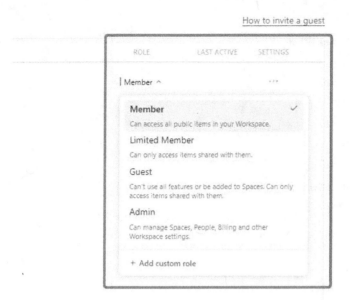

You can also filter users by role, which is helpful in large organizations with many team members.

Organizing with Teams and User Groups

If you're using the Business Plan or higher, you'll gain access to **Teams (a.k.a. User Groups)**. This feature allows you to bundle users together and assign tasks, comments, or permissions to an entire group rather than individuals.

Examples:

- Marketing Team

- Engineering Team

- Freelance Contractors

This is especially useful for:

- Assigning tasks to a rotating group

- Mentioning a department

- Controlling access across large Spaces or Folders

To create a Team:

1. Go to **Workspace Settings > Teams**

2. Click **"+ New Team"**

3. Name the team and add members

4. Save and start using the group across your Workspace

Best Practices for Member Management

ClickUp is powerful, but like any system, it can get messy if not managed with intention. Here are some best practices for smooth member management:

1. Onboard with Purpose

Ensure every new user knows:

- What Spaces they're working in

- Their responsibilities

- How to use core ClickUp features Use templates or onboarding projects to guide them.

2. Limit Access When Appropriate

- Use Guests for external collaborators (clients, freelancers).

- Use permissions carefully to prevent accidental data loss or unwanted edits.

- Assign view-only access when needed.

3. Audit Regularly

Periodically review:

- Who is in your Workspace

- Their access level and roles

- Inactive users who no longer need access

ClickUp doesn't charge for deactivated users, so it's fine to remove or pause access temporarily.

4. Keep Teams Updated

When people change roles or leave the company, reflect those changes immediately in ClickUp. Update their Teams or remove them to maintain security and organization.

5. Communicate Expectations

Make it clear how you expect users to interact within ClickUp:

- How often should they check notifications?

- Are tasks updated daily or weekly?

- Should comments be formal or informal?

ClickUp is flexible—but that flexibility needs clear team standards.

Handling Common Scenarios

Scenario 1: You're Collaborating with a Client

Use **Guest Access** and limit them to only see tasks related to their project. Set view/comment permissions depending on their involvement level.

Scenario 2: A New Employee Joins the Company

Invite them as a Member, assign them to the correct Teams, and enroll them in your ClickUp onboarding list.

Scenario 3: Someone Leaves the Organization

Remove them from the Workspace entirely to revoke access. If they owned tasks or lists, reassign ownership to another user beforehand.

Troubleshooting Member Issues

- **Invitation Not Received?**

  o   Have the user check spam folders.

o   Try resending the invite or using a different email address.

- **Can't Change a Role?**

  o   Only Owners can promote other users to Admin or change their roles in some cases.

- **Exceeding User Limits on Plan?**

  o   ClickUp will prompt you to upgrade or remove existing members to stay within your current plan's user cap.

Conclusion: People First, Tools Second

While ClickUp is a sophisticated tool, its true value lies in how well your team uses it together. Adding members is the starting point, but managing them thoughtfully—giving the right access, maintaining clear roles, and ensuring efficient onboarding—will determine whether your workspace feels like a hub of clarity or a source of chaos.

Remember: **the more intentional you are with your team structure, the smarter your entire system becomes.**

In the next section, we'll take a closer look at **user roles and permission levels**, so you can confidently control access across your workspace.

3.1.2 Roles and Access Levels

Effective team collaboration in ClickUp starts with understanding how to manage **roles and access levels** properly. Whether you're onboarding a new team member, assigning responsibilities, or safeguarding sensitive information, ClickUp's role-based permissions ensure that everyone sees only what they need and is empowered to do what they must — no more, no less.

This section will take a deep dive into:

- The core **roles** available in ClickUp

- What **each role can and cannot do**

- How to **customize access at different hierarchy levels**

- Real-world **use cases and best practices**

Let's explore the building blocks of user control and team structure in ClickUp.

🔐 Understanding Roles in ClickUp

ClickUp provides a flexible permission system structured around **user roles**. These roles determine the capabilities a user has within a Workspace, Space, Folder, or List. Here are the primary roles you need to know:

1. Owner

- The **creator of the Workspace** or someone transferred ownership by an existing owner.

- Has **full access** to all settings, billing, integrations, and Workspace-wide configurations.

- Can manage members, delete Spaces, and remove other users (including admins).

- Only **one owner** per Workspace.

2. Admin

- Assigned by the Owner.

- Can access most **Workspace-level settings** including integrations and member management.

- Cannot transfer ownership or delete the Workspace.

- Suitable for IT managers, team leads, or operations specialists who help manage the platform.

3. Member

- A regular user with access to create, manage, and interact with tasks, views, and documents.

- Can create Spaces (depending on settings), manage personal tasks, and participate fully in collaboration.

- Cannot manage billing or administrative settings.

4. Guest

- External collaborators (e.g., freelancers, clients, partners).

- Access is restricted to specific **Tasks**, **Lists**, or **Folders** shared with them.

- Cannot access Workspace-wide features or Spaces unless specifically invited.

- Ideal for situations where a lightweight, read-or-comment access is necessary.

5. Read-Only (Guest or Member)

- This optional setting gives a user the ability to **view** content without making any edits.

- Useful for upper management or stakeholders who only need oversight.

📝 **Note:** ClickUp also allows you to fine-tune permissions on a **per-user** or **per-role** basis inside individual Folders, Lists, and even views — a powerful feature for larger teams or complex projects.

📊 Comparing Role Capabilities

To clarify the distinctions, here's a simplified comparison table:

Feature / Role	Owner	Admin	Member	Guest
Access billing	✓	✓	✗	✗
Manage integrations	✓	✓	✗	✗
Create/edit Spaces	✓	✓	✓	✗
Invite users	✓	✓	✓	✗
Access all tasks	✓	✓	✓	✗ (only shared)
Comment on tasks	✓	✓	✓	✓
Change task status	✓	✓	✓	✓ (if allowed)

Feature / Role	Owner	Admin	Member	Guest
Delete tasks	☑	☑	☑	✕
Share public links	☑	☑	☑	☑
Create automation	☑	☑	☑	✕

Granular Permissions Across the Hierarchy

ClickUp's hierarchy — from Workspace to Spaces, Folders, Lists, Tasks, and Views — allows for **role-based access control** at each level.

Workspace-Level Permissions

- **Control over the entire environment.**
- Owners/Admins can set default permission settings for new users.
- Ideal for large organizations with multiple departments.

Space-Level Permissions

- Assign who can view, create, edit, or delete within a Space.
- For example, give the Marketing team full access to the "Campaigns" Space while giving Finance read-only access.

Folder/List-Level Permissions

- Highly useful for collaborative projects with outside clients.
- You may want to:
  - Share a single List (e.g., "Deliverables") with a Guest.
  - Hide other Lists in the same Folder to protect sensitive planning docs.

Task-Level Permissions

- Assign individual tasks to Guests without sharing the entire List or Folder.
- Enable granular collaboration on specific deliverables.

👥 Assigning and Managing Roles

Assigning roles is straightforward:

1. Navigate to your **Workspace settings**.

2. Select the **"People"** tab.

3. Click the dropdown beside the user's name to assign a **role** (Owner, Admin, Member, Guest).

4. To manage **permissions**, click the gear icon to configure **custom access** at each level.

For Guests, simply:

- Share a specific List/Folder/Task.

- Choose what they can do: **View**, **Comment**, or **Edit**.

You can **revoke access** at any time by removing them from the shared item or Workspace.

🧩 Use Cases and Scenarios

✅ Use Case 1: Managing Internal Teams

- **Team Leads**: Assigned as Admins.

- **Team Members**: Given Member access.

- **Executives**: May have read-only Member access or Guest access to dashboards.

✅ Use Case 2: Working with Freelancers

- Add them as **Guests** to specific Lists (e.g., "Design Tasks").

- Allow **Comment** or **Edit** access depending on project needs.

- Remove access after the contract ends.

✅ Use Case 3: Client Collaboration

- Add clients as **Guests** with view-only access to progress dashboards.

- Let them comment on deliverables without exposing internal discussions.

💡 Best Practices for Managing Roles & Permissions

- **Follow the Principle of Least Privilege**: Only give users access to what they truly need. This minimizes risk and keeps the workspace clean.

- **Use Spaces to Group Permissions Strategically**: Assign permissions at the Space level to group departments, teams, or clients logically.

- **Audit Roles Regularly**: Every quarter, review user access and remove any outdated permissions — especially for ex-employees or former contractors.

- **Use Custom Roles for Advanced Control**: On ClickUp's Business Plus and Enterprise plans, you can create **custom roles** to define specific permissions — ideal for organizations with unique workflows.

🔍 Troubleshooting Role Issues

If users report not seeing tasks or being unable to complete actions:

- Double-check **their role** (are they a Guest when they should be a Member?)

- Ensure they have access to the correct **Space/List/Task**

- Make sure **permissions haven't been overwritten** at a sub-level

Use the **"What They See"** feature (on certain plans) to preview the interface from another user's perspective — a helpful tool for debugging.

⊛ Final Thoughts

The power of ClickUp lies not just in what it allows you to do — but **who** you allow to do **what**.
Understanding and mastering **Roles and Access Levels** empowers your team to work confidently, independently, and securely. It also enables leaders to delegate responsibility without compromising control or transparency.

Whether you're running a startup, managing a remote team, or handling sensitive client projects, using roles strategically will help you **scale your collaboration** with confidence.

3.1.3 Sharing Tasks and Lists

Effective collaboration is the heart of any successful team, and in ClickUp, one of the most powerful tools to enable that collaboration is **sharing**. Whether you're managing a small team or an enterprise-scale operation, the ability to control **who sees what**, **who can do what**, and **how tasks and lists are shared** is crucial to your workflow. This section will walk you through everything you need to know about **sharing tasks and lists** in ClickUp, from the basics to advanced use cases.

🔑 Understanding Sharing in ClickUp

In ClickUp, sharing is how you **grant access** to others—whether they are team members, stakeholders, or external collaborators. You can share:

- Individual **Tasks**
- Entire **Lists**
- Higher-level structures like **Folders** or **Spaces**
- **Dashboards**, **Docs**, and more (though we'll focus on Tasks and Lists here)

ClickUp's sharing capabilities allow for granular control, meaning you can **fine-tune access and permissions** based on the sensitivity of the content and the needs of your team.

✳ Why Sharing Matters

Here are some of the key benefits of using ClickUp's sharing features:

- **Real-time collaboration** on tasks and projects
- **Transparency** across departments or teams
- **Better delegation** by sharing with the right roles

- **Streamlined communication** through contextual comments
- **Controlled access**, ensuring only the right people can make changes

---

◆ Sharing a Task in ClickUp

Tasks are the atomic units of ClickUp. Sharing tasks allows other users to **view**, **comment**, or **edit** based on their permission levels.

📌 How to Share a Task:

1. **Open the Task** you want to share.

2. Click on the **"Share"** icon (a person with a plus sign).

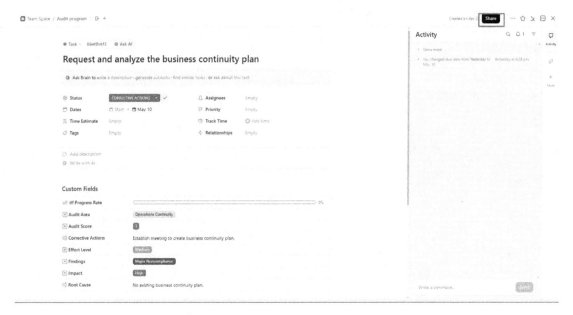

3. Choose who you want to share it with:

   o   Members of your Workspace

   o   Guests (with restricted permissions)

   o   Public links (if enabled)

4. Set the **permission level** (more on this below).

5. Confirm by clicking "Share".

🔒 Permissions When Sharing a Task:

ClickUp provides four main types of permissions:

- **View only** – The user can view the task but cannot make changes.

- **Comment** – The user can view and leave comments.

- **Edit** – The user can view, comment, and edit the task content.

- **Full** – The user can edit, delete, assign, and change statuses.

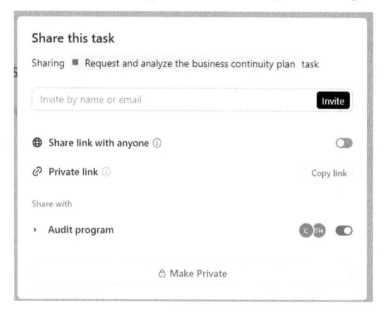

💡 **Tip:** Be cautious when granting "Full" access to tasks, especially if sharing outside your core team.

◆ Sharing Lists in ClickUp

A **List** is a container for tasks grouped by a theme, project, or goal. Sharing an entire List gives collaborators access to **all tasks within it**.

🦋 How to Share a List:

1. Open the desired List.

2. Click the **"Share"** icon at the top-right of the List view.

3. Invite members or guests by email or select from your Workspace.

4. Set access level per user:

   o View

   o Comment

   o Edit

   o Full

5. Click **"Invite"** to finalize sharing.

🗨 **Best Practice:** Use List-level sharing when you want to involve someone in a complete project or workflow, not just a single task.

👥 Sharing with Guests

Guests are users who are not full Workspace members. You might invite a guest when working with:

- A client who needs access to specific deliverables

- A freelancer contributing to one project

- A stakeholder who only needs visibility

Guest Permissions include:

- View Only

- Comment

- Edit (depending on your plan)

- They are **free**, but limited by plan and feature availability.

🔒 **Security Tip:** Guests cannot access anything outside what you explicitly share with them. This makes it ideal for external collaborators.

🔁 Inheriting Permissions

ClickUp uses a **hierarchical permission model**. Here's how it works:

- Sharing a **Folder** grants access to all Lists and Tasks inside it.
- Sharing a **List** gives access to all Tasks in that List.
- Sharing an individual **Task** overrides inherited access.

This flexibility allows you to **create exceptions**. For example:

- Your client can see a task within a shared List but can't see other tasks.
- A team member can be given full access to just one critical task without viewing others.

📌 **Note:** Inherited access can be customized by overriding it at the task level, offering precise control over visibility and collaboration.

✗ Managing Shared Access

If you've already shared a Task or List and want to **change access**, here's how:

1. Open the Task/List.
2. Click on the **"Share"** icon.
3. You'll see a list of users who currently have access.
4. Click the **ellipsis (:)** next to their name to:
   - Change permission level
   - Remove access
   - Reassign access to another user

This is useful when team members leave, roles change, or you want to reduce clutter.

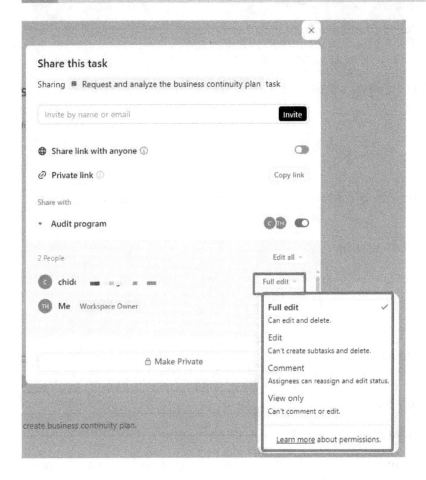

🗄 Sharing via Public Links

ClickUp also allows you to **generate public sharing links**, especially useful when:

- Sharing a report or update with clients

- Creating a public roadmap or changelog

- Collaborating on documents without requiring a ClickUp login

To generate a public link:

1. Open the item you wish to share.

2. Click "Share" and go to the **"Public Link"** tab.

3. Enable the toggle to generate a link.

4. Set optional link permissions (e.g., view-only or allow comments).

⚠ **Caution:** Public links can be forwarded, so avoid using them for sensitive or internal content unless secured.

🔍 Use Case Examples

Let's break down some real-world use cases to illustrate how sharing can be applied effectively.

☑ Use Case 1: Team Collaboration

You're managing a product launch. You create a List called "Product Launch Tasks" and share it with:

- Designers (Edit access)

- Marketing team (Full access)

- Sales manager (View only access) Everyone sees the same tasks but interacts with them based on their roles.

☑ Use Case 2: Client Updates

You're working with a client on a campaign. You create a List called "Client Campaign Tasks," but only share:

- A few client-facing tasks with the client (View or Comment access)

- The full list with your internal team (Full access)

☑ Use Case 3: Department-Level Collaboration

You lead the IT department. You create a Folder called "IT Projects" with several Lists:

- "Website Maintenance"

- "Security Upgrades"

- "Internal Tools" You share each List only with the relevant team members for that sub-project. This ensures focus and security.

💡 Best Practices for Sharing in ClickUp

1. **Start with Least Privilege**: Always start by granting the lowest necessary permission and escalate only if needed.

2. **Use Lists for Contextual Sharing**: Don't share individual tasks unless it's for quick, limited collaboration.

3. **Document Sharing Rules**: Especially in large teams, document your sharing policy to avoid confusion or permission chaos.

4. **Audit Regularly**: Periodically review who has access to sensitive Lists and Tasks.

5. **Train New Team Members**: Teach them how to share responsibly and avoid permission errors.

📃 Wrapping Up

Sharing in ClickUp isn't just about access—it's about enabling **efficient teamwork**, fostering **accountability**, and driving **project visibility**. When done right, sharing tasks and lists ensures everyone knows what to do, when to do it, and how it contributes to the bigger picture.

With ClickUp's detailed permission controls, team members get just the right amount of access—no more, no less. Whether you're a startup founder, a project manager, or a freelance designer, mastering ClickUp's sharing features empowers you to work smarter, not harder.

In the next section, we'll look at **communication within ClickUp**—where collaboration truly comes to life through comments, assigned discussions, and integrations.

3.2 Communication in ClickUp

3.2.1 Comments and Mentions

Effective communication is the cornerstone of any successful project, and ClickUp has made it a core element of its design philosophy. While many project management platforms focus heavily on task tracking and workflow optimization, ClickUp recognizes that **communication within tasks** is equally essential. That's where **Comments** and **Mentions** come in.

In this section, we'll dive into how comments and mentions work in ClickUp, how to use them strategically, and how they can transform the way your team collaborates—whether you're in the same office or scattered across different time zones.

Understanding Comments in ClickUp

At its core, a **comment** is a message added to a task, subtask, document, or any item in ClickUp that supports collaboration. Think of it as an in-line chat feature—but one that's **contextually tied to specific work**.

Types of Comments in ClickUp

1. **Task Comments**: These are added directly to individual tasks. Team members use them to:

    o   Provide updates or clarification

    o   Ask questions

    o   Share ideas or solutions

    o   Log decisions

2. **Subtask Comments**: Each subtask has its own comment thread, separate from the parent task. This keeps detailed conversations focused and relevant.

3. **Doc Comments**: Comments can also be made on documents within ClickUp Docs. These are similar to Google Docs-style comments and are particularly useful for team editing and feedback.

4. **Assigned Comments**: One of ClickUp's most powerful features, **assigned comments**, allow you to assign a comment like a mini-task within a task. More on that shortly.

Where You'll Find Comments

- On every **task page**, typically in the Activity or Comments tab

- Within **Docs** in the right-hand comment bar or inline

- Inside **Whiteboards**, where notes can include comments

- In **notifications**, where replies to comments appear for easy access

How to Use Comments Effectively

ClickUp's comments system is built for **real-time collaboration**, but it also encourages **asynchronous work**, allowing teams in different time zones to stay updated without missing context.

1. Provide Context

Never assume your teammates know what you're referring to. A comment like:

"Please update this."

...is much less helpful than:

"Please update the due date on this task to align with the client's new timeline."

Include links, screenshots, or even attach files directly in the comment box to provide deeper clarity.

2. Use Threads for Clarity

ClickUp allows for threaded replies to comments. This helps avoid the all-too-familiar "lost in the scroll" problem. Threaded comments:

- Keep conversations organized

- Help readers follow the flow of discussion

- Allow multiple discussions within a task to coexist

3. Be Action-Oriented

When discussing tasks, frame comments around **action**, not just status.
Instead of:

"This looks late."

Try:

"Can we push the deadline to Friday to allow for final review?"

This promotes solution-focused thinking and prevents frustration or confusion.

Using Mentions in ClickUp

Mentions bring attention to specific people, tasks, or documents. When you **@mention** a team member, they're notified instantly. This ensures your message doesn't get lost and the right people are pulled into the loop.

Types of Mentions

1. **@Teammember**
   Example: @JohnDoe

   ○ Notifies a specific user

   ○ Great for clarifying ownership or asking for input

2. **@Team or @Everyone**
   Use @TeamName or @Everyone to notify groups.
   Caution: Overuse of @Everyone can lead to notification fatigue.

3. **@Here**
   Notifies all active users currently online.

4. **@Task**
   Mentions a specific task—great for referencing related work.

5. **@Doc, @List, @Folder, @Space**
   These allow you to point others directly to ClickUp content.
   Example:

"Refer to @MarketingPlan2024 Doc before finalizing the ad copy."

Mention Best Practices

☑ Tag with Purpose

Only tag people who are relevant to the conversation. Avoid tagging the entire team unless necessary.

☑ Combine with Assigned Comments

For added clarity, tag someone and then assign the comment to them to indicate that **action is required**, not just awareness.

☑ Use for Updates

Mention stakeholders when:

- A milestone is completed
- A deadline changes
- A decision is made

This keeps everyone aligned and reduces the need for external emails or Slack pings.

Assigned Comments: Turning Communication into Action

One of ClickUp's signature features is the **ability to assign comments**. Instead of creating a new subtask or chasing someone to act on a note, you simply turn the comment into a mini-assignment.

How to Assign a Comment

- Type the comment
- Click the checkmark icon (✔)
- Assign it to a team member
- Set an optional due date

The comment becomes a **resolvable item**. Once the person completes the task, they check it off, and the conversation continues.

Benefits of Assigned Comments

- Keeps tasks clean (no cluttering with micro-tasks)
- Ensures follow-up on suggestions or questions
- Reduces the need for meetings and follow-up messages
- Gives visibility to outstanding issues

Comment Formatting and Tools

ClickUp allows rich formatting inside comments, so your messages can be clear and visually organized.

Supported Features:

- **Bold**, *Italic*, Code, and ~~Strikethrough~~
- Bullet and numbered lists
- Inline checkboxes
- File attachments and images
- Emojis and reactions
- Threaded replies
- Hyperlinks

Use these tools to make your comments:

- Easier to read
- More actionable
- Less likely to be ignored

ClickUp Inbox: Where Comments Live

ClickUp's **Inbox** centralizes all activity, including comments you're mentioned in or assigned to. This acts like a filtered feed that lets you:

- Catch up on mentions and replies

- Mark items as read or resolved

- Prioritize work without switching between tasks

The **Inbox** helps users stay on top of communication **without context-switching**, which is one of the biggest productivity killers.

Managing Notifications for Comments

ClickUp gives users full control over what types of comment notifications they receive.

You can:

- Choose to be notified only when mentioned

- Opt for browser, desktop, email, or mobile push notifications

- Mute tasks, lists, or entire spaces

Encourage team members to customize notifications so they **don't miss important mentions**, but also avoid notification overload.

Common Mistakes and How to Avoid Them

✕ Overusing @everyone

This leads to team members ignoring alerts or turning off notifications entirely.

✕ Not Assigning Comments

Mentioning someone isn't enough if you expect action. Assign the comment.

✕ Being Too Vague

"Please review this" isn't helpful. Specify what needs to be reviewed and by when.

✕ Letting Threads Get Too Long

Break up long discussions into separate threads or, when needed, move to Docs or Whiteboards for deeper collaboration.

Real-World Example: Communication Done Right

Let's imagine a content team working on a product launch.

- Task: "Finalize Product Landing Page"
- Comment Thread:
    - @Designer: "Can you update the hero image with the new branding assets?"
        - ✔ Assigned Comment with Due Date
    - @Copywriter: "Please refine the headline. We want it to be more benefit-driven."
    - @Manager: "I'll review the page after both of you are done. Let me know when it's ready."

By keeping everything in the task comments, the entire team has a **centralized record of decisions, action items, and status**. No Slack threads. No lost emails.

Summary: Why Comments and Mentions Matter

ClickUp's comment and mention system is more than just a chatbox—it's a dynamic **collaboration layer** that makes it possible to:

- Replace scattered communications with centralized updates
- Hold team members accountable
- Document decisions in context
- Encourage asynchronous workflows
- Keep work and communication tightly integrated

By mastering comments and mentions, your team can reduce miscommunication, shorten feedback loops, and maintain momentum—no matter where or when they're working.

3.2.2 Assigned Comments

Introduction to Assigned Comments

Effective communication is the lifeblood of any successful team, and in the fast-paced world of task and project management, clarity and accountability are non-negotiable. ClickUp understands this need and offers a robust communication feature that stands out: **Assigned Comments**.

Unlike traditional commenting systems where comments can get buried in threads or overlooked in notifications, Assigned Comments give teams a direct and actionable way to ensure that important messages don't just get noticed—they get done. This feature turns communication into a workflow tool, tightly integrated with your task management system.

In this section, you'll learn exactly what Assigned Comments are, how they function, when to use them, and best practices to avoid clutter and confusion. Whether you're managing a small project or leading a large cross-functional team, mastering Assigned Comments will sharpen your collaboration and prevent tasks from falling through the cracks.

What Are Assigned Comments?

An **Assigned Comment** in ClickUp is a comment that includes a specific action and is assigned to a particular user. Unlike standard comments, which serve more for discussion or clarification, Assigned Comments function like **mini action items**. They are:

- Tied to a specific **user**
- Appear in the **Inbox** and **Notification Center** of that user
- Persist until **marked as resolved**
- Help track accountability for comments within a task or subtask

Think of them as an in-context to-do list, embedded within your task communication. This bridges the gap between conversation and execution.

How to Create an Assigned Comment

Creating an Assigned Comment is simple:

1. **Open any task** (or subtask).

2. Navigate to the **Comments** section.

3. Write your comment as you normally would.

4. Highlight the part of the text you want to assign (optional but useful).

5. Click the **"Assign" icon (the checkbox + profile image)** that appears near the comment editor.

6. Choose the **teammate** you want to assign the comment to.

7. Click **"Comment"** or **"Comment & Assign"**.

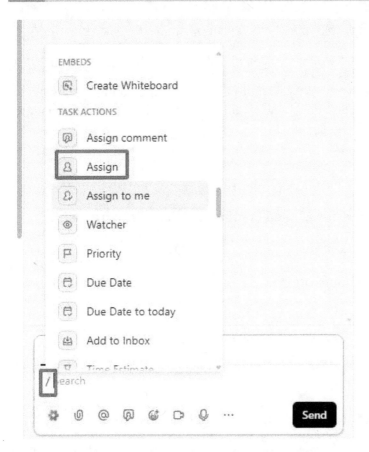

Once assigned, the comment will:

- Show the assignee's avatar next to it.
- Move to their **Inbox** until resolved.
- Have an option to **resolve** or **reassign**.

Real-World Use Cases

Here are some common scenarios where Assigned Comments can make a difference:

- ☑ **Requesting Feedback**: "@Anna Can you review the new wireframes by Friday?"

- ✕ **Assigning Micro Tasks**: "@David Please fix the typo in paragraph three."

- 🔍 **Flagging a Follow-up**: "@Sophie Let's revisit this in next week's meeting."

- 📄 **Clarification Needed**: "@John Can you explain the numbers in cell B12?"

By assigning these comments directly, the relevant person is notified and responsible for following up. This avoids confusion about who is doing what and removes the need for external follow-up emails or messages.

Assigned Comments vs. Regular Task Assignments

It's important to distinguish between **Assigned Comments** and **assigning a task**:

Feature	Assigned Comment	Assigned Task
Primary Purpose	Micro communication or requests	Full ownership of a task or subtask
Visibility	Inbox and comments section	Task list and board views
Resolution Mechanism	Mark as Resolved	Change task status
Used for	Small actions, follow-ups	Major deliverables

Use Assigned Comments for **quick interactions**, not to replace the full task assignment. They complement each other beautifully.

Managing Assigned Comments

Managing your Assigned Comments is easy, thanks to ClickUp's UI integrations:

 Inbox

Your **Inbox** is the primary hub for all Assigned Comments. You can:

- View all your assigned comments in one place.
- Filter by task, due date, or Workspace.
- Resolve directly from the Inbox interface.

☑ Resolving Comments

When you've completed the requested action:

- Click **"Resolve"** on the comment.

- It disappears from your Inbox but stays in the task for historical reference.

- It gets visually marked as resolved (usually grayed out and checked off).

🔄 Reassigning or Unassigning

If a comment was assigned to the wrong person, you can:

- Reassign it to another team member.

- Unassign it if no longer relevant.

This flexibility ensures that action items never stagnate.

Team Accountability and Visibility

Assigned Comments enhance **team accountability** in several ways:

- Everyone knows **who is responsible** for a specific issue or question.

- Project managers or team leads can **quickly scan** a task's comments to check on progress.

- You can trace **communication history**, showing what was requested and by whom.

This creates a culture of transparency and responsibility, which is invaluable in distributed or asynchronous teams.

Best Practices for Using Assigned Comments

Here are some expert tips to make the most of this feature:

☑ Be Clear and Concise

Write action-oriented comments that clearly describe the expectation. Avoid vague phrases like "take a look" without context.

✕ "Check this out."

☑ "Please confirm if the images are properly optimized for web."

☑ Use Mention Tags Smartly

Always use **@mentions** when assigning comments. This reinforces clarity and ensures notifications are routed correctly.

☑ Don't Overuse

Not everything needs to be an Assigned Comment. Use them sparingly and intentionally— if everything becomes a mini-task, they lose significance.

☑ Pair with Due Dates When Needed

Although Assigned Comments don't have built-in due dates, you can mention deadlines in the text or link them to subtasks for clarity.

☑ Use Emojis or Labels for Quick Context

A simple 🔴 or ⚠ can help highlight urgency.

Advanced Tactics and Pro Tips

- 💡 **Use Assigned Comments as Review Checklists**: Create a running comment thread for each project stage and assign them out as deliverables become ready.

- **Integrate Assigned Comments with Automations**: If someone resolves a comment, you can trigger an automation like changing the task status.

- 🐞 **Use with Custom Views**: Filter tasks that contain unresolved Assigned Comments to quickly identify communication bottlenecks.

Common Pitfalls to Avoid

- 🚫 **Assigning to Multiple People in One Comment**
  This can dilute ownership. It's better to break the comment into separate ones for each user.

- 🚫 **Ignoring the Resolution Step**
  If comments aren't marked as resolved, they'll linger in the Inbox, causing clutter and confusion.

- 🚫 **Using Comments for Major Task Instructions**
  If the action requires multiple steps or coordination, it's better to create a subtask.

Recap: Why Assigned Comments Matter

- Turn messages into actions

- Clarify responsibility

- Reduce missed follow-ups

- Centralize collaboration

- Enhance accountability

Assigned Comments are a deceptively simple feature with enormous impact. By using them wisely, you not only enhance team collaboration but also prevent communication breakdowns that can derail even the most organized projects.

What's Next

In the next section, we'll look at **ClickUp Chat and Integrations (3.2.3)**, where we explore real-time messaging, Slack/Teams integration, and how to streamline communication across tools.

But for now, go ahead—**start assigning comments** and see how much smoother your team's communication becomes!

3.2.3 ClickUp Chat and Integrations

Effective communication is at the heart of every successful team. While email and third-party messaging apps still have their place, many modern organizations are shifting toward integrated, centralized platforms that combine task management and communication.

ClickUp not only allows teams to manage their work in one place but also empowers seamless internal communication through **ClickUp Chat** and a wide range of **integrations** with other tools like Slack, Microsoft Teams, Zoom, and more.

In this section, we'll dive into **ClickUp Chat** — what it is, how it functions, when to use it — and then explore **popular integrations** that can help unify your workflows and reduce app-switching. By the end, you'll have a full understanding of how to use ClickUp as your team's communication hub.

What Is ClickUp Chat?

ClickUp Chat is a built-in messaging system designed to help team members communicate without leaving the platform. Unlike comments, which are typically tied to specific tasks or documents, Chat allows for real-time conversation within designated locations in your workspace.

Chat in ClickUp comes in **two primary forms**:

- **Chat View**: A standalone view where users can create dedicated chat spaces for discussion.

- **Task/Comment Threads**: While technically not part of Chat View, comment threads serve as discussion spaces tied to specific tasks.

For the purpose of this section, we're focusing on the **Chat View**, which acts as your team's internal message board.

Setting Up a Chat View

To add a Chat View:

1. Navigate to the Space, Folder, or List where you want the chat to live.

2. Click the **"+"** sign next to your views.

3. Choose **"Chat"** from the view options.

4. Name the chat (optional) and set it as a personal or shared view.

Once added, you'll see a familiar messaging interface, complete with avatars, timestamps, and text formatting tools.

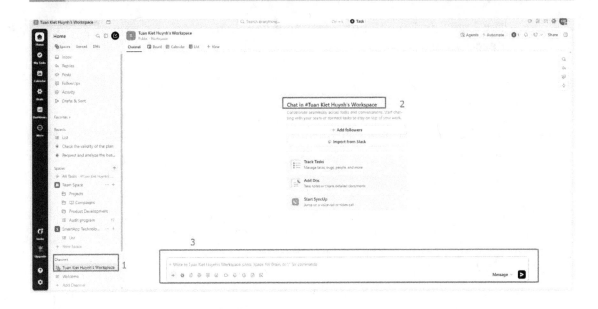

When and How to Use ClickUp Chat

ClickUp Chat isn't meant to replace all your communication tools — rather, it centralizes conversation **in context** with your work. Here are some practical use cases and best practices:

Best Use Cases

- **Project Discussions**: Create a chat view within a Folder or List related to a specific project, so all discussions stay contextually relevant.

- **Team Check-ins**: Use a Space-level Chat for your department or team's casual updates and coordination.

- **Brainstorming**: Create chat channels for idea-sharing, inspiration, and cross-functional dialogue.

- **Quick Questions**: Replace internal emails with a faster, more informal exchange.

When Not to Use Chat

- Avoid using Chat for task-specific discussions — use **task comments** instead to ensure clarity.

- For formal documentation, meeting notes, or decision logs, rely on **Docs** or **task descriptions**.

Chat Features Overview

ClickUp Chat is simple but powerful. Let's explore some features that make it an effective collaboration tool:

◯ Message Threading

While ClickUp Chat doesn't yet support Slack-style threading, you can mention tasks, documents, or even other chat messages to create context.

🖇 File Attachments

Attach files (e.g., PDFs, images, spreadsheets) directly to your chat messages for quick sharing. ClickUp stores them alongside your messages for easy retrieval.

🔗 Task Linking

Use **@** to mention a teammate and **/task** to link to a specific task. This creates direct connections between conversations and action items.

🧠 Slash Commands

ClickUp supports markdown-style shortcuts:

- *text* or _text_ = *italic*
- **text** = **bold**
- ~~text~~ = ~~strikethrough~~
- /task, /doc, or /link = create embedded references

👥 Chat Participants and Permissions

Chat views can be **shared** or **private**:

- **Shared Chat Views**: Available to everyone with access to the parent Space/Folder/List.
- **Private Chat Views**: You can restrict access to specific people — great for leadership or sensitive discussions.

Integrating with External Communication Tools

Sometimes, you'll need to communicate across platforms. ClickUp offers integrations with several popular messaging and meeting platforms to ensure fluid workflows.

Let's take a closer look at **Slack, Microsoft Teams, Zoom,** and **Google Chat** integrations.

Slack Integration

ClickUp's integration with Slack is among its most powerful. Here's what it enables:

🔄 Two-Way Communication

- **Create tasks from Slack messages** using the ClickUp shortcut.
- **Receive ClickUp notifications** (task updates, mentions, new assignments) directly in Slack channels.
- **Attach Slack threads** to ClickUp tasks for context.

🚀 Setup Instructions

1. Go to **ClickUp Settings > Integrations > Slack**.
2. Authorize the connection and choose which Workspaces and Slack channels to sync.
3. Customize notification rules — for example, only tasks with high priority or status changes.

Microsoft Teams Integration

ClickUp also integrates with **Microsoft Teams**, enabling real-time collaboration inside your existing communication stack.

Key Features:

- Embed ClickUp tasks inside Teams conversations.

- Use **ClickUp's Teams bot** to get notifications, assign tasks, or update statuses directly from chat.

- Pin ClickUp dashboards to Teams tabs for visibility.

Setup:

1. Install the ClickUp app from the Microsoft Teams App Store.

2. Connect your ClickUp account and authorize the workspace.

3. Choose what notifications and functions you want Teams to access.

Zoom Integration

For teams relying on Zoom for virtual meetings, ClickUp's Zoom integration helps document conversations and keep work moving.

What You Can Do:

- Start a Zoom meeting directly from a ClickUp task.

- Link Zoom recordings to tasks for reference.

- Create tasks from meeting action items.

How to Enable:

1. Navigate to **Integrations > Zoom**.

2. Log in with your Zoom credentials and authorize the integration.

3. Use the **Zoom button** within tasks to start meetings.

Google Chat (via Webhooks or Zapier)

ClickUp doesn't have a native Google Chat integration, but you can set up automated workflows using **Zapier** or **Make** (formerly Integromat).

Example Automation:

- When a new task is created in ClickUp, post a message in a Google Chat room.

- When a task status is changed, send a notification to a team chat.

This setup allows you to keep your Google ecosystem aligned with ClickUp activity, even without a direct native app.

Best Practices for Unified Communication

To use ClickUp effectively as your communication command center, keep these principles in mind:

1. Define Boundaries

- Use **Chat Views** for ongoing team discussions.
- Use **task comments** for work tied to specific deliverables.
- Avoid mixing chat types to reduce confusion.

2. Establish Norms

- Agree on where and how to communicate: e.g., "All project decisions go in task comments," or "Status updates happen in Chat every Friday."

3. Minimize Notification Fatigue

- Customize notifications (especially from Slack or Teams) to reduce noise.
- Educate your team on muting unnecessary alerts and using filters like Assigned Comments or @mentions.

4. Link, Don't Repeat

- Rather than rewriting task details, link to them using @ or /task commands.
- This keeps communication short, relevant, and traceable.

Summary: Bringing It All Together

ClickUp offers a flexible yet powerful internal communication system. Through **Chat Views**, you can centralize real-time discussions without leaving your project environment. And with integrations like **Slack, Teams, and Zoom**, you ensure that conversations across platforms connect directly to your ClickUp tasks and projects.

Instead of scattering communication across apps, ClickUp encourages a **single source of truth** — where your conversations support your work, and your work supports your team.

When you build a culture of effective, integrated communication inside ClickUp, you unlock its full potential: faster decision-making, fewer silos, and greater clarity for everyone involved.

3.3 Managing Notifications

3.3.1 Notification Settings

In the modern digital workplace, where teams collaborate across different locations, time zones, and work styles, **notifications** play a crucial role in maintaining awareness, responsiveness, and flow. However, without proper control, they can quickly become overwhelming and disruptive.

ClickUp understands this balance and offers **robust, customizable notification settings** that help you stay informed **without the noise**. In this section, we'll take a deep dive into ClickUp's notification system, how to configure it effectively, and best practices for managing your alert environment for **maximum productivity and minimal distraction**.

🔔 Understanding the Purpose of Notifications in ClickUp

Notifications in ClickUp serve several essential purposes:

- **Keeping you informed of updates** to tasks, comments, mentions, and status changes.

- **Helping you respond quickly** when someone requests action or needs your input.

- **Tracking your involvement** across multiple spaces, projects, and teams.

But while being informed is necessary, **too many alerts** can lead to fatigue, missed updates, and general disorganization. That's why ClickUp gives you control over **what kind of notifications you receive, how you receive them, and when they're triggered**.

⚙ Where to Find Notification Settings

There are **two main locations** where you can manage your notification settings in ClickUp:

1. **Personal Settings (User-Level Notifications)**

   o Click your **avatar** (bottom left of the sidebar).

   o Choose **Settings → Notifications**.

o   Here, you can manage email, mobile, desktop, and in-app notifications.

2. **Workspace Settings (Admin Settings)**

o   If you're an Admin or Owner, go to **Workspace Settings**.

o   Navigate to **People**, and manage default notification preferences across users.

Each user can fine-tune notifications independently unless limited by a workspace-wide setting.

Types of Notifications Available

ClickUp allows notifications across **multiple channels**, ensuring you receive updates where and how you prefer. These include:

- Email notifications

- In-app notifications

- Desktop (browser) notifications

- Mobile push notifications (iOS and Android)

- ClickUp Inbox

Let's look at each type more closely.

---

1. Email Notifications

These are ideal for users who prefer getting updates outside of ClickUp or who are heavily reliant on their email inbox.

You can choose to receive emails when:

- You're assigned to a task

- Someone comments or replies to your comment

- A task you're watching is updated

- Someone mentions you

Email notification tips:

- Disable email alerts for minor updates (like status changes) if you already receive in-app or mobile notifications.

- Use email filters in Gmail or Outlook to sort ClickUp updates into folders.

2. In-App Notifications

These appear in the **"Notifications" panel** inside ClickUp, accessible from the bell icon in the top-right corner.

They are perfect for:

- **Staying in the loop** without checking your email constantly

- Reviewing everything in one place

Key features:

- **Mark as read/unread**

- **Filter by type** (mentions, task changes, etc.)

- **Direct links to relevant tasks**

Pro tip: Visit this panel once or twice a day as part of your workflow to stay updated in a non-disruptive way.

3. Desktop Notifications (Browser-Based)

These are **real-time pop-up alerts** in your desktop environment, commonly used when:

- You're actively working in ClickUp

- You need to be immediately notified of urgent updates

Enable desktop notifications via:

- Your browser settings (e.g., allow notifications in Chrome or Firefox)

- ClickUp notification settings (toggle on Desktop Notifications)

Caution: These can be distracting if left unchecked. Consider enabling only for **assigned comments** or **mentions**.

---

4. Mobile Notifications

Great for remote teams, freelancers, or users who often work on the go. ClickUp's mobile app can notify you of:

- Assigned tasks

- Mentions

- Reminders

- Comments and updates

Customization options:

- Choose which actions trigger alerts

- Set "Do Not Disturb" hours to avoid off-hour interruptions

---

5. ClickUp Inbox

Think of the **Inbox** as your command center. It shows:

- Assigned comments

- Reminders

- Task activity that requires attention

Inbox is **action-based**—you can resolve, dismiss, or snooze items. It's perfect for managing **what matters now**.

Configuring Your Notification Preferences

ClickUp allows deep customization so you can avoid overload and focus only on what's relevant.

Steps to Customize Notifications:

1. Go to your **User Settings** → **Notifications**

2. For each type (Email, Mobile, In-App, Desktop):

    o Toggle specific events like:

        ▪ "Task assigned to me"

        ▪ "Someone mentions me"

        ▪ "Comment added"

        ▪ "Due date changed"

        ▪ "Task status updated"

        ▪ and more...

3. Adjust preferences per workspace or even **per Space** (available on Business Plan or higher)

4. Set **frequency** for emails (e.g., immediate, daily digest)

Best Practices for Managing Notifications

1. **Start Minimal**: Begin with core updates like mentions and assigned tasks, then expand based on need.

2. **Use Watching Wisely**: You're automatically set to watch tasks you're involved in—unwatch tasks where you don't need updates.

3. **Snooze Notifications**: In your inbox, snooze lower-priority updates for later review.

4. **Batch Notification Checks**: Avoid constant interruptions by setting times of day to check notifications (e.g., once in the morning, once after lunch).

5. **Leverage Roles**: Managers may need broader visibility (e.g., status updates), while contributors may prefer only action-based alerts.

6. **Use Automation to Reduce Alerts**: Automate routine updates instead of manually triggering comments or changes that generate noise.

🧠 Use Case Examples

Use Case 1: A Team Manager

- Wants to be notified of every task status change and overdue task

- Enables in-app + desktop notifications for task progress

- Uses ClickUp Inbox to manage daily follow-ups

Use Case 2: A Developer

- Gets overloaded with notifications

- Disables email notifications

- Keeps only "assigned to me" and "mentioned" alerts via mobile

Use Case 3: A Remote Freelancer

- Checks ClickUp once daily

- Uses email digest and mobile notifications for mentions

- Customizes mobile push to turn off after 7 PM

🚧 Troubleshooting Notification Issues

Sometimes, you may not receive the updates you expect. Here are a few common issues and fixes:

- **Not getting desktop notifications?**
  → Check browser permissions and system settings

- **Email notifications not arriving?**
  → Check spam folder or ensure email is verified

- **Too many updates?**
  → Review tasks you're watching and turn off unnecessary triggers

- **Multiple workspaces?**
  → Configure notifications individually for each one

🎯 Wrapping Up: Be in Control, Not Controlled

ClickUp's notification system is one of the most **flexible and powerful** in any project management platform. By customizing your preferences, setting boundaries, and understanding your needs, you can transform notifications from a source of anxiety into a **tool of awareness and focus**.

In the next section, we'll explore how to avoid overload by using **best practices for managing notification volume** and building notification-friendly workflows.

➡️ Continue reading: **3.3.2 Inbox and Activity Feed**

3.3.2 Inbox and Activity Feed

ClickUp is more than just a task management tool — it's a central communication hub designed to help you stay on top of your team's activities without being overwhelmed. Among its most powerful tools for this are the **Inbox** and **Activity Feed**. These features ensure that you never miss a comment, task update, mention, or notification that's relevant to your work — while also giving you control over how much information you want to see.

In this section, we'll explore the functionality, customization, and best practices for using the Inbox and Activity Feed in ClickUp. You'll learn how to stay informed without getting distracted, how to organize your notifications like a pro, and how to use these features for better collaboration and decision-making.

Understanding the ClickUp Inbox

What is the Inbox?

ClickUp's Inbox is your **personal notification center**. It shows you a chronological list of all updates, tasks, mentions, comments, and reminders that are specifically related to you — not the entire workspace. Think of it as your to-do and attention list for collaboration updates.

This is **not your email inbox** — rather, it's a workspace-native center that gives you direct links to the work items where changes or communications occurred.

Why the Inbox Matters

- Keeps you focused on what requires your attention

- Consolidates communication into a manageable stream

- Encourages prompt action on comments, tasks, and mentions

- Reduces reliance on external communication platforms like Slack or email

Whether you're a team leader, individual contributor, or project manager, mastering the Inbox can help you **prioritize** and **respond effectively**.

Components of the Inbox

The Inbox contains different types of updates categorized as:

- **Assigned to You**: Tasks newly assigned to you

- **Mentions**: Comments or tasks where you're @mentioned

- **Comments**: Threads you're participating in

- **Reminders**: Personal or task-linked reminders

- **Assigned Comments**: Comments that have been turned into actionable items

- **Task Updates**: Changes to tasks you're following (e.g., due date, status)

Each item is **clickable**, taking you directly to the task or comment, so you can take action or respond without digging through folders or lists.

Managing Your Inbox Efficiently

Here are some of the **best practices** and settings to manage your Inbox effectively:

1. Use Filters and Focus Mode

- ClickUp allows you to **filter** by notification type (e.g., only show mentions or reminders).

- You can also **snooze items** or **mark them as done**, which helps you keep the Inbox clean and focused.

- **Focus Mode** lets you hide completed tasks and only display actionable items.

2. Mark as Done or Archive

Each notification comes with a " ✔ " checkmark to mark it as **Done** or **Archived**, depending on your role or preference. This is not the same as completing a task — it's only clearing the item from your view.

Marking updates as done helps with:

- Reducing clutter

- Showing progress in communication follow-ups

- Keeping your mental workspace clean

3. Using Assigned Comments

When a comment is assigned to you, it becomes part of your Inbox. These are great for:

- Quick follow-ups

- Minor tasks that don't require a full task entry

- Decision tracking within threads

Once completed, these can be marked as "resolved," clearing them from your Inbox.

Using the Activity Feed

While the Inbox is user-specific, the **Activity Feed** is like a **workspace-wide audit trail**. It shows a live timeline of everything happening across your workspace (or within a Space, Folder, or List, depending on your view). It's a powerful way to see the pulse of your team's operations.

What You Can Track in the Activity Feed

- Task creation, deletion, and updates

- Status changes

- Time tracking entries

- Comment additions and deletions

- Subtask creation or updates

- File attachments

- Custom field changes

The Activity Feed helps team leads, project managers, or workspace owners **monitor progress and accountability** across projects.

Where to Find the Activity Feed

You can access the Activity Feed from several locations:

- **Global Activity**: From your home screen or workspace overview

- **List View**: View activity specific to a particular list

- **Task View**: See history related to a single task

- **Dashboard Widgets**: Create activity feed widgets for specific spaces or projects

This contextuality allows you to **zoom in or zoom out**, depending on how granular your information needs to be.

Customizing Your Notifications

To avoid notification fatigue, ClickUp offers **granular notification settings**. You can choose what shows up in your Inbox or email for:

- Task assignments
- Comments
- Status changes
- Due date reminders
- Dependencies or relationships updates
- Mentions in tasks or documents

You can modify these settings from:

Avatar > Notifications

There, you can tailor notifications for **email**, **browser**, **mobile**, or **in-app** experiences.

Inbox vs. Activity Feed: Which to Use When?

Purpose	Use the Inbox	Use the Activity Feed
Personal task tracking	☑	✕
Responding to mentions	☑	✕
Viewing workspace-wide changes	✕	☑
Monitoring project health	✕	☑
Resolving assigned comments	☑	✕
Auditing user activity	✕	☑

The Inbox is **your** tool. The Activity Feed is **the team's** record.

Tips for Staying on Top of Notifications

1. **Check your Inbox twice a day**, like email: morning and before end-of-day.

2. **Clear out notifications** by marking them as done. Don't let it pile up.

3. **Use Assigned Comments** for small collaborative tasks.

4. **Avoid notification overload** by muting tasks or lists you don't need.

5. **Use filters** to focus only on critical updates.

6. **Train your team** to tag people responsibly — don't @mention the entire team unless necessary.

Common Mistakes to Avoid

- **Ignoring the Inbox completely**: You'll miss key mentions and deadlines.

- **Letting it get too cluttered**: A messy Inbox is a mental load.

- **Over-notifying your team**: Be selective when assigning comments or mentions.

- **Relying only on email**: ClickUp's notifications are faster and directly linked to tasks.

Real-World Use Case: A Marketing Team

Let's say you're on a **marketing team** working on a campaign:

- The copywriter gets tagged in a task comment to review ad text.

- The designer assigns a comment to the copywriter asking for new CTA suggestions.

- A PM changes the campaign task's due date.

- These updates all appear in the **copywriter's Inbox**.

- Meanwhile, the PM watches the **Activity Feed** to ensure that the whole campaign list is active, comments are happening, and tasks are changing statuses.

This shows how the Inbox and Activity Feed **complement each other** in day-to-day work.

Conclusion: Own Your Workflow

Both the **Inbox** and **Activity Feed** in ClickUp are essential tools for modern productivity and communication. By using these tools effectively, you ensure:

- Nothing important slips through the cracks

- You're not overwhelmed by irrelevant updates

- You're fully in control of your personal and team-level notifications

In the fast-paced world of collaborative work, clarity is power. And with ClickUp's notification system, you get the clarity you need — without the chaos.

3.3.3 Best Practices to Avoid Overwhelm

ClickUp is a powerful productivity tool designed to help you manage complex projects and collaborate effectively. However, with great flexibility comes the potential for information overload—especially when it comes to notifications. From email updates to in-app alerts and mobile push notifications, it's easy to get overwhelmed if your system isn't properly tuned.

In this section, we'll explore **best practices to manage ClickUp notifications** so you can stay focused on meaningful work instead of being pulled into a whirlwind of constant pings. You'll learn how to fine-tune your settings, use built-in features smartly, and design notification habits that align with your productivity style.

Why Notification Overload Happens

Before diving into solutions, let's understand the common causes of notification fatigue:

- **Default notification settings are too broad.** By default, ClickUp may notify you about every comment, task change, or update—even if it's not immediately relevant to your work.

- **Lack of role clarity.** When multiple team members are involved in tasks without defined responsibilities, notifications may get scattered to everyone.

- **Overuse of mentions.** @Mentions are powerful for drawing attention—but overusing them can desensitize your team.

- **Too many watchers.** If you or your team are "watching" too many tasks, you'll receive every minor update about them.

- **Cross-platform duplication.** You might receive the same update via email, mobile, and desktop, creating a noisy feedback loop.

Core Principles of Notification Management

To manage ClickUp notifications effectively, you must approach it from a **strategic, layered perspective**. That means:

1. **Define your priorities.** What truly requires your attention? Focus on notifications tied to your role and high-impact responsibilities.

2. **Be proactive.** Don't wait until you're overwhelmed—configure your settings as you start using ClickUp.

3. **Segment by context.** Use Spaces, Folders, Lists, and Views strategically to group related notifications together.

4. **Train your team.** Establish communication norms around when and how to notify team members.

Let's now walk through actionable best practices and tools to implement these principles.

☑ Best Practices to Avoid Notification Overwhelm in ClickUp

1. Audit and Adjust Your Notification Settings

ClickUp gives you granular control over how and when you receive alerts. You can access these settings by navigating to:

User Profile → Notifications Settings

Here are the main areas to adjust:

a. Choose Your Channels Wisely

You can receive notifications via:

- In-app alerts

- Email

- Mobile push notifications

- ClickUp Inbox

Avoid redundancy. For example, if you're always working with the ClickUp desktop app, you might **disable email and push notifications** to reduce noise.

b. Customize Event Triggers

Disable notifications for events you don't need:

- Uncheck items like "Task closed," "Task moved," or "Task created" if they're not directly relevant to your workflow.

- Focus on task assignment, mentions, and due date changes if those are your priorities.

c. Set Workspace-Wide Preferences

If you're a Workspace Admin, you can standardize certain notifications across the team to ensure consistency.

---

2. Use Assigned Comments Instead of Generic Mentions

Assigned comments are an underrated way to **cut through noise** and ensure accountability.

Instead of tagging someone in a general comment:

- Use the **"Assign Comment"** feature to convert it into an action item.

- The assignee will get a dedicated notification in their Inbox.

- Once done, they can check it off and clear the notification—keeping their feed tidy.

This practice avoids unnecessary back-and-forth tagging and makes communications more intentional.

3. Watch Only What Matters

Watching a task or list means you'll get updates on everything that happens in it. Be selective:

- Watch tasks where you're directly involved.

- Unwatch tasks once your role in them is done.

- If you need visibility without constant updates, create a **custom dashboard widget** instead of watching.

Pro tip: Use the **"Unwatch All"** feature periodically to reset and prevent notification overload.

4. Leverage ClickUp Inbox Strategically

ClickUp's **Inbox** is a powerful tool for centralized notifications and personal task management. It filters the noise and keeps only **actionable alerts**.

Best practices for Inbox:

- Set aside 2–3 times per day to check your Inbox (like checking email).

- **Clear out irrelevant alerts** as soon as you review them.

- Use the **"Done" and "Snooze"** features to organize your Inbox.

- Avoid Inbox multitasking—batch process it like email.

5. Train Your Team on Notification Etiquette

Without a team-wide understanding of communication etiquette, even well-configured settings can be undermined. Define ground rules like:

- Use @mentions **only when a direct action is required.**

- Don't spam the whole team with list-wide updates unless necessary.

- Use status updates and task fields to communicate progress—avoid comment overuse.

- Before tagging someone, ask: *"Would I say this in a meeting, or can it wait until the next check-in?"*

You can also create a short internal guide or ClickUp doc titled **"Team Notification Guidelines"** for quick reference.

6. Use Automations to Reduce Manual Updates

ClickUp Automations can reduce the need for constant manual updates that trigger alerts. Examples:

- Automatically assign a task when a status changes.

- Automatically unassign watchers when a task is marked "Complete."

- Create silent task moves that don't notify the whole team.

This reduces redundant updates and streamlines the workflow without overwhelming the team.

7. Create a "Low-Priority" Space or View

Some updates are good to monitor—but don't require immediate action. To filter them out:

- Create a dedicated "Low-Priority" Space or View.

- Mute notifications for that area or set a routine time to review it.

- Use filters (like "Status is On Hold" or "Tag is Internal") to separate updates that don't need alerts.

This way, updates aren't lost—but also don't demand instant attention.

8. Segment Notifications by Role or Function

If you're managing a large team or complex project, create **notification segments** by:

- Job role (e.g., designers only watch design tasks)

- Phase of work (e.g., dev team gets alerts in the development folder)

- Urgency or priority (e.g., only high-priority tasks trigger pings)

This prevents team members from being flooded with updates that aren't relevant to their job scope.

9. Use Dashboards to Monitor Progress Without Notifications

Dashboards allow you to monitor progress, workload, and updates **passively**—without needing constant notifications.

- Create a dashboard with widgets like "Tasks due this week," "Tasks by assignee," or "Workload overview."

- Check the dashboard during daily or weekly planning, rather than reacting to every ping.

- Share dashboards with team members instead of tagging them repeatedly in updates.

10. Regularly Review and Refine

Notification needs evolve as your team grows or your project scales. Set a **monthly or quarterly notification review** to:

- Check if current settings are still effective.

- Prune watchers on old tasks or lists.

- Adjust automation rules and triggers.

- Update internal communication policies if needed.

✏️ Summary: From Chaos to Clarity

Managing notifications in ClickUp isn't just about turning things off—it's about **tuning your system to your brain**. With the right settings, habits, and team norms, notifications become valuable signals—not distractions.

Key Takeaways:

- Audit and adjust your notification settings regularly.

- Use assigned comments, roles, and watchers with purpose.

- Rely on the ClickUp Inbox and Dashboards for centralized control.

- Train your team in notification etiquette to build a healthy communication culture.

- Automate repetitive updates to reduce manual noise.

ClickUp is designed to support **deep work and collaboration**, but only if you make the system work for *you*—not the other way around.

In the next section, we'll explore how to take your workflow even further by automating and customizing your ClickUp environment.

CHAPTER IV
Automating and Customizing Your Workflow

4.1 Using Templates

4.1.1 Creating Task and List Templates

In the fast-paced world of modern work, efficiency is everything. Repetition is the enemy of innovation—and when your workday is filled with recurring projects, repeated checklists, or standard team processes, you need a way to save time and reduce errors. That's where **ClickUp Templates** come in.

ClickUp allows you to create powerful, reusable **Task** and **List Templates** to streamline your work, maintain consistency, and make onboarding, scaling, or launching projects a breeze. In this section, we'll explore **why templates matter**, how to **create them effectively**, and how to **ensure your templates support your workflow** without becoming cluttered or outdated.

🔍 What Are Task and List Templates in ClickUp?

In ClickUp, **templates are pre-configured structures** that can be applied to new tasks, lists, projects, or even entire spaces. These templates save you from having to re-create the same elements each time. Templates can include:

- Task names and descriptions
- Checklists and subtasks
- Assignees, priorities, and tags

- Custom fields

- Dependencies

- Comments or assigned comments

- Task statuses and due dates (or relative due dates)

Templates are especially useful when your work is **repeatable** (e.g., onboarding workflows, editorial calendars, bug reports, sprint planning, etc.).

Why Use Templates?

Let's explore a few compelling benefits:

1. **Consistency Across Teams**: Templates ensure everyone is following the same process and nothing important is missed. Whether it's a client onboarding checklist or a product launch plan, templates help standardize success.

2. **Faster Task Creation**: Instead of creating every subtask, field, or checklist from scratch, you can apply a template and start working immediately.

3. **Improved Collaboration**: Shared templates reduce ambiguity. Team members know what to expect, where to find things, and how to contribute.

4. **Onboarding and Training**: New team members can quickly get up to speed using templates as blueprints for standard work.

How to Create a Task Template in ClickUp

Step 1: Set Up Your Base Task

Before you can save a template, you need a **well-structured task** to base it on. Here's how to do it:

1. **Create a new task** (or edit an existing one).

2. Add relevant details:

   o Title and description

   o Subtasks or checklists

- o Due date or start/due date range

- o Assignee (optional)

- o Priority and tags

- o Attachments or reference materials

- o Custom fields (e.g., project type, client name, estimated hours)

💡 *Tip: Use placeholders like [CLIENT NAME] or [DUE DATE] to remind users to personalize the task once it's created from the template.*

☑️ Step 2: Save as a Template

Once your task is set up:

1. Click the **three-dot menu (:)** in the upper right corner of the task window.

2. Select **"Template Center"** > **"Save as Template."**

3. Name your template clearly (e.g., "Weekly Team Sync Checklist" or "Client Onboarding – Basic").

4. Choose whether to include:

   o Subtasks

   o Attachments

   o Comments

   o Assignees (you may want to leave this off unless it's always the same)

   o Custom fields and values

5. Click **Save Template**.

Your task template is now available to reuse from the Template Center or directly when creating new tasks.

How to Create a List Template in ClickUp

While task templates work for individual pieces of work, **List Templates** give you control over entire processes, including:

- Multiple tasks

- Custom statuses

- List-level settings

- View configurations (Board, Calendar, Gantt, etc.)

This is perfect for repeatable projects like marketing campaigns, product launches, or client workflows.

Step 1: Create a Base List

1. Go to the **Folder or Space** where you want to create the list.

2. Click **"+ New List"**, name it, and set your desired statuses (To Do, In Progress, Complete, etc.).

3. Add all tasks that are part of the process.

4. Configure:

   o   Views (e.g., List, Board, Gantt)

   o   Custom fields

   o   Automations (optional)

   o   Task templates within the list (if desired)

The more complete and polished your base list is, the better your template will be for future use.

Step 2: Save the List as a Template

1. Click the **List settings menu (⋮)** in the upper-right corner of the list.

2. Choose **"Save as Template."**

3. Name your template.

4. Choose what to include:

   o   Tasks and subtasks

   o   Comments and attachments

   o   Assignees and due dates

   o   List settings and views

5. Optionally, **set sharing permissions** so others on your team can access and apply the template.

6. Click **Save.**

Your List Template is now saved and can be applied to any folder or space in the future.

📋 Best Practices for Creating Templates

Creating a template is more than just saving a structure—it's about designing something that works again and again. Follow these best practices to make your templates efficient and user-friendly:

✅ 1. Use Descriptive Names

Name templates clearly and consistently. For example:

- ✅ "Weekly Marketing Review Checklist"

- ✕ "New Template 3"

Group them logically if you're managing many templates (e.g., prefix all campaign templates with "Campaign - ").

✅ 2. Keep Templates Updated

As your workflow evolves, revisit templates regularly to update outdated information, remove irrelevant steps, and add any improvements.

✅ 3. Use Placeholders and Comments

Add notes in the description or comments with instructions. For example:

"Replace [CLIENT NAME] with actual client before assigning."

✅ 4. Avoid Including Too Much

Not every field needs to be filled. Only include what's essential and repeatable. Let users customize the rest when applying the template.

✅ 5. Centralize Access

Use the **Template Center** or create a centralized **ClickUp Docs page** to list available templates, when to use them, and how to apply them.

💬 Use Cases: When to Create a Template

Here are some common workflows where task and list templates shine:

Use Case	Recommended Template Type
Client onboarding	List Template
Weekly check-ins	Task Template
Bug reporting	Task Template
Marketing campaigns	List Template
Employee onboarding	List Template
Monthly reporting	Task Template
Product feature requests	Task Template

🫥 Should You Use Tasks or Lists as Templates?

Consideration	Use Task Template	Use List Template
One recurring item	✅	❌
Multiple tasks in a sequence	❌	✅
Simple processes/checklists	✅	❌
Complex workflows	❌	✅
Needs task dependencies	❌	✅

🚀 Next Steps: Applying Templates Across Workflows

Now that you know how to create task and list templates, the next section (4.1.2) will show you **how to apply them effectively** across different parts of your workspace. From building repeatable projects to onboarding new clients or team members, templates can become your secret weapon for consistency, speed, and clarity.

4.1.2 Applying Templates Across Workflows

One of ClickUp's most powerful and time-saving features is its **template system**. Once you've built a solid structure for your task, list, folder, or even space, you don't need to start from scratch each time you manage a new project. Instead, you can apply templates to ensure **consistency**, **efficiency**, and **scalability** across all your workflows.

This section will guide you through how to **apply templates effectively**, whether you're managing daily operations, running sprints, onboarding new clients, or launching marketing campaigns. The key to mastering ClickUp is learning not only how to build great templates—but how and **where** to apply them in context.

Why Use Templates Across Workflows?

Templates allow you to save a predefined structure and reapply it as often as you need. This is especially useful when:

- You manage **repetitive projects** (weekly meetings, monthly reports, agile sprints)

- Your team follows **standardized processes** (content production pipelines, development cycles)

- You want to **ensure quality and consistency** across teams or departments

- You're **scaling** your business and need to duplicate success quickly

Using templates effectively helps you reduce the time spent on setup and enables you to focus on execution. Now, let's dive into how to apply templates at different levels.

Where Can You Apply Templates in ClickUp?

In ClickUp, templates can be applied at multiple levels:

Template Type	Where It Applies	Example Use Case
Task Templates	Inside any task	Sales call checklist

Template Type	Where It Applies	Example Use Case
List Templates	Inside folders or spaces	Monthly content calendar
Folder Templates	Inside spaces	Client onboarding
Space Templates	Workspace-wide	Department-level structure

We'll now go through the process of applying each of these templates and how they can be integrated into workflows.

Applying Task Templates

Step-by-Step Guide:

1. **Open the task** where you want to apply a template.
2. Click the **ellipsis (...)** in the top-right corner of the task modal.
3. Select **"Templates" > "Browse Templates"**.
4. Choose the template you want to use.
5. Click **"Use Template"**.
6. Choose what elements to include (e.g., attachments, assignees, checklists).
7. Confirm to apply.

Use Cases:

- **Client Follow-Up Call**: Pre-filled task with talking points, checklist, and due date.
- **Bug Report**: Template with subtasks for validation, triage, fix, and testing.

Tips for Workflow Efficiency:

- Attach automations to template-based tasks (e.g., auto-assign based on status).
- Use custom fields in templates to capture key task metadata (e.g., priority level, client name).

Applying List Templates

List templates are incredibly useful when you manage recurring processes that require a set of predefined tasks.

How to Apply a List Template:

1. Navigate to the **folder or space** where you want the new list.

2. Click the **"+"** button to create a new list.

3. Choose **"Use Template"** from the menu.

4. Select the desired template from your library or ClickUp's built-in options.

5. Configure options (e.g., include tasks, due dates, assignees).

6. Click **"Create List"**.

Common Use Cases:

- Weekly Blog Production Schedule

- Product Feature Launch Checklist

- Event Planning Timeline

Workflow Integration:

- Apply templates for each sprint during your development cycle.

- Use templates for standardized team meetings (e.g., agendas, task tracking).

- Pair with recurring reminders to automate workflow creation.

Applying Folder Templates

Folder templates help you organize multiple lists under one project. They're ideal for **multi-phase processes** or **project types** that have a fixed structure.

Steps to Apply a Folder Template:

1. In the sidebar, navigate to the space where you want to create the folder.

2. Click **"+ New Folder"**.

3. Select **"Use Template"**.

4. Choose from saved folder templates.

5. Configure import settings.

6. Click **"Create Folder"**.

Use Case Examples:

- **Client Onboarding Folder**

  o List 1: Pre-Discovery Tasks

  o List 2: Kickoff Checklist

  o List 3: 30-60-90 Day Plan

- **Marketing Campaign**

  o List 1: Strategy

  o List 2: Execution

  o List 3: Review & Analytics

Workflow Tips:

- Embed automations at the list or folder level to assign tasks or set due dates automatically.

- Tag folders with custom fields like client names, project type, or region for better reporting.

Applying Space Templates

A **space template** is the most extensive template type in ClickUp. It includes everything from folders, lists, tasks, custom fields, automations, views, and more.

How to Apply a Space Template:

1. Go to your workspace sidebar and click **"New Space"**.

2. Select **"Use Template"**.

3. Choose from saved space templates or ClickUp's library.

4. Customize the import (select which elements to include).

5. Click **"Create Space"**.

When to Use:

- When onboarding **new departments or teams**

- When launching a new **company initiative**

- When duplicating a **proven business process** across business units

Example Space Templates:

- **HR Department**

    o Folders: Recruitment, Onboarding, Employee Reviews

- **Creative Agency**

    o Folders: Client Work, Internal Projects, Marketing

    o Automations: Tag client project managers on kickoff

    o Views: Calendar, Board, and Gantt

Tips for Applying Templates Across Workflows

1. Combine Templates with Automations

Once you've applied a template, enrich it with automations like:

- When task is created → assign to user

- When status is "In Progress" → set due date for 2 days later

- When list is complete → notify project owner

This allows every workflow to move forward automatically without manual intervention.

2. Use Custom Fields and Views

After applying a template, tailor it with views like:

- **Board View** for agile task management

- **Calendar View** for event or content planning

- **Workload View** for balancing team capacity

Pair these with **custom fields** (e.g., budget, department, client type) to filter and report efficiently.

3. Keep Templates Updated

Don't let your templates go stale. Schedule regular reviews to:

- Add or remove steps based on new team processes

- Update assignees or due dates for relevance

- Incorporate feedback from users to improve clarity

4. Use Naming Conventions

A clear naming convention makes template management easier.

Examples:

- [Template] Weekly Sprint Plan

- [Template] Product Launch Checklist

- [Template] Sales Onboarding Folder

Common Mistakes to Avoid

Mistake	Better Practice
Applying a template with old assignees	Always review before applying
Not checking custom field compatibility	Align field structure before applying
Using too many templates	Consolidate when possible for simplicity
Forgetting to test a new template	Always run a dry test with a small project

Final Thoughts

ClickUp's template system is one of its greatest strengths. Applying templates across workflows helps your team stay organized, aligned, and productive—even as your projects scale. Whether you're building repeatable processes, managing client work, or coordinating internal teams, templates give you a strategic edge.

Use them wisely. Review them often. And build a library that reflects your team's way of working—efficiently and intelligently.

4.1.3 Template Best Practices

Templates are one of the most powerful and underutilized features in ClickUp. While creating a task or list from scratch is always an option, leveraging templates can save you hours of work, reduce errors, and ensure consistency across your workflows—especially when working with teams or recurring processes. In this section, we'll explore best practices for building, maintaining, and evolving templates to maximize their effectiveness.

Why Templates Matter

Templates are not just time-savers—they're system-builders. They allow you to:

- **Ensure Consistency:** Keep team workflows aligned with standardized steps, labels, and formats.

- **Save Time:** Eliminate repetitive setup by applying pre-made structures in seconds.

- **Reduce Human Error:** Avoid forgetting essential steps or details.

- **Scale Efficiently:** Onboard new team members or launch projects faster using repeatable systems.

However, not all templates are created equal. A poorly built template can cause confusion, bottlenecks, or even workflow failure. That's why having best practices is essential.

Best Practices for Creating Effective ClickUp Templates

1. Design Before You Template

Before you hit the "Save as Template" button, spend time designing the optimal structure. Consider:

- **The goal of the template** – Is it for a content calendar, software sprint, hiring process, event planning, or client onboarding?

- **The scope and scale** – Will this template be used for solo projects or by cross-functional teams?

- **Workflow complexity** – Identify stages, steps, dependencies, and required information in advance.

Tip: Sketch your process on paper or use a whiteboarding tool like Lucidchart or Miro before translating it into ClickUp.

2. Use Descriptive Naming Conventions

Naming matters. A vague title like "Template 1" or "Task Template" leads to confusion, especially when you have many templates in your workspace. Use a clear, descriptive name that reflects its purpose.

Examples:

- ✅ *Content Creation Template – Blog Posts*

- ✅ *Client Onboarding – Agency Model*

- ✅ *Weekly Team Meeting Checklist*

Also, consider versioning if templates are updated regularly (e.g., *Product Launch v2.1*).

3. Document Template Usage Instructions

Even the best-designed template can be misused if people don't understand how to apply it. Always include internal documentation or instructions in the template itself.

Ways to do this:

- Add an introductory task or checklist titled **"Start Here"**

- Use task descriptions or comment threads to explain what each section is for

- Embed Loom videos or links to SOPs (standard operating procedures)

This helps with onboarding and ensures consistent application across your team.

4. Keep Templates Lean and Modular

A common mistake is trying to cram every possible detail into a single template. While it might seem efficient, this can overwhelm users.

Instead:

- Create modular templates for specific purposes
- Break down complex workflows into parts (e.g., *"Sprint Planning Template"* + *"Daily Standup Template"*)
- Link related templates via task relationships or documentation

This modular approach also makes it easier to maintain and update specific workflows without disrupting others.

---

5. Pre-Fill Strategically (But Not Too Much)

ClickUp templates allow you to pre-fill tasks with due dates, custom field values, assignees, priorities, statuses, and more. This is incredibly useful—but use it wisely.

Best practices include:

- Only assign tasks in a template if roles never change
- Avoid setting hard due dates unless they are relative (e.g., "X days after start")
- Pre-fill custom fields and tags only if they're universal across use cases

Remember: The goal is to give users a solid starting point—not a rigid structure they must always modify.

---

6. Use Relative Dates and Dynamic Elements

ClickUp supports **relative due dates** and **automations**, which can enhance the flexibility of your templates.

Examples:

- A content planning template can auto-set "Outline Due" 3 days after creation, and "Publish Due" 10 days after.

- Use **Automations** to auto-assign tasks, change statuses, or move items when a task is created from a template.

Always test these elements before rolling out templates across your team.

7. Build Templates at the Right Hierarchy Level

You can save templates at different levels:

- **Task**

- **List**

- **Folder**

- **Space**

Each has its use case:

- **Task Templates** are great for simple repeatable items (e.g., "Interview Follow-Up").

- **List Templates** work well for grouped items like sprints or weekly plans.

- **Folder/Space Templates** are ideal for managing large projects or entire departments.

Choose the appropriate level based on how complex and recurring your process is.

8. Test Templates Before Launch

Before you let your team use a new template:

- Create a test project using it

- Run through each step

- Evaluate whether anything is unclear, redundant, or missing

Get feedback from others. A 15-minute dry run can save you hours of confusion later.

9. Set a Review Schedule for Templates

Workflows evolve. That means your templates should too.

- Set reminders every 3–6 months to review major templates
- Archive or update outdated versions
- Collect feedback from users on what's working and what's not

This ensures your templates grow with your business, not against it.

10. Control Access and Template Governance

When multiple users can create or edit templates, you risk inconsistency or clutter.

To manage this:

- Define a **template governance policy** (Who can create? Who approves?)
- Store official templates in a dedicated "Templates" Space or Folder
- Use naming prefixes like **[Official]**, **[Draft]**, or **[Team-Specific]**

This prevents redundancy and ensures only high-quality templates are in use.

Use Case Examples

Use Case 1: Marketing Content Calendar

Template Includes:

- Pre-set statuses: Draft, Review, Scheduled, Published
- Custom fields: Content Type, Channel, Owner
- Automations: Notify editor when status changes to "Review"
- Relative due dates: Review set 3 days after creation

Use Case 2: Client Onboarding

Template Includes:

- Checklists for documents, calls, and contracts

- Placeholder tasks for kickoff and setup

- Linked Docs: Welcome guide, internal SOP

- Assigned to onboarding specialist by default

Use Case 3: Product Launch Campaign

Template Includes:

- Folder template with marketing, design, and dev Lists

- Timeline View configured

- Dependencies set between content creation and dev milestones

- Custom Dashboards for tracking campaign KPIs

Common Mistakes to Avoid

- ✗ Creating too many similar templates without naming conventions

- ✗ Hard-coding dates or assignees that change every project

- ✗ Overcomplicating a template with unnecessary elements

- ✗ Forgetting to update or test a template after making changes

---

Final Thoughts

Templates aren't just about efficiency—they're about **building systems that scale**. Whether you're a solo entrepreneur or a manager at a 100-person company, templates allow you to offload repeatable work and focus on what really matters: strategy, creativity, and results.

By following the best practices outlined above, you'll be well-equipped to build ClickUp templates that are flexible, intuitive, and effective. Don't just use ClickUp—**optimize it.**

4.2 ClickUp Automations

4.2.1 Setting Up Automations

Introduction to ClickUp Automations

In the modern workplace, time is a currency—and wasting it on repetitive actions can cost more than we realize. Whether you're marking tasks as "complete," assigning team members, or changing priorities based on due dates, many of these actions can and should be automated. That's where **ClickUp Automations** come in.

ClickUp's automation engine allows users to set up powerful **trigger-action** workflows that reduce manual input, enhance accuracy, and ensure consistency across projects. In this section, you'll learn how to set up your first automation, explore different types of triggers and actions, and understand best practices for using automation effectively.

What is an Automation in ClickUp?

In ClickUp, **automations** are predefined rules that follow a basic logic pattern:

When [Trigger] happens, then [Action] occurs.

For example:

When a task status changes to "In Progress", then assign it to John.

This "if-this-then-that" logic helps automate repetitive steps, saving time and reducing human error. ClickUp provides **dozens of pre-built automation recipes**, and also allows you to create **custom automations** to match your workflow.

Benefits of Using Automations

Before diving into setup, it's helpful to understand the key advantages of automation:

- **Saves Time**: No need to manually assign people or change statuses.

- **Increases Accuracy**: Reduces the risk of human error and forgotten steps.

- **Streamlines Workflow**: Keeps your projects flowing with minimal intervention.

- **Improves Team Coordination**: Automatically alerts the right people at the right time.

- **Scales with You**: As your projects grow, automations keep things manageable.

Accessing the Automation Panel

To begin creating an automation in ClickUp:

1. Open the **Space**, **Folder**, or **List** where you want the automation to live.

2. Click on the **Automation** button at the top of your view.

3. You'll be presented with:

    o   A list of **pre-built automation templates** (e.g., "Assign task when status changes")

    o   An option to **Create Custom Automation**

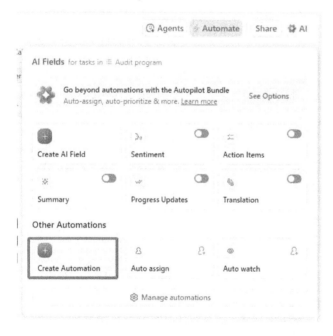

💡 *Note: Automations created in a Folder or List only apply to that scope. To apply across multiple areas, you must duplicate the automation or use Workspace-wide ClickApps (available in Business+ plans).*

Step-by-Step: Creating a Custom Automation

Let's walk through the process of creating your own automation from scratch.

Step 1: Choose a Trigger

Triggers are the "when" part of the automation—what event starts the chain. ClickUp offers a wide array of triggers such as:

- **Task Created**

- **Status Changed**

- **Priority Changed**

- **Due Date Arrives**

- **Assignee Added**

- **Custom Field Changes**

- **Time Tracked**

- **Checklist Completed**

☑ *Example: When a task status changes to "Review"...*

You can only choose one trigger per automation, but it can be customized with conditions (we'll cover this below).

Step 2: Choose an Action

Actions are the "then" part—what you want ClickUp to do when the trigger occurs. Common actions include:

- **Assign Task**

- **Change Status**

- **Move to Another List**

- **Add a Comment**

- **Set Due Date**

- **Apply Template**

- **Set Priority**

- **Add Watchers**

- **Post to Slack (via Integration)**

☑ *Example: ...then assign the task to Sarah and add a comment "Please review by EOD."*

You can add **multiple actions** to a single automation.

Step 3: Add Conditions (Optional but Powerful)

Conditions allow for more specific targeting within your automation. Examples:

- **Only apply if the assignee is empty**

- **Only run if priority is High**

- **Exclude subtasks**

- **Apply only to specific Custom Fields**

🔍 *Use Case:* Only assign a task to "QA Team" when the status changes **and** the task priority is **High**.

These filters help ensure that automations don't trigger unnecessarily or create conflicts.

Step 4: Test and Enable

Once your automation is configured:

1. **Name it clearly** (e.g., "Assign QA for High-Priority Reviews")

2. Click **Create Automation**

3. You'll see it listed under the **"Active Automations"** tab

4. You can toggle it on/off at any time, or edit/delete it if needed

To test it, simply trigger the action manually (e.g., change a status or assign a task) and see if the automation fires as expected.

Using Pre-Built Automation Templates

ClickUp provides **dozens of ready-to-use templates** that are ideal for beginners. Some examples include:

- ☑ *When a task is created, assign to [User]*

- ☑ *When status changes to "Done", mark due date as complete*

- ☑ *When due date passes, change status to "Overdue"*

To use a template:

1. Open the Automation Panel

2. Click **"Browse Recipes"**

3. Choose a template and customize it

4. Save and activate

Templates can be modified just like custom automations, so they're a great starting point.

Common Use Cases for Automations

Here are real-world scenarios where automations shine:

Onboarding Tasks

- When a new task is created in the "New Hire" list, apply the "Employee Onboarding" template, assign HR, and set the due date to 5 days later.

Bug Tracking

- When a bug report is marked "High Priority", assign the tech lead and notify QA via comment.

Marketing Campaigns

- When a campaign task moves to "Ready to Launch", schedule a due date, tag the team, and send a Slack alert.

Freelance Client Work

- When invoice task is marked "Sent", change status to "Waiting for Payment" and add reminder after 7 days.

Automation Limits and Considerations

While powerful, automations have some limits depending on your plan:

Plan	Monthly Automations	Features
Free	100/month	Basic rules only
Unlimited	1,000/month	Custom automations
Business	10,000/month	Advanced filters, multiple actions
Business Plus/Enterprise	Custom	Priority support, workload automations

You can check your usage by visiting **Workspace Settings > Automations Usage**.

Other important considerations:

- Automations **do not retroactively apply** to existing tasks (they only work from the moment they are active).

- Be cautious with **looping automations** (e.g., Task status changes trigger another automation which loops back).

- Automation logs can be viewed under each task's **Activity Feed** for troubleshooting.

Automation Best Practices

To get the most from ClickUp automations:

- **Start small**: Automate one or two core actions before expanding.

- **Use clear naming** conventions for easier tracking.

- **Avoid redundancy** by reviewing existing rules before adding new ones.

- **Train your team**: Ensure everyone knows which automations are active and how they function.

- **Regularly review and refine** your automations as workflows evolve.

Conclusion: Let ClickUp Work for You

Automations are one of the most valuable features in ClickUp—and once you start using them effectively, you'll wonder how you ever worked without them. Whether you're a solo user managing personal projects or a team lead running a multi-layered department, automations can save time, improve consistency, and eliminate bottlenecks.

In the next section (**4.2.2 Automation Triggers and Actions**), we'll break down each trigger and action type in more detail, helping you become even more confident in building workflow automations tailored to your unique needs.

4.2.2 Automation Triggers and Actions

One of the most powerful time-saving features in ClickUp is **Automations**. With the right automations in place, you can reduce manual tasks, ensure consistency in your processes, and build workflows that quite literally run themselves. At the heart of ClickUp Automations are two critical components: **triggers** and **actions**.

In this section, we'll take a deep dive into these components. You'll learn what each of them means, how they work together, and how to use them effectively to optimize your productivity.

Understanding the Logic of Automations: "When This Happens, Do That"

Automations in ClickUp operate on a simple **IF–THEN** logic:

"When [Trigger], then [Action]."

This structure makes automations intuitive even for users who have no coding or scripting experience. The platform provides a wide array of triggers and actions to choose from, allowing for an impressive level of flexibility.

Before we examine specific examples, let's break down what **triggers** and **actions** really are.

What Is a Trigger?

A **trigger** is the event that initiates the automation. It's what ClickUp listens for. When the trigger condition is met, the system springs into action.

ClickUp supports a variety of triggers across different work contexts. These can range from simple events like a task status changing to more specific actions like assigning a task to a user or updating a custom field.

Here are the main categories of **Triggers** in ClickUp:

🔄 Status Changes

These are the most common automation triggers.

- **Task status changes**
  Example: When a task moves from "In Progress" to "Review".

- **Task moves to a specific status**
  Example: When a task enters the "Done" status.

Use Case: Automatically assign a QA reviewer when a task enters the "Review" stage.

👤 Assignee Changes

Automate tasks based on who is assigned or unassigned.

- **Task is assigned**
  Example: When a task is assigned to anyone or a specific person.

- **Task is unassigned**
  Example: When a task becomes unassigned, notify the team lead.

Use Case: When a task is assigned to John, automatically set a due date 2 days later.

🕐 Date-Based Triggers

ClickUp can act when a due date, start date, or other date field reaches or passes.

- **Due date arrives**

- **Start date arrives**

- **Date custom field changes**

Use Case: Send a reminder when a task's due date is today.

Task Property Changes

These triggers relate to task fields or attributes.

- **Priority changes**
  Example: When priority becomes "Urgent".

- **Custom field changes**
  Example: When a dropdown field is updated to "Client Approved".

Use Case: When a custom field "Stage" changes to "Final", send a Slack message.

Checklist or Subtask Completion

Track checklist items and subtasks as triggers.

- Checklist item is completed

- All checklist items are completed

- All subtasks are completed

Use Case: Automatically move parent task to "Done" when all subtasks are completed.

Location-Based Triggers

React to changes in folder or list location.

- Task is moved to another list

- Task is created in a specific list

Use Case: When a task is moved to "Archive" list, remove all assignees.

Recurring or Creation Triggers

Great for process-based workflows.

- Task is created

- Task is created from a template

Use Case: When a task is created, auto-assign to a default team member and set due date.

What Is an Action?

Once a trigger fires, ClickUp performs an **action**. Actions are the tasks ClickUp does for you — they are the "then" in the automation formula.

There's a robust selection of built-in actions you can use to manipulate tasks, notify users, and shape your workflows.

Here are the main categories of **Actions**:

Task Property Updates

Modify the task's attributes automatically.

- **Change status**
  Example: Set task status to "Done".

- **Change priority**
  Example: Set priority to "High".

- **Set due/start date**
  Example: Set due date 3 days from now.

- **Change custom field value**
  Example: Set dropdown to "Awaiting Approval".

Use Case: Automatically escalate priority when a task remains in "In Progress" for over 5 days.

Assignment Actions

Modify who is assigned to the task.

- **Assign task to...**
  Example: Assign to a specific person or team.

- **Remove assignee**
  Example: Clear current assignee after task completion.

Use Case: Auto-assign newly created tasks to the team lead.

Checklist and Subtask Management

Manage internal task components.

- **Add checklist**
  Example: Insert a predefined QA checklist.

- **Create subtasks**
  Example: Add 3 subtasks for standard onboarding steps.

Use Case: When a task enters the "Hiring" stage, add interview subtasks.

Notifications and Communication

Keep your team informed.

- **Send email**
  Example: Email team lead when a task is overdue.

- **Send ClickUp notification**
  Example: Notify assignee when priority changes.

- **Send webhook (advanced)**
  Example: Trigger external systems or custom integrations.

Use Case: When a task is marked as "Client Ready," notify the sales team via email.

Templates and Movement

Help maintain structure and flow.

- **Apply task template**
  Example: Apply "Product Launch" template on creation.

- **Move task to another list**
  Example: Move to "Done" list upon completion.

Use Case: When a new task is created, apply the "Bug Report" template and move it to QA list.

Combining Triggers and Actions: Creating Workflows

You can mix and match triggers and actions to create layered workflows. For example:

When a task is moved to the "Review" status
Then assign it to Jane, set due date to 2 days from now, and notify the project manager.

This simple combination eliminates 3 manual steps, saving time and ensuring consistency.

Advanced Automation Options

Multiple Triggers and Conditional Logic

ClickUp currently supports one trigger per automation, but with creative structuring and multiple automations, you can simulate conditional logic (e.g., "If this AND that").

Use linked automations across multiple statuses, fields, or actions to mimic more complex workflows.

Automation Conditions

Some actions can be refined further with conditions — such as only sending a notification if a certain field equals a value.

Example:

- **Trigger:** Task enters "Waiting for Review"

- **Condition:** Only if assignee is "John"

- **Action:** Send notification to QA lead

Tips for Using Automations Effectively

1. **Start simple.** Don't try to automate everything at once. Focus on repetitive actions that waste time.

2. **Name automations clearly.** Use descriptive titles like "Auto-assign QA Reviewer" or "Move to Done When All Subtasks Complete".

3. **Test before scaling.** Always test your automation in a sandbox or with a sample task to ensure it works as intended.

4. **Avoid automation loops.** Be cautious of creating workflows where two automations keep triggering each other endlessly.

5. **Document your automation logic.** Especially for teams, keep track of what automations are running and why.

Real-World Use Case Examples

Here are a few automation setups used by teams across industries:

Marketing Campaign Workflow

- **Trigger:** Task status changes to "Approval Needed"
- **Action 1:** Assign to Marketing Director
- **Action 2:** Notify via ClickUp comment
- **Action 3:** Set due date to 2 days from now

Bug Tracking System

- **Trigger:** Task is created with tag "Bug"
- **Action 1:** Apply Bug Template
- **Action 2:** Assign to Developer Team
- **Action 3:** Set priority to "High"

Client Onboarding Process

- **Trigger:** Task created in "Onboarding" list

- **Action 1:** Add "Onboarding Checklist"

- **Action 2:** Create 3 subtasks

- **Action 3:** Assign to Account Manager

Conclusion: Automate the Busywork, Focus on the Big Work

Mastering **Automation Triggers and Actions** in ClickUp is like hiring a tireless virtual assistant who ensures nothing falls through the cracks. The more thoughtfully you configure these automations, the more you unlock the true potential of ClickUp as a productivity powerhouse.

By reducing human error, saving time, and standardizing your processes, automations help you and your team **focus on what matters most** — solving problems, creating value, and achieving goals.

4.2.3 Sample Use Cases

ClickUp Automations allow you to eliminate repetitive work, reduce human error, and streamline collaboration by letting the system take care of routine actions. While creating an automation may sound technical or complicated, ClickUp makes it intuitive with a simple **"Trigger → Condition → Action"** model. Once you understand the basics, the real power lies in applying automations to real-world situations.

In this section, we will explore **practical sample use cases** across different roles, teams, and industries to help you envision how automations can bring order and efficiency to your workflow.

Use Case 1: Onboarding New Clients (for Agencies or Freelancers)

Goal:

Create a standardized onboarding workflow for every new client with automated task creation, assignee, and deadlines.

Setup:

- **Trigger:** When a task is moved to the "Client Onboarding" list

- **Condition:** If status is "In Progress"

- **Actions:**

  - Create subtasks: "Send welcome email", "Schedule kickoff call", "Share access to portal"

  - Assign subtasks to relevant team members

  - Set due dates 1–3 days from trigger

☑ Outcome:

The moment a new client project is moved into onboarding, all essential steps are triggered automatically. This ensures consistency and prevents steps from being missed—especially important when scaling operations or delegating to junior staff.

Use Case 2: Bug Tracking and Escalation (for Tech Teams)

🐛 Goal:

Ensure urgent bugs get flagged, assigned, and prioritized without delays.

💡 Setup:

- **Trigger:** When priority is set to "Urgent"

- **Condition:** If status is "Open"

- **Actions:**

  - Assign to "Lead Developer"

  - Change status to "Needs Review"

  - Add comment: "Auto-flagged as urgent. Please review ASAP."

  - Notify QA team via email

☑ Outcome:

By automating the routing and communication around urgent bugs, developers save time and bugs are handled swiftly. No need for manual Slack messages or endless pings.

Use Case 3: Auto-Closing Stale Tasks (for Managers)

🗓 Goal:

Keep the workspace clean by automatically closing tasks that haven't been updated in weeks.

💡 Setup:

- **Trigger:** When a task is inactive for 30 days
- **Condition:** If status is "To Do" or "In Progress"
- **Actions:**
    - Change status to "Archived"
    - Add comment: "This task was automatically archived due to inactivity. Reopen if needed."
    - Move to "Backlog" list

✅ Outcome:

Helps teams maintain a healthy, updated board and avoid accumulating irrelevant tasks. It also encourages accountability—people will either act on tasks or let them go.

Use Case 4: Sales Pipeline Management (for Sales Teams)

💼 Goal:

Ensure that prospects are properly nurtured and follow-ups are never missed.

💡 Setup:

- **Trigger:** When a lead moves to "Proposal Sent"
- **Actions:**
    - Create subtask: "Follow up in 3 days"
    - Assign to sales rep

- o Set due date 3 days from today

- o Change priority to "High"

☑ Outcome:

Automates sales follow-up, which is crucial for closing deals. Every sales rep gets reminded to check in with prospects, reducing drop-offs in the sales funnel.

Use Case 5: HR – Employee Offboarding Checklist

🖐 Goal:

Make sure that all tasks related to offboarding (e.g., returning equipment, removing access, conducting exit interview) are completed on time and assigned to the correct departments.

💡 Setup:

- **Trigger:** When status changes to "Offboarding Started"

- **Actions:**

  - o Create subtasks: "Collect company laptop", "Disable email account", "Exit interview"

  - o Assign to relevant departments

  - o Add checklist: "Confirm all accounts disabled", "Collect ID badge"

  - o Notify IT and HR via email

☑ Outcome:

Nothing falls through the cracks, and every offboarding process is consistent and auditable. This is especially useful for growing teams and remote-first companies.

Use Case 6: Creative Workflow – Content Publishing

✍ Goal:

Streamline the steps of reviewing, approving, and publishing a blog post or video content.

Setup:

- **Trigger:** When a task moves to "Ready for Review"
- **Actions:**
    - Assign to Editor
    - Change status to "Under Review"
    - Set due date for review: 2 days from today
- **Trigger:** When status changes to "Approved"
- **Actions:**
    - Assign to Content Manager
    - Move task to "Ready to Publish"
    - Post comment: "Content approved. Schedule for publishing."

Outcome:

The team doesn't need to manually tag or notify editors and content managers—it happens instantly. This keeps content moving smoothly down the pipeline.

Use Case 7: Weekly Task Reset (for Operations Teams)

Goal:

Each week, recurring operational tasks should be reset with fresh due dates and status.

Setup:

- **Trigger:** Every Monday at 9 AM (Recurring trigger)
- **Condition:** If task has tag "Weekly"
- **Actions:**
    - Change status to "To Do"
    - Set new due date (Next Friday)

      o   Add comment: "This task has been reset for the new week."

✅ Outcome:

Perfect for teams managing routine checklists or operational reviews. This removes the need for creating fresh tasks each week—just reset and go.

Use Case 8: Task Approval Workflow (for Marketing Teams)

✅ Goal:

Create a simple approval process for social media posts or designs.

💡 Setup:

- **Trigger:** When status changes to "Awaiting Approval"
- **Actions:**
  - Assign to "Marketing Manager"
  - Add checklist: "Review copy", "Check image resolution", "Confirm branding"
  - Set due date in 1 day
- **Trigger:** When checklist is completed
- **Actions:**
  - Change status to "Approved"

✅ Outcome:

Instead of chasing approvals over email or chat, the process is automated with clear visibility and accountability.

Use Case 9: Sprint Planning (for Agile Teams)

🏃 Goal:

Automate the setup of new sprints including recurring ceremonies like stand-ups and retrospectives.

💡 Setup:

- **Trigger:** When a task named "Start Sprint" is marked complete
- **Actions:**
  - Create tasks: "Daily Standups", "Sprint Demo", "Retrospective"
  - Assign each to team leads
  - Set relative due dates (e.g., +1 day, +7 days)
  - Move user stories from "Backlog" to "Sprint" list

☑ Outcome:

Agile teams can maintain a reliable cadence without manual setup for each sprint. Less time planning, more time building.

Use Case 10: Auto-Reminders for Overdue Tasks

🕐 Goal:

Send reminders to task assignees when due dates are missed.

💡 Setup:

- **Trigger:** When due date arrives
- **Condition:** If status is not "Complete"
- **Actions:**
  - Add comment: "Reminder: This task is overdue."
  - Change priority to "High"
  - Send notification to assignee and project manager

☑ Outcome:

Keeps accountability high and ensures that deadlines are taken seriously—without the need for a manager to check manually.

Final Thoughts on Use Cases

The examples above are just the tip of the iceberg. Whether you're in marketing, design, software development, customer service, HR, or finance—**ClickUp Automations can be tailored to match your team's rhythm**.

Some additional tips when designing your own automations:

- **Start small.** Try a simple automation before building complex flows.

- **Test before scaling.** Use test spaces or dummy tasks to ensure your logic works.

- **Combine automations.** Chain multiple triggers and actions together to cover end-to-end workflows.

- **Review regularly.** Automation needs evolve. Keep them updated as your team grows or pivots.

By using the right automations, you're not just saving time—**you're building a system that works for you even when you're offline or asleep**.

4.3 Custom Fields and Statuses

4.3.1 Designing Custom Workflows

ClickUp's greatest strength lies in its **customizability**. Unlike many productivity tools that force users into a rigid format, ClickUp empowers you to **design workflows that align with your team's specific needs**, whether you're managing a content pipeline, a product roadmap, a client onboarding system, or an internal ticketing process.

This section will guide you through the process of **designing custom workflows** using **Custom Fields** and **Custom Statuses**, two of the most powerful features in ClickUp. Whether you're a team leader building processes from scratch or a solo freelancer seeking more structure, learning how to map your work into ClickUp's framework can transform the way you plan, track, and deliver projects.

What Is a Workflow in ClickUp?

A workflow is a **series of repeatable steps** that guide how work gets done—from idea to completion. In ClickUp, workflows are represented through:

- **Tasks and Subtasks**
- **Statuses** (e.g., To Do, In Progress, Complete)
- **Custom Fields** (e.g., Budget, Priority, Client Name)
- **Views** (e.g., Kanban Board, List, Calendar, Gantt)

By customizing these elements, you can **mirror real-life processes**, ensure consistency, and enable team members to work more effectively.

The Role of Custom Fields in Workflow Design

Custom Fields allow you to add additional data to your tasks that are specific to your workflow. Think of them as columns in a spreadsheet—but built directly into your task management system.

Some use cases include:

- **Marketing**: Campaign type, client name, target platform

- **Product development**: Feature priority, release version, status label

- **Sales**: Deal value, lead source, stage in pipeline

- **HR**: Candidate stage, job title, interview date

ClickUp supports several types of Custom Fields, including:

- Text (Single-line or Multi-line)

- Dropdown

- Date

- Number

- Checkbox

- People (User Assignment)

- Labels

- Phone/Email/Website

- Currency

- Progress Bar or Slider

🔧 **Steps to Add Custom Fields:**

1. Navigate to the **List, Folder, or Space** where you want the custom field.

2. Click the **+** icon next to existing columns.

3. Select the **type of Custom Field** you want.

4. Name it and choose whether to make it **private or shared**.

5. Optionally, set **default values** or color code labels.

Once a Custom Field is created, it can be **reused across tasks**, and you can **sort, filter, or group by these fields** in your views.

The Importance of Custom Statuses

ClickUp's status system is flexible and designed to fit **your unique process**, not the other way around. Traditional task apps often use simple status sets like "To Do," "Doing," and "Done." With ClickUp, you can define your **own stages**, for example:

- For a content team:
  Ideas → Drafting → Editing → Scheduled → Published

- For a software team:
  Backlog → In Progress → QA → Staging → Released

- For a service business:
  New Request → Under Review → Waiting for Client → Approved → Completed

You can **customize statuses at the List, Folder, or Space level**, meaning different departments or projects can use completely different workflows.

Creating Custom Statuses:

1. Open the settings menu for your Space, Folder, or List.

2. Go to **Statuses**.

3. Select **Custom Statuses**.

4. Add, remove, or rename statuses to match your process.

5. Use **colors** to visually differentiate stages (e.g., red for blocked, green for done).

Statuses help team members know **exactly where a task is**, and can be tied to **Automations**, such as "When status changes to 'Completed,' move task to archive."

Mapping Out Your Workflow

Before diving into ClickUp and adding statuses or custom fields, take time to **analyze your current workflow**. Ask these questions:

- What are the **repeatable stages** of your task or project?

- What **data** do you track for each task?

- Are there **dependencies** or **decision points** that should be visualized?

- Who is responsible at each stage?

Once you've mapped out the answers, you can begin implementing them inside ClickUp.

🔄 Real-World Workflow Examples

1. Content Creation Workflow

Custom Statuses: Idea → Outline → Drafting → Editing → Scheduled → Published

Custom Fields:

- Content Type (Dropdown: Blog, Video, Podcast)
- Target Audience (Text)
- Assigned Editor (User)
- Publish Date (Date)
- Distribution Channels (Labels)

View Setup: Use a **Board View** grouped by status, with **Calendar View** for scheduling.

---

2. Client Onboarding Workflow

Custom Statuses: Initial Contact → Kickoff Call → Proposal Sent → Agreement Signed → Onboarded

Custom Fields:

- Client Company (Text)
- Contract Value (Currency)
- Onboarding Date (Date)
- Main Contact (User)

Automations:

- When status is "Agreement Signed", create onboarding checklist.
- When onboarding date arrives, assign task to onboarding lead.

3. Bug Tracking Workflow (for Development Teams)

Custom Statuses: New → Assigned → In Progress → QA → Closed

Custom Fields:

- Severity (Dropdown: Low, Medium, High)

- Platform (Label: iOS, Android, Web)

- Related Feature (Text)

- Assigned Developer (User)

Gantt or Timeline View: Use to visualize priority bugs and sprint timing.

🚀 Scaling Your Workflow

As your team grows, or as you manage multiple workflows, ClickUp gives you options to **standardize and scale**:

- **Templates**: Once you finalize a workflow, save it as a List or Folder Template for future reuse.

- **Custom Field Manager**: Use this to manage, rename, or delete custom fields across your Workspace.

- **Permissions**: Control who can edit statuses, add fields, or modify processes.

- **ClickApps**: Activate enhancements like "Multiple Assignees," "Time Estimates," or "Sprints" for more powerful workflows.

🔄 Iterate and Improve

Your first workflow isn't set in stone. Use ClickUp's reporting and feedback mechanisms to see what's working and what isn't.

- Ask team members: **Is this field helpful? Are the statuses clear?**

- Review metrics: Are tasks stuck in certain stages? Are due dates frequently missed?

- Adapt: Add automation, remove unused fields, consolidate steps.

Remember, the best workflow is the one your team **actually uses**.

✅ Best Practices for Designing Workflows

- **Start simple**: Don't add 10 statuses or 15 custom fields unless truly necessary.

- **Use consistent naming conventions** for fields and statuses.

- **Color-code** statuses for better visual understanding.

- **Test** workflows with a small group before rolling out to everyone.

- Use **Automations** to support, not replace, human logic.

- Document the workflow so all users know how to use it properly.

❄ Conclusion: Building a System That Works for You

Designing custom workflows in ClickUp allows you to **own your process**. Whether you're an agile software team or a marketing agency juggling clients, the combination of **Custom Fields** and **Statuses** lets you **create a visual, trackable, and repeatable system** for getting things done.

Remember: ClickUp is a blank canvas. By investing time to set up smart workflows, you're not just organizing tasks—you're designing **how your business operates**.

4.3.2 Custom Field Types Explained

One of the standout features of ClickUp that sets it apart from other project and task management platforms is its **powerful customization** capabilities. Among the most vital of these are **custom fields**, which allow users to tailor ClickUp to fit almost any workflow or business model.

In this section, we'll explore the **types of custom fields** available in ClickUp, explain **how and when to use each**, and provide **real-world examples** to inspire your workflow optimization.

What Are Custom Fields?

Custom fields in ClickUp are flexible data containers that can be added to tasks, lists, or folders. Unlike built-in fields such as "Assignee" or "Due Date," custom fields are entirely user-defined. They give you the power to **track virtually anything**—from budget, hours worked, and client names, to approval statuses, invoice numbers, and beyond.

You can think of custom fields as the building blocks for making ClickUp *your* system, not just a standard to-do list.

How Custom Fields Work in ClickUp

Each custom field is associated with a particular **field type**, which determines what kind of data it can store and how it can be interacted with. You can apply custom fields at multiple levels (e.g., list level, folder level), and they will cascade to all tasks beneath that level unless otherwise specified.

You can add custom fields by clicking the **"+" button** at the top of your task view or within your settings for a specific list, folder, or space.

Why Field Types Matter

Field types control both the **form** and **function** of the data. For instance, a "Dropdown" field ensures consistent tagging across tasks, whereas a "Number" field allows for calculations and reporting. Choosing the right field type directly affects your ability to:

- Filter and sort tasks

- Generate meaningful dashboards

- Create automations

- Export structured reports

- Ensure data consistency

Now let's explore each of the available field types in ClickUp and understand their use cases.

Common Custom Field Types Explained

1. Text Field

- **Purpose:** To store short pieces of text, like names, tags, or notes.
- **Use Cases:**
  - Client Name
  - Campaign Title
  - Order ID
- **Limitations:** Cannot be used for sorting numerically or linking across tasks.
- **Tip:** Great for identifiers or when you need something human-readable and short.

2. Text Area (Long Text)

- **Purpose:** To store longer blocks of text.
- **Use Cases:**
  - Task Descriptions (if more detail is needed beyond default description)
  - Meeting Notes
  - Status Updates
- **Ideal For:** Teams that prefer capturing detailed written content within structured task views.

3. Dropdown

- **Purpose:** To provide a set of predefined options.
- **Use Cases:**
  - Priority Levels

- o Task Category (Design, Marketing, Development, etc.)
- o Department Assignment
- **Best Practices:**
  - o Keep dropdowns concise and avoid duplications.
  - o Use color-coding to add quick visual cues.
- **Pro Tip:** Dropdowns are perfect for standardizing team-wide data input.

4. Labels (Multi-select)

- **Purpose:** Similar to dropdowns but allows multiple selections.
- **Use Cases:**
  - o Feature Tags (Bug, Enhancement, Urgent)
  - o Campaign Channels (Email, Social, Paid)
  - o Project Phases
- **Best For:** Situations where one task belongs to multiple categories.

5. Number

- **Purpose:** Stores numerical data.
- **Use Cases:**
  - o Estimated Hours
  - o Budget Amount
  - o Revenue or Sales Value
- **Advanced Use:** Can be used in formulas and reporting widgets in dashboards.
- **Tip:** Set decimal places based on the field's purpose (e.g., whole numbers for hours, 2 decimals for currency).

6. Currency

- **Purpose:** Similar to number fields but formatted as monetary values.
- **Use Cases:**
  - Invoices
  - Budget Tracking
  - Client Payments
- **Tip:** Set the appropriate currency symbol and decimal precision.

7. Date

- **Purpose:** Store additional dates beyond the default due date.
- **Use Cases:**
  - Review Dates
  - Contract Expiration
  - Event Dates
- **Smart Use:** Combine with automations to trigger status changes or reminders.

8. Checkbox

- **Purpose:** Create a simple binary value (checked/unchecked).
- **Use Cases:**
  - Approval Status
  - QA Checked?
  - Legal Reviewed?
- **Best Practices:** Pair with automations to move tasks to the next stage upon check.

9. People

- **Purpose:** Assign additional team members beyond the main assignee.
- **Use Cases:**
  - Reviewer
  - Stakeholder
  - Backup Owner
- **Note:** Allows better team tracking when tasks have multiple stakeholders.

10. Email

- **Purpose:** Store email addresses in structured format.
- **Use Cases:**
  - Client Contact Email
  - Vendor Email
  - Assigned Support Agent
- **Advanced Use:** Can be linked to email integrations (e.g., sending direct messages).

11. Phone

- **Purpose:** Structured field for phone numbers.
- **Use Cases:**
  - Client Contact Info
  - Delivery Numbers
  - Internal Helpdesk Lines

12. Website/Link

- **Purpose:** For URLs.
- **Use Cases:**
    - Client Website
    - Project Resources
    - Social Media Links
- **Helpful Feature:** Automatically opens in a new tab when clicked.

13. Formula Field

- **Purpose:** Calculates values based on other fields using formulas.
- **Use Cases:**
    - Time Remaining (Due Date - Today)
    - Cost Estimations (Hours * Rate)
    - Completion Score (% of Checklists Done)
- **Skills Needed:** Basic formula logic, similar to spreadsheets.
- **Note:** Read-only field; auto-calculated.

14. Progress Bar

- **Purpose:** Visual representation of progress (based on numerical input or checklist completion).
- **Use Cases:**
    - Task Completion %
    - Stage Completion
    - Subtask Coverage
- **Tips:** Make it visible in List View for real-time updates.

15. Rating (Stars)

- **Purpose:** 1–5 star rating system.

- **Use Cases:**

  o   Task Complexity

  o   User Satisfaction

  o   Priority Visual

- **Bonus Tip:** Great for UX teams doing feature scoring or feedback tracking.

16. Location

- **Purpose:** Stores geographical locations or addresses.

- **Use Cases:**

  o   Office Locations

  o   Event Venues

  o   Site Visits

17. Milestone (via Status or Tag)

- **Purpose:** Though not technically a field, many teams use Tags or Statuses as milestones.

- **Use Cases:**

  o   "Launch Complete"

  o   "Contract Signed"

  o   "Final Review"

- **Recommendation:** Combine with custom statuses for clarity.

🛠 Using Custom Fields Effectively

It's not just about **adding custom fields**—it's about **designing your system for clarity, consistency, and reporting**. Here are some best practices:

- **Avoid clutter**: Only use fields you'll consistently track.

- **Standardize field names**: Especially across different teams or spaces.

- **Re-use fields across lists**: Instead of creating a new "Budget" field in each project, create one global field.

- **Make fields visible in views**: ClickUp allows you to show or hide fields in List, Board, or Calendar view.

- **Use with Automations**: Trigger actions when a field value changes (e.g., "When Priority = High → Move to Urgent List").

◎ Real-World Use Case Examples

Marketing Team

- **Fields Used:** Campaign Name (Text), Channel (Dropdown), Budget (Currency), Live Date (Date), Owner (People), Approval Status (Checkbox)

Product Development Team

- **Fields Used:** Feature Name (Text), Status (Dropdown), Complexity (Rating), QA Complete (Checkbox), Dev Estimate (Number)

HR Team

- **Fields Used:** Candidate Name (Text), Position (Dropdown), Interview Date (Date), Contact (Phone), Status (Dropdown)

▣ Field Management and Permissions

Admins and members with edit access can manage custom fields. You can also **lock fields** so only specific roles can change them—this is useful for financial or compliance-related data.

☑ Wrapping Up

Custom fields in ClickUp allow you to transform a simple task manager into a **robust, tailored system** for tracking exactly what your team needs. Whether you're managing creative projects, product development, marketing campaigns, or client services, choosing and configuring the right custom field types ensures:

- Better visibility

- More consistent workflows

- Easier automation

- Higher team productivity

In the next section (4.3.3), we'll take these concepts a step further and explore how to **group, color-code, and organize statuses** to create fully customized workflows that align with your team's process.

4.3.3 Status Groups and Colors

When managing multiple tasks, especially across different teams or complex workflows, clarity becomes essential. ClickUp's **Status Groups and Colors** provide a powerful way to visually communicate task progress, stages, or categories—at a glance. This section walks you through how to effectively use and customize status groups and colors to reflect your unique workflow, improve collaboration, and streamline project tracking.

What Are Status Groups in ClickUp?

Status Groups in ClickUp are **collections of related task statuses** that fall under broader categories. These groups provide context and structure, letting users know whether a task is just starting, in progress, completed, or blocked.

There are four core types of **default status groups** in ClickUp:

- ☑ **To Do** – Tasks that haven't started yet.

- 🔄 **In Progress** – Tasks that are actively being worked on.

- ⬦ **Complete** – Tasks that are finished.

- ⬡ **Closed** – Tasks that are done and archived or no longer needed.

You can **rename, add, or customize** these groups to fit your use case. For example, a marketing team might use:

- To Do: "Not Started"

- In Progress: "Writing", "Editing", "Reviewing"

- Complete: "Published"

- Closed: "Archived"

Each of these statuses can be color-coded for **instant visual clarity**.

Why Use Status Groups?

Using status groups can:

- **Organize tasks** more effectively, especially in complex workflows.

- **Simplify automation**, as rules can be triggered based on group transitions.

- **Improve team communication**, ensuring everyone knows what stage a task is in.

- **Enable better reporting**, since Dashboards and Views can filter by status groups.

How Status Groups Work in Practice

Imagine you're leading a **product development project**. Your team includes designers, developers, QA testers, and product managers. Instead of just "To Do → In Progress → Done", you might need:

- **To Do**: Backlog, Sprint Planning

- **In Progress**: Design, Development, QA Testing

- **Complete**: Ready for Release

- **Closed**: Released, Deprecated

In this case, the **In Progress** group helps you track exactly *which* phase the task is in, while the **Complete** and **Closed** groups clearly separate active work from work that's entirely done or no longer relevant.

Setting Up Status Groups in ClickUp

You can set up or modify status groups by following these steps:

1. **Navigate to the Space, Folder, or List** you want to customize.

2. Click on the **Settings (gear icon)** next to the Space or Folder name.

3. Choose **Statuses** from the sidebar.

4. You'll see options to:

   o **Add New Status**

   o **Edit Existing Status**

   o **Drag and Drop** statuses into different groups

   o **Change Colors** of individual statuses

ClickUp uses **drag-and-drop** grouping to place statuses under the To Do, In Progress, Complete, or Closed headings.

Best Practices for Grouping Statuses

1. **Keep It Intuitive**: Users should immediately understand what each status means without needing explanation.

2. **Match Your Workflow**: Don't just use generic labels. Instead, tailor your statuses to reflect the exact steps in your process.

3. **Limit Statuses**: Too many statuses can create confusion. Stick to 4–7 within a group to keep things manageable.

4. **Use Parallel Structures**: For example, in a content pipeline:

   o Draft → Review → Finalize (all "In Progress")

   o Approved → Published (both "Complete")

5. **Color-Code Strategically**: Use meaningful and consistent colors to convey urgency or phase (e.g., Red for "Blocked", Green for "Approved").

Understanding Status Colors

Color is a powerful visual tool, and ClickUp lets you assign a unique color to each status label. This helps users:

- Instantly recognize the current stage of a task.
- Spot bottlenecks (e.g., lots of "In Review" tasks stuck in yellow).
- Prioritize visually by urgency or task type.

Here are some common **color conventions**:

Color	Meaning (Suggested)
Red	Blocked, Urgent, Needs Fixing
Orange	In Review, Needs Feedback
Yellow	In Progress, Waiting
Green	Complete, Approved, Ready
Blue	Scheduled, Planning
Purple	Backlog, Draft
White	Neutral, General, Default
Black	Deprecated, Canceled, Closed

You can also **use brand colors** or team-specific color schemes for visual consistency across teams.

Example: A Marketing Workflow with Custom Status Groups and Colors

Let's say your marketing team uses the following statuses in a campaign folder:

To Do:

- Backlog (Purple)

- Assigned (Blue)

In Progress:

- Writing (Yellow)

- Reviewing (Orange)

- Editing (Yellow-Orange)

Complete:

- Approved (Green)

- Scheduled (Light Green)

Closed:

- Published (Dark Green)

- Archived (Gray)

This structure makes it extremely easy for a manager or team member to open the board and instantly know what's happening—without digging into each card.

Using Status Groups in Views and Filters

Once you've defined your status groups and colors, you can:

- **Filter views** (List, Board, Calendar, Gantt) by group (e.g., only show tasks "In Progress").

- **Create Dashboards** showing how many tasks are in each group.

- **Automate workflows**, e.g.:

  o If status changes to "Published", then move to "Archived" after 30 days.

  o When task enters "QA Testing", assign it to the QA team lead.

Status Groups and Agile or Scrum Workflows

If your team uses Agile, you can align ClickUp status groups with sprint cycles:

- **To Do**: Sprint Backlog

- **In Progress**: Active Sprint, Dev, QA

- **Complete**: Ready for Release

- **Closed**: Released, Retrospective

These groupings make sprint planning meetings and daily standups far easier to manage and track.

Troubleshooting Common Status Group Issues

Here are a few common problems and how to resolve them:

- **Too many statuses?** Simplify or merge redundant ones.

- **Statuses don't reflect current workflow?** Revisit your team's actual process and adjust accordingly.

- **Confused users?** Add documentation or onboard your team with a quick tour of what each status means.

- **Automations not triggering correctly?** Double-check that the automation logic aligns with the status group transitions (e.g., "when a task moves from 'Writing' to 'Reviewing'...").

When to Use Default vs. Custom Status Groups

Scenario	Use Default	Use Custom
Simple project with one phase	☑	
Multi-step workflow (e.g., DevOps)		☑

Scenario	Use Default	Use Custom
Team needs visual cues	☑	☑
Complex automations required		☑
Company-wide standardization needed	☑	☑

Collaborating Across Teams with Shared Status Groups

If different teams use different terminology, try to **standardize status groups** across spaces when possible to:

- Align expectations

- Make reporting easier

- Enable cross-team automations

For instance, Sales might use "Negotiating" and "Signed," while Customer Success might use "Onboarding" and "Live." But they can all fall under common groups like **In Progress** and **Complete**.

Tips for Scaling with Status Groups

As your workspace grows:

- **Document your status systems** (a shared wiki or doc works well).

- Use **Templates** with pre-configured status groups.

- Audit your status lists quarterly to remove clutter.

- Train new members on your team's naming conventions and colors.

Conclusion: Bring Structure to Chaos

ClickUp's **Status Groups and Colors** are more than visual aids—they are foundational elements of a smart, scalable workflow. By thoughtfully customizing and consistently using them, you reduce confusion, promote transparency, and make it easier for your team to stay on the same page.

In a world filled with competing tasks and priorities, clear, structured statuses give you a **language of progress**—a visual, intuitive way to say *"Here's where we are, and here's what's next."*

CHAPTER V
Tracking Time, Goals, and Productivity

5.1 Time Tracking Features

5.1.1 Built-In Time Tracker

Time is one of the most valuable resources in any professional setting. Whether you're a freelancer billing by the hour, a project manager keeping your team accountable, or a business owner measuring team efficiency, accurate time tracking is essential. ClickUp recognizes this need and offers a **built-in time tracker** to help users monitor their work in real-time without the need for third-party integrations.

This section explores the **native time tracking tool** within ClickUp—how it works, how to use it effectively, and the practical value it offers for personal productivity and team operations.

Why Use ClickUp's Built-In Time Tracker?

ClickUp's native time tracking offers a unified, seamless experience. Unlike third-party tools like Toggl or Harvest (which ClickUp also supports via integration), the built-in tool is fully integrated into tasks, dashboards, reports, and goals.

Key benefits include:

- ☑ Direct tracking from any task

- ☑ Centralized reporting

- ☑ Billable vs. non-billable hours

- ☑ Manual and automatic entry

- ☑ Easy aggregation for payroll, invoicing, or performance analysis

Whether you're a solo user or managing multiple teams, built-in time tracking ensures your work is not only organized but also **measurable**.

How to Enable the Time Tracking Feature

Before you can start tracking time, ensure the feature is enabled in your workspace.

1. **Go to Workspace Settings**

2. Click on **ClickApps**

3. Search for and **Enable "Time Tracking"**

4. Optionally, enable sub-options such as:

   o Time estimates

   o Billable time

   o Required time before completion

Once enabled, the time tracking widget will appear in every task by default, and other time-related options will become available across your ClickUp views.

Tracking Time on a Task

To track time on a task:

1. **Open the Task**: Navigate to any task where you want to track time.

2. **Click the Time Tracker Icon**: Look for the **"clock" icon** in the top task toolbar.

3. **Start the Timer**: Simply press **Start**, and the timer begins. It records time in real-time until you stop it.

4. **Pause or Stop the Timer**: You can pause and resume the timer as needed or stop it once the task is completed.

5. **Review and Edit Logs**: After stopping the timer, you can adjust the duration, add notes, and categorize the time as **billable** or **non-billable**.

Manual Time Entry

If you forgot to start the timer or prefer to log hours retroactively, ClickUp allows for **manual entries**.

- From the task's time tracking widget, click **"+ Add time"**

- Choose:

    o The date

    o Start and end times (or total duration)

    o Notes for the entry

    o Billable status

Manual entries are useful for:

- Logging meetings or calls

- Recording offline work

- Time corrections

Billable vs. Non-Billable Time

ClickUp lets users differentiate between **billable** and **non-billable** hours—especially useful for consultants, agencies, or service teams.

- Toggle the **"Billable" switch** when logging or editing a time entry.

- Billable hours appear in **separate reports** and can be used for client invoicing.

This distinction helps companies analyze profitability per project or client and ensures accurate billing.

Time Tracking in the Global Timer Widget

ClickUp also provides a **Global Time Tracker Widget**, which you can access from:

- The **bottom-left corner** of the screen on desktop
- Or from the **Command Center** (Cmd/Ctrl + K → search "Time Tracker")

From the Global Tracker, you can:

- Start/pause timers from any task
- Switch between tasks without opening each one
- View daily and weekly summaries
- Access a log of all tracked sessions

This is especially useful for:

- Multi-tasking professionals
- Users who switch contexts frequently
- Managing parallel projects

Time Tracking Across Projects and Teams

Time entries aren't limited to a single task. Admins and managers can use time data to:

- Review time spent across **folders, lists, spaces, or the entire workspace**
- Filter by user, date range, task status, or billability
- Analyze trends, identify bottlenecks, and improve future planning

Visualizing Time Data: The Time Reporting View

ClickUp includes a **Time Reporting View**, available in dashboards and list views.

To create a report:

1. Go to a **Dashboard**
2. Add a new **Time Reporting Widget**

3. Choose filters: assignee, date, billable status

4. Choose display mode: list, bar chart, or pie chart

Use this to:

- Generate weekly productivity reports

- Monitor team workloads

- Prepare payroll summaries

- Track hours for client billing

Time Estimates vs. Actual Time Tracked

ClickUp allows you to set **Time Estimates** for each task. This helps compare planned vs. actual effort:

- Add a time estimate field to your task

- Track actual time worked using the timer

- Use the **Time Tracked vs. Estimated Report** to evaluate accuracy

This feature supports:

- Agile teams estimating story points/hours

- Project managers optimizing workload distribution

- Teams improving estimation skills over time

Best Practices for Time Tracking in ClickUp

1. **Use Tags or Custom Fields to Classify Time**
   Example: "Client Work", "Admin Tasks", "Creative", "Research"

2. **Encourage Real-Time Tracking**: Logging time as you work ensures accuracy and better context.

3. **Review Weekly Logs**: Teams should have a habit of reviewing and updating time logs weekly.

4. **Automate Time Reminders**: Use ClickUp Automations to remind team members to log their time at the end of the day.

5. **Set a Time Tracking Policy**: Especially in team settings, define when and how time should be tracked to avoid confusion.

Common Use Cases by Role

Role	Use Case
Freelancer	Logging billable hours per client
Manager	Reviewing team workload and efficiency
Developer	Tracking time across tasks and sprints
Consultant	Billing time spent on each service
Agency	Generating client-ready time reports

Limitations of the Built-In Tracker (and Workarounds)

While the built-in time tracker is powerful, it may not be a one-size-fits-all tool for every organization. Some limitations include:

- No built-in invoicing feature (can be integrated with tools like QuickBooks)
- No automated time rounding
- Limited permissions (everyone can see time entries unless restricted)

Workarounds:

- Use **custom fields** for greater control
- Export reports to CSV for client billing
- Combine with **Dashboards** for better visibility and summaries

ClickUp vs. External Time Trackers

Feature	ClickUp Time Tracker	Toggl / Harvest (via integration)
Native Task Integration	☑	✗ (requires mapping)
Reporting in Dashboards	☑	✗
Invoicing	✗	☑
Advanced Analytics	●	☑
Simplicity for Teams	☑	●
Cost	Included	Additional fees

In many cases, ClickUp's native tracker is **more than sufficient** for teams and freelancers—especially if combined with other native features like goals and dashboards.

Conclusion: Making Time Count

Tracking time is not about micromanagement—it's about visibility, improvement, and accountability. ClickUp's built-in time tracking makes it easy to know where time is going, where it's being lost, and how to optimize future work. Whether you're a solo entrepreneur or part of a 100-person team, this feature—when used properly—can be a game-changer in improving **productivity, transparency, and results**.

5.1.2 Manual vs. Automatic Time Logging

Effectively managing your time is one of the most important aspects of productivity in any project management system. ClickUp offers both **manual** and **automatic time tracking** tools that allow users to log hours spent on tasks with flexibility and accuracy. Understanding the difference between these two logging methods—and how and when to use them—is critical to taking full advantage of ClickUp's time management capabilities.

This section breaks down the features, use cases, benefits, and potential pitfalls of manual and automatic time logging in ClickUp. Whether you're a freelancer billing clients by the hour, a team manager monitoring team output, or simply someone trying to understand where your time goes, you'll find a method that suits your working style.

What Is Time Logging in ClickUp?

Time logging in ClickUp refers to recording the amount of time spent on a task. Time can be tracked either by:

- Manually entering the time worked

- Automatically tracking time in real-time using ClickUp's built-in timer or integrations

All time entries are attached to specific tasks and include metadata such as the user, time spent, date of entry, and optional notes. These logs can then be visualized in time reports, workload dashboards, and productivity reviews.

Understanding Manual Time Logging

Manual time logging means entering time worked after the fact. This is particularly useful in scenarios where:

- You forgot to start the timer

- You worked offline or away from your computer

- You prefer to track time mentally or on a separate app before logging it

- You need to enter bulk time at the end of the day or week

How to Manually Log Time in ClickUp

1. **Open a Task**: Navigate to the task you want to log time against.

2. **Click the Time Tracking Icon**: Usually represented by a clock.

3. **Select "Log Time"**: Instead of "Start Timer", choose the option to manually log.

4. **Enter the Duration**: You can log minutes or hours (e.g., "2h 30m").

5. **Choose the Date**: If you're logging for a past day, you can backdate the entry.

6. **Add Notes (Optional)**: Record what was accomplished during this time.

7. **Click "Save"**: Your log is now attached to the task and visible in reports.

Advantages of Manual Time Logging

- **Flexibility**: You can log time retroactively, even days later.

- **Freedom from Distraction**: No need to remember to start or stop a timer.

- **Better for Planning-Based Workflows**: Ideal if you estimate your time and reflect later.

- **Offline Compatibility**: Great when working in non-digital environments.

Disadvantages of Manual Time Logging

- **Prone to Human Error**: Relying on memory may result in inaccurate entries.

- **No Real-Time Insight**: Managers can't track time in progress.

- **Inconsistent Logs**: Without habit, users might skip logging entirely.

Understanding Automatic Time Logging

Automatic time logging tracks time as you work in real-time. ClickUp includes a built-in timer and integrations with popular time-tracking tools (like **Toggl**, **Harvest**, or **Everhour**). With the built-in timer, you simply hit "Start" when beginning a task and "Stop" when you're done.

How to Automatically Track Time in ClickUp

1. Navigate to a Task.

2. Click on the Time Tracking Icon.

3. Click "Start Timer".

4. Work on Your Task.

5. Click "Stop Timer" when finished.

6. Review or Edit Time Log: You can always adjust the duration or add notes afterward.

You can also **start timers from ClickUp's Chrome Extension**, which allows for background tracking even when ClickUp is minimized or closed.

Advantages of Automatic Time Logging

- **Accuracy**: Tracks time to the minute, reducing over- or underestimation.

- **Real-Time Monitoring**: Great for transparency within teams.

- **Productivity Awareness**: Encourages time-consciousness while working.

- **Integrated Workflows**: Syncs directly with task progress and completion.

Disadvantages of Automatic Time Logging

- **User Dependence**: Requires you to remember to start and stop the timer.

- **Interruptions Cause Issues**: If you forget to stop the timer, the time may be inflated.

- **Less Flexible**: Not ideal for fragmented, jumpy workflows.

Comparison Table: Manual vs. Automatic Logging

Feature	Manual Logging	Automatic Logging
Best for	Post-task recording	Real-time activity tracking
Ease of Use	Easy but requires memory	Easy with habit
Accuracy	Depends on estimation	Highly accurate
Offline Compatibility	Yes	No (requires connection)
Transparency	Low	High (can be seen live)
Ideal User	Reflective worker	Active time tracker

Use Cases: When to Use Each Method

Use Manual Time Logging When...

- You're reflecting on your work at the end of the day

- You forgot to track your time in the moment

- You were working offline or during meetings

- You estimate time for recurring or routine tasks

Use Automatic Time Logging When...

- You work on long, focused tasks

- You need to prove time worked to clients

- You're trying to build self-awareness around how time is spent

- You're collaborating in teams where transparency is valued

Combining Both Methods

Many ClickUp users find the ideal workflow is a **hybrid** approach:

- Start your day with automatic timers for deep work

- Use manual entries to fill in time for calls, meetings, or forgotten logs

- Rely on dashboards and time reports to identify gaps and adjust your habits

ClickUp makes it easy to edit time entries later, so combining both styles doesn't create data fragmentation.

Tips for Consistent and Effective Time Logging

1. **Use the Chrome Extension**: It allows quick access to start/stop timers from anywhere.

2. **Review Time Daily**: Build a habit of end-of-day review and logging.

3. **Add Descriptions**: Notes attached to time logs help track your focus and output.

4. **Train Your Team**: Encourage standardized logging practices across all members.

5. **Integrate Tools**: If you already use Toggl or Harvest, connect them to ClickUp for continuity.

6. **Use ClickUp's Time Reports**: Weekly and monthly views will help you spot trends and inefficiencies.

Final Thoughts on Manual vs. Automatic Time Logging

Time logging is not just about tracking billable hours—it's about **awareness**, **accountability**, and **improvement**. Whether you prefer the flexibility of manual input or the precision of automatic timers, ClickUp gives you the tools to create a system that works for you.

Start with one method, observe how it fits your workflow, and evolve your practice as you get more comfortable. With consistent use, ClickUp's time tracking features will help you become more productive, intentional, and ultimately, more successful in your personal and team goals.

5.1.3 Time Reports

Time is one of the most precious resources in any workflow, and in a fast-paced digital workspace, tracking how time is spent can mean the difference between meeting goals or falling behind. In ClickUp, **Time Reports** offer an insightful and data-driven way to measure productivity, evaluate project efficiency, and make strategic improvements across your team or individual tasks. This section will walk you through everything you need to know about generating and using time reports in ClickUp.

What Are Time Reports in ClickUp?

Time Reports in ClickUp are analytical summaries that collect and display time entries logged by users across tasks, lists, folders, or even entire workspaces. These reports allow you to:

- Understand **how much time** has been spent on a project

- See **who** has logged time and **where**

- Evaluate **billable vs. non-billable** hours

- Generate **custom reports** by filtering based on assignees, tasks, time ranges, tags, and more

They serve as a foundation for understanding team efficiency, billing clients, managing payroll, and identifying time-related bottlenecks.

Accessing Time Reports in ClickUp

To view Time Reports in ClickUp:

1. **Go to the "Time Tracking" section** from the Sidebar (or open the Dashboard where a Time Reporting widget is configured).

2. If using Dashboards, **add a "Time Reporting" widget**.

3. Click the **"Time Tracked"** tab or use the "Reports" feature if your plan supports it (available in **Business** and higher tiers).

🔒 **Note**: Time tracking and reports are limited or unavailable in some lower-tier plans unless enabled through the Time Tracking ClickApp.

Key Components of a Time Report

Let's break down the main elements you'll encounter when analyzing a Time Report in ClickUp:

1. Time Entries

Each time report is built from individual **time entries**, which include:

- The **task name** associated with the entry
- **Start and end times**
- **Duration**
- **User who logged the time**
- **Billable or non-billable** flag (if enabled)
- Any **notes** or descriptions added to the entry

2. Filters

Filters are the backbone of customized reporting. You can tailor your reports using options like:

- **Date range**: Today, This Week, Last 7 Days, Custom

- **Assignee**: Show time tracked by specific team members

- **Task, Folder, or List**

- **Billable status**: Filter for only billable or non-billable hours

- **Tags**: View time entries associated with specific tags

- **Task status or priority** (great for active project reviews)

3. Group By Options

You can group your report data by:

- **Assignee**

- **Task**

- **List**

- **Tag**

- **Client (if using custom fields)**

Grouping allows you to quickly compare where time is going and who is contributing the most.

4. Total Time Summary

At the top or bottom of the report, ClickUp often shows:

- **Total time logged**

- Time grouped by user or task

- **Time spent per day/week/month**

- **Aggregate billable time**

This makes invoicing and review easier for teams managing client-based work.

Use Cases for Time Reports

Let's explore practical ways to utilize time reports for both teams and solo users:

👨‍💼 **Project Managers**

- Monitor how long tasks actually take vs. the estimates
- Identify time-draining activities or unproductive trends
- Balance workload across team members more effectively

Freelancers and Consultants

- Track client work for accurate billing
- Provide transparent time logs to clients
- Measure profitability per project or task type

Team Leaders and HR

- Understand time allocation for performance evaluations
- Review billable vs. non-billable ratios for profitability
- Track hours for payroll processing

Executives and Stakeholders

- Gain insights into departmental productivity
- Compare time spent across business units or roles
- Inform decisions around hiring, outsourcing, or budgeting

Creating Custom Time Reports with Dashboards

For advanced users, ClickUp Dashboards allow you to create **real-time custom reports** using widgets. Here's how to build a simple time report dashboard:

Step 1: Create a New Dashboard

- Go to Dashboards > "+ New Dashboard"
- Name your dashboard appropriately, such as "Weekly Time Tracking"

Step 2: Add a Widget

- Choose **"Time Reporting"** or **"Time Tracked"** widget

- Configure filters:
  - Assignees
  - Projects
  - Date range
  - Grouping method

Step 3: Add More Widgets (Optional)

- **Pie Charts** for time per project
- **Bar Charts** to show daily logged time
- **Line Charts** for productivity trends over time

✅ Pro Tip: Save common time reports as templates to reuse across clients or projects.

Exporting Time Reports

ClickUp allows you to export time data for further processing or documentation. To do this:

1. Go to the **Time Reporting widget** or Time section
2. Click the **"Export"** or **"..."** menu
3. Choose your format:
   - CSV
   - PDF (via dashboard exports)
4. Choose your filters and download

Exporting is especially useful for:

- Client invoicing
- Performance audits
- Backup logs
- Importing into external tools like Excel or Power BI

Integrating Time Reports with External Tools

For businesses using accounting, invoicing, or HR platforms, time data from ClickUp can be pushed or synced via:

- **Zapier/Make**: Automate export or sync to Google Sheets, QuickBooks, or Slack.

- **ClickUp API**: Build custom solutions for advanced use cases.

- **Third-Party Tools**: Apps like Everhour, Harvest, or Toggl integrate directly with ClickUp.

These integrations enable:

- Seamless billing

- Payroll integration

- Centralized reporting across platforms

Tips for Using Time Reports Effectively

Here are some best practices to maximize the benefits of Time Reports in ClickUp:

1. Train Your Team on Consistent Logging

If people forget to log time or don't do it correctly, reports become meaningless. Encourage logging time:

- At the end of each task

- Using the timer for real-time tracking

- Via mobile for field work

2. Use Tags and Descriptions

Add context to entries by tagging them with project phases or adding detailed notes. This improves audit trails and client transparency.

3. Set Weekly Reporting Habits

Automate delivery of weekly time reports to managers or team leads. Review logged hours every Friday or Monday for ongoing performance checks.

4. Combine Time and Task Reports

For deeper insights, compare time reports with task completion data. This shows whether tasks are taking longer than expected and why.

5. Analyze Trends Over Time

Using dashboards and charts, identify time trends like:

- Repetitive overtime

- Project phases with long durations

- Peaks and drops in daily output

Common Pitfalls to Avoid

- **Not enabling Time Tracking ClickApp** before logging entries

- **Lack of structure** in naming tasks or categorizing time entries

- **Over-relying on manual entries**, which are prone to errors

- **Poor access control**—ensure only permitted users can edit time data

- **Ignoring billable/non-billable separation**, leading to inaccurate invoicing

Conclusion: Turning Time Into Insight

ClickUp's Time Reporting capabilities transform raw time logs into actionable insights. Whether you're a team of two or two hundred, understanding how time is used helps you work smarter—not harder.

By regularly using time reports, you'll:

- **Make better staffing decisions**

- **Improve client relationships through transparency**

- **Optimize workflows**

- **Set realistic project timelines**

- **Stay accountable to your goals**

In the next section, we'll explore how to set and track goals within ClickUp—and how those goals align with the time you're investing.

Ready to move from tracking time to achieving big milestones? Let's dive in.

5.2 Goals and Milestones

5.2.1 Creating and Linking Goals

One of ClickUp's most powerful features is its **Goals** system — a centralized space where users can track high-level objectives and break them down into smaller, manageable targets. Whether you're a solopreneur looking to stay focused or a team leader managing quarterly OKRs, ClickUp Goals provide the framework to connect your daily tasks with long-term outcomes. In this section, we'll explore how to create goals effectively in ClickUp, how to link them to your workflow, and how to make them actionable for real productivity.

What Are Goals in ClickUp?

Goals in ClickUp represent measurable, time-bound achievements that help teams and individuals align their efforts. Each goal can include one or multiple **Targets**, which are measurable sub-items that support the main objective. These targets can be tied to tasks, numbers, currency, or even simple checklists. This makes ClickUp Goals both flexible and powerful — suited for everything from revenue growth tracking to task completion metrics.

Types of Targets:

- **Number** (e.g., increase monthly subscribers to 1,000)
- **True/False** (e.g., Launch new website = True/False)
- **Currency** (e.g., Reach $50,000 in Q2 sales)
- **Task** (e.g., Complete 15 out of 20 tasks)
- **List** (e.g., Checklist of milestones or deliverables)

Benefits of Using Goals

Before diving into the creation process, let's look at why you should use ClickUp Goals:

1. **Alignment** – Keep everyone focused on what truly matters.

2. **Transparency** – Share goal progress with stakeholders in real-time.

3. **Motivation** – Celebrate milestones and see the finish line more clearly.

4. **Measurement** – Attach real numbers and metrics to your goals.

5. **Accountability** – Assign owners, set due dates, and track every step.

Creating Goals in ClickUp

Let's walk through how to create your first goal in ClickUp, step by step:

Step 1: Accessing the Goals Feature

To start working with goals, go to the left-hand sidebar in ClickUp and click on the **"Goals"** icon (represented by a flag). This opens your goals dashboard — a centralized view for everything you're aiming to achieve.

📌 **Tip:** If you don't see the Goals feature, ensure it's enabled in your workspace under **ClickApps**.

Step 2: Creating a New Goal

Click the **"+ New Goal"** button in the top right-hand corner of the Goals dashboard. A modal window will open prompting you to input several key elements:

Name Your Goal

- Choose a short, clear, and outcome-driven name.
- Example: "Increase Customer Retention Rate Q3"

Add a Description (Optional)

- Give context to your team or collaborators.
- Explain the *why*, *what*, and *how* behind the goal.

Set an Owner

- Assign one or more responsible users.

- Owners receive updates and are accountable for progress.

Set a Due Date

- Define the deadline by which this goal should be completed.

- Can be tied to quarterly planning, sprint cycles, etc.

Set a Visibility Level

- Choose who can view this goal: Everyone, Members, or Private.

Step 3: Adding Targets

Once the goal is created, you'll be prompted to **Add Targets** — these are the action points that make up your goal. Targets are where the real tracking happens.

Choosing a Target Type

1. **Number**
   Useful for tracking progress that can be quantified.
   Example: Increase email list size to 5,000 subscribers.

2. **True/False**
   Binary targets – either done or not.
   Example: Finish brand guidelines = True.

3. **Currency**
   Monetary objectives like revenue or savings.
   Example: Earn $100,000 from product sales.

4. **Tasks**
   Link specific tasks in ClickUp to track as progress.
   Example: Complete 10 marketing deliverables.

5. **List**
   Manual checklist format — you define items.
   Example: [ ] Launch webinar, [ ] Collect feedback, [ ] Publish case study

Target Details to Input

- **Name**: Clear label for each target.

- **Start and End Value** (where applicable)

- **Assign an Owner** (can be different from the goal owner)

- **Start and Due Dates**

- **Link Tasks (for task-based targets)**

You can add multiple targets to one goal — allowing you to track a broad objective through different types of data points.

Linking Goals to Tasks and Workflows

Once your goals and targets are set, the real magic begins: **integration with your daily work**. You can link tasks from across any workspace in ClickUp to your targets.

How to Link Tasks:

1. Create or open a task.

2. Click the "..." menu in the top-right corner.

3. Choose **"Add to Goal"**.

4. Select the goal and target you wish to link the task to.

This turns every day-to-day effort into something measurable. When you mark the task as complete, the target updates automatically.

Using Goals in Your Weekly and Monthly Planning

ClickUp Goals should not be "set and forget." Integrate goal reviews into your planning routine:

- **Weekly Check-ins:** Review goal progress in team meetings.

- **Monthly Reports:** Use Dashboards or Goal overviews to share metrics.

- **Quarterly Reviews:** Reassess or update goal relevance and completion.

📌 **Pro Tip:** Pin your most important goals to the sidebar or Dashboard for easy access and motivation.

Organizing Goals with Folders

If you're managing multiple objectives — especially in a team or organization setting — it helps to **organize goals into folders**. This is especially useful for:

- Department-specific goals

- Personal vs. team goals

- Short-term vs. long-term objectives

To create a goal folder:

1. Go to the Goals section.

2. Click **"+ New Folder"**

3. Name the folder and set visibility options.

You can drag and drop goals into folders to keep your goals area clean and intuitive.

Goal Progress and Tracking

Each goal will show a **percentage completion** based on how your targets are progressing. Here's how ClickUp calculates it:

- Each target contributes equally to the goal's overall progress.

- Completion is determined by the % achieved within each target.

You can also view:

- **Progress graphs**

- **Target status indicators**

- **Team activity logs** related to goal updates

These tracking insights give stakeholders visibility into performance, helping with decision-making and resource allocation.

Best Practices for Effective Goal Setting in ClickUp

Here are some guidelines to help you make the most of the Goals feature:

1. Make Goals SMART

- Specific
- Measurable
- Achievable
- Relevant
- Time-bound

2. Assign Clear Ownership

Don't leave goals ownerless. Assign individuals or small teams to maintain momentum.

3. Keep Visibility in Mind

Make goals public when alignment matters across teams. Use private goals for personal objectives or sensitive targets.

4. Review Goals Frequently

Incorporate goal tracking into your weekly or biweekly routines.

5. Tie Goals to Strategy

Always ask: how does this goal support our bigger mission or KPIs?

Common Mistakes to Avoid

- **Setting Too Many Goals** – It dilutes focus. Stick to 3–5 high-impact goals.
- **Ignoring Updates** – Letting goals sit idle won't yield results.
- **No Alignment with Workflows** – Failing to link goals to tasks or projects makes them abstract.
- **Vague Targets** – Avoid unclear descriptions or generic objectives.

Goal Templates (Bonus Tip)

ClickUp allows you to **create templates** for frequently used goal types. For example:

- Quarterly OKRs

- Marketing Campaign Metrics

- New Product Launch Milestones

Templates save time and ensure consistency across teams or departments.

Summary

Creating and linking goals in ClickUp allows you to turn vague aspirations into structured, trackable, and collaborative achievements. With the ability to assign ownership, set due dates, and connect real tasks, Goals become more than motivational quotes — they become measurable pathways to success.

Whether you're leading a startup or managing your personal development, ClickUp's Goals feature puts your ambitions front and center, helping you and your team stay aligned and accountable every step of the way.

5.2.2 Tracking Progress with Targets

In any project, understanding **where you are** and **how far you have to go** is vital to success. ClickUp's **Goals and Targets** feature transforms this process from guesswork into a clear, trackable system. In this section, we'll dive deep into **how to track progress using Targets**, explore best practices, and help you unlock the power of ClickUp's goal-tracking features.

What Are Targets in ClickUp Goals?

In ClickUp, a **Goal** is a high-level objective—something you or your team wants to achieve, such as "Launch Product X by Q3" or "Grow YouTube Channel to 10,000 Subscribers."

A **Target**, on the other hand, is a **measurable milestone or component of that goal**. You can think of Targets as the building blocks of the overall Goal. Each Target contributes toward completing the Goal and can be tracked independently.

There are four types of Targets in ClickUp:

- **Number**: Perfect for metrics like revenue, subscriber count, tasks completed, etc.

- **True/False**: A simple binary completion (e.g., "Create marketing strategy – Yes or No").

- **Task**: Linked to actual ClickUp tasks that must be completed.

- **Currency**: For goals that involve money (e.g., "Raise $100,000 in funding").

Why Tracking Targets Matters

Without measurable targets:

- Progress is hard to assess.

- Motivation can dwindle due to lack of visible movement.

- Teams can lose alignment and direction.

By tracking progress through **well-structured targets**, you:

- Create **transparency** across the team.

- Reinforce **accountability**.

- Establish a culture of **continuous improvement**.

Setting Up Targets in ClickUp: A Step-by-Step Guide

Let's walk through the process of tracking progress using Targets in a real-world example.

📌 Step 1: Create a Goal

1. Navigate to **Goals** from the left sidebar.

2. Click **+ New Goal**.

3. Name your goal (e.g., "Improve Customer Satisfaction").

4. Add collaborators (optional).

5. Set a due date.

📌 Step 2: Add Targets

ClickUp allows you to break down your goal into specific, measurable targets. After creating the goal:

1. Click **+ Add Target**.

2. Choose the **type of target**:

   ○ For example, choose **Number** if you're tracking a metric like "Reduce support ticket response time to under 6 hours."

3. Name the target and set:

   ○ **Start value**

   ○ **Target value**

   ○ **Current value** (if applicable)

   ○ **Unit label** (e.g., "hours", "tickets")

You can add multiple targets to the same goal. For example:

- Target 1: "Reduce average response time from 12h to 6h" (Number)

- Target 2: "Implement new helpdesk system" (True/False)

- Target 3: "Complete training for support team" (Task)

📌 Step 3: Link Tasks to Targets (for Task-Based Targets)

If your Target is task-based:

- You can **search and link tasks** from any Space or Folder within ClickUp.

- Tasks can be **automatically updated** as they are marked complete.

This ensures your target progress is tied directly to real work being done—no manual updates required.

Visualizing Progress

Once Targets are created and connected to your actual work:

- Each Target displays a **progress bar** or percentage.

- You'll see **individual Target progress** as well as **overall Goal progress**.

- Color indicators (green, yellow, red) offer a visual snapshot of what's on track and what needs attention.

ClickUp also shows:

- Due dates and progress trends.

- Who's assigned to each Target.

- Notes and updates added by collaborators.

Best Practices for Tracking with Targets

Here are some practical tips to make the most of your progress-tracking:

✅ Set SMART Targets

Make sure your targets are:

- **[S]pecific**

- **[M]easurable**

- **[A]chievable**

- **[R]elevant**

- **[T]ime-bound**

Example:
Bad target – "Improve marketing"
Good target – "Increase monthly website visits from 20K to 40K by end of Q2"

✅ Use Multiple Target Types

Don't stick with just one type of target. Mix it up:

- Use **Number targets** for performance metrics.

- Use **Task targets** for action steps.

- Use **True/False** for one-off milestones.

- Use **Currency targets** for financial tracking.

This gives you a **360-degree view** of goal progress.

☑ Keep Goals Manageable

Avoid stuffing too many targets into a single goal.
Focus on **4–6 meaningful targets** per goal to maintain clarity and focus.

☑ Assign Responsibility

Make sure every Target has an **owner**.
Someone should be accountable for updating the target (if needed) and driving progress.

☑ Review Weekly

Set a **weekly or biweekly goal review cadence** with your team to:

- Check progress

- Adjust targets if needed

- Unblock stalled work

Use this opportunity to **celebrate wins** and refocus efforts.

Advanced Tip: Using Goals with Dashboards

Want to take your goal-tracking to the next level?

Create a **Dashboard** in ClickUp that pulls in:

- A "Goal Tracking" widget

- Task progress widgets tied to goal-related lists

- Time tracking charts

- Workload visualizations

This creates a **single source of truth** for everything related to your project goals. You can even create **Client Dashboards** if you want to report progress externally.

Example Use Case: Marketing Team Campaign Goal

Goal: "Launch and Promote New Product in Q3"
Due Date: July 1 – September 30
Targets:

1. "Publish 10 blog posts" (Task)

2. "Reach 1,000 pre-registrations" (Number)

3. "Create and distribute email campaign" (True/False)

4. "Spend $20,000 on ads" (Currency)

5. "Reduce bounce rate on landing page to <40%" (Number)

The Marketing Manager can log into ClickUp, check this Goal, and see exactly where the team stands across content, traffic, budget, and conversion metrics.

Common Mistakes and How to Avoid Them

Mistake	How to Avoid
Creating vague or broad targets	Use specific, measurable metrics
Not updating progress regularly	Set weekly check-ins or use automation
Assigning no ownership	Always assign an owner per Target
Too many unrelated targets	Keep Goals cohesive and focused
Forgetting due dates	Set target-level deadlines

Leveraging Automations to Track Targets

Did you know? You can combine **Automations + Goals** for powerful effects:

- Automatically update a Target when a task is completed.

- Trigger a Slack or email alert when a Goal is 80% complete.

- Update task statuses when a milestone Target is reached.

This allows your ClickUp instance to **self-update and inform your team**, so you're not bogged down with manual check-ins.

When to Archive or Adjust Targets

Not all Targets stay relevant. If:

- The underlying project shifts

- Team priorities change

- Metrics evolve

...you can **edit**, **pause**, or **archive** a Target.
ClickUp gives you full control without losing historical progress.

Final Thoughts: Progress with Purpose

Tracking progress with Targets in ClickUp is more than a feature—it's a mindset.

It helps you:

- Connect daily tasks to big-picture goals

- Measure what matters

- Align your team

- Adjust course before it's too late

In the fast-moving world of modern work, being able to clearly **see progress** at every level—from individual tasks to company-wide objectives—can be a game-changer.

Set your Targets. Track them often. And let your success build itself, one milestone at a time.

5.2.3 Using Goals for Team Alignment

In any organization, alignment is everything. Whether you're managing a five-person startup or overseeing departments across multiple continents, keeping everyone rowing in the same direction is the secret sauce to success. This is where **ClickUp's Goals feature** becomes a true game-changer. Not just a simple checklist or task counter, ClickUp Goals provide a **dynamic, measurable, and collaborative framework** to ensure your team is not only productive—but strategically aligned with your company's bigger picture.

In this section, we'll dive deep into how you can use ClickUp Goals for **team alignment** by:

- Understanding what team alignment really means

- Creating shared goals that map to company objectives

- Assigning ownership and visibility across the team

- Using Targets to measure success in real-time

- Leveraging Milestones for motivation and tracking

- Incorporating ClickUp Dashboards and Automations

- Adopting best practices for maintaining alignment over time

What is Team Alignment and Why It Matters

Team alignment is the degree to which team members share a common understanding of:

- Company mission and vision

- Team priorities and strategic objectives

- Individual responsibilities and expectations

- What success looks like—quantitatively and qualitatively

When teams lack alignment, productivity may not translate to progress. A team can be busy without being effective. By contrast, a well-aligned team knows exactly what they're working toward—and why.

ClickUp's Goals feature enables teams to make strategic objectives visible, measurable, and actionable.

Setting Shared Goals in ClickUp

✳ Strategic Goal Setting Starts at the Top

Begin by defining **macro-level goals** that reflect organizational priorities. These could be OKRs (Objectives and Key Results), quarterly KPIs, or department milestones.

Examples:

- Increase product adoption by 25% in Q2
- Launch a new marketing campaign by June 15
- Reduce churn rate to below 5% by year-end

In ClickUp, you can **create a Goal** and give it:

- A name
- A due date
- A description or context
- An owner (individual or shared)

Once created, this top-level goal becomes a **shared reference point** that keeps all sub-tasks and team activities anchored to real outcomes.

👥 Making It a Team Effort

When building goals for alignment, collaboration is key. Assign team members as **contributors or co-owners**. You can:

- Set **shared targets**
- Tag stakeholders in comments
- Link associated tasks from different teams

The goal should act as a **central dashboard** for progress. Any team member should be able to check in and see:

- What the goal is

- Who's responsible

- What progress has been made

- What remains to be done

Using Targets for Transparent Progress

Each Goal in ClickUp is made up of **Targets**, which are individual measurable components of progress. Targets can be one of four types:

1. **Number** – e.g., Grow newsletter to 10,000 subscribers

2. **Currency** – e.g., Generate $100,000 in revenue

3. **Task** – e.g., Complete 50 onboarding tickets

4. **True/False** – e.g., Launch event site by deadline

By using Targets, you shift from vague aspirations to **concrete deliverables**.

Real-Time Tracking

As contributors update tasks or enter values manually, Targets update **automatically** (if linked) or via **manual input**. This lets everyone:

- See live progress

- Celebrate milestones

- Spot bottlenecks

You can also filter by **completed, overdue, or at-risk targets**, allowing for better mid-course corrections and communication.

Incorporating Milestones and Dependencies

Milestones are major moments that matter—like the halfway mark in a campaign or the go-live of a website. While not a separate ClickUp entity like Goals, **Milestones can be created using tasks marked with a milestone tag**.

🗏 Aligning Work with Milestones

Use Milestones to:

- Segment long-term goals into meaningful phases
- Align teams across departments (e.g., content + development)
- Motivate progress through **visual checkpoints**

Combine Milestones with **task dependencies** so that everyone knows:

- What needs to happen first
- Who's waiting on what
- Where the blockers are

When used together, Goals, Targets, and Milestones form a **strategic backbone** for team activity.

Enhancing Team Alignment Through Dashboards

While Goals give structure, **Dashboards bring visibility.** A custom Dashboard can include widgets that show:

- Progress toward team goals
- Time tracked against specific tasks
- Burndown charts
- Workload by team member
- Priority breakdowns

You can use a **Goals widget** to display one or more active goals, and a **Task list widget** filtered by related goals or priorities. Share Dashboards with:

- Project teams
- Executives
- Cross-functional groups

This transparency ensures that everyone stays on the same page—**without needing a daily meeting.**

Automation for Alignment

ClickUp allows you to set up **automations** that connect goal-related activity with alerts, assignments, or updates. Examples include:

- When a task is marked as complete → update a goal target
- When a subtask is overdue → notify the goal owner
- When a milestone task is reached → auto-tag for visibility

These small automations can dramatically improve follow-through, minimize human error, and help managers **stay proactive** instead of reactive.

Best Practices for Using Goals to Align Teams

Here are a few proven methods to get the most from your Goals in ClickUp:

1. Link Tasks, Don't Duplicate Them

Rather than creating new tasks under the Goal, link existing tasks from team workflows. This keeps everything connected and avoids confusion.

2. Make Goals a Standing Agenda Item

In team meetings, pull up your ClickUp Goal and review progress live. It keeps goals top-of-mind and reinforces ownership.

3. Review and Reset Quarterly

Team priorities evolve. Review your goals regularly, archive completed goals, and create new ones to reflect changing business needs.

4. Keep Goal Owners Accountable

Assign each goal a clear owner, and define their responsibilities—not just "being in charge" but communicating, tracking, and reporting status.

5. Celebrate Milestones Publicly

Use ClickUp's celebration features (like confetti on task completion), shout-outs in team channels, or even reward systems to build morale.

Case Study: How a Marketing Team Aligned Using ClickUp Goals

A mid-size marketing agency used ClickUp to unify their content, design, and SEO teams around quarterly goals.

Their approach:

- Created a Goal for each major campaign
- Linked all creative tasks as targets
- Assigned contributors and added milestones
- Built a dashboard showing campaign readiness in real-time
- Automated reminders for weekly goal check-ins

Result:

- Project delivery time improved by 27%
- Internal communication friction dropped
- Clients received deliverables ahead of schedule

Conclusion: Empowering Teams with Shared Purpose

Goals are more than numbers—they're statements of intention and direction. When your team understands what they're aiming for, why it matters, and how progress is measured, they're more likely to:

- Stay focused
- Be motivated
- Collaborate better
- Deliver higher-quality work

ClickUp's robust Goals system makes this possible. By connecting day-to-day tasks to long-term targets, it transforms productivity into **purposeful progress.**

5.3 Reporting and Dashboards

5.3.1 Creating Dashboards

In any project management system, the ability to visualize data is a game-changer. Dashboards in ClickUp provide a customizable, real-time snapshot of your projects, workload, goals, and overall team performance. They act as mission control—giving users access to insights that help them make data-driven decisions quickly and effectively. Whether you're a team lead tracking performance metrics, a project manager monitoring timelines, or a business owner keeping an eye on company objectives, Dashboards can be tailored to meet your exact needs.

This section will guide you through everything you need to know to **create, customize, and use dashboards** in ClickUp—from the basics to advanced best practices. By the end, you'll be able to build a dashboard that transforms raw data into actionable insight.

What Is a Dashboard in ClickUp?

A **Dashboard** is a highly visual and flexible interface that aggregates data from across your ClickUp workspace into one centralized location. Unlike individual task views or project lists, Dashboards let you see metrics from multiple projects and spaces at once. They can include widgets such as charts, tables, task lists, time tracking summaries, workload distributions, and even embedded documents or websites.

Dashboards serve different purposes depending on the user:

- A **project manager** might use it to track timelines, task statuses, and blockers.

- A **team lead** might use it to monitor team workload and overdue tasks.

- A **business executive** might want a high-level overview of goal progress or client delivery.

In short, Dashboards give clarity where complexity exists.

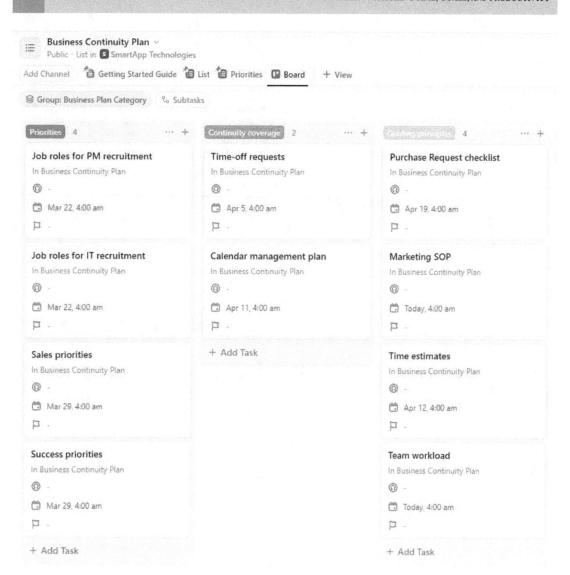

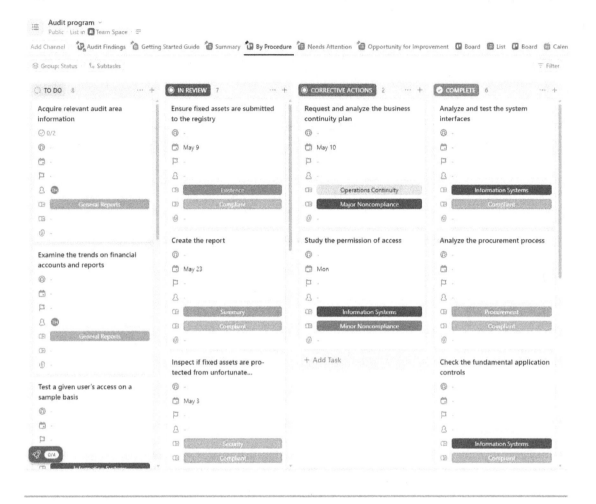

Why Use Dashboards in ClickUp?

Here are just a few of the reasons Dashboards are essential:

- **Centralized Data:** Pull data from across spaces, folders, and lists to create a unified overview.

- **Custom Visualization:** Choose from dozens of widgets to tailor the dashboard to your exact needs.

- **Real-Time Updates:** As work is done, your dashboards update instantly—no need to refresh or manually track.

- **Collaboration-Ready:** Share dashboards with your team or clients to ensure transparency and alignment.

- **Track Key Metrics:** From time spent on tasks to progress on goals, dashboards bring visibility to the KPIs that matter most.

Getting Started: How to Create a Dashboard

Creating a dashboard in ClickUp is straightforward, and it's accessible even for beginners. Follow these steps to set up your first dashboard:

Step 1: Navigate to the Dashboards Page

1. From the main sidebar, click on the **Dashboards** tab. If you don't see it, click **More** to expand your options.

2. Click **+ New Dashboard** in the top-right corner.

Step 2: Name and Configure the Dashboard

1. Choose a name for your dashboard. Make it descriptive and relevant to its purpose (e.g., "Marketing Overview" or "Team Performance Tracker").

2. Select who can access it:

   o Private: Only you.

   o Shared with specific users or teams.

   o Public within your Workspace.

You can also set it as a **Favorite** for quick access later.

Step 3: Add Widgets

ClickUp Dashboards are built using **Widgets**—modular blocks that display different types of data. When you create your dashboard, you'll be prompted to add your first widget. Don't worry—you can always add or rearrange them later.

We'll explore widget types in detail below.

Widget Types and Their Uses

There are over 50 different widgets to choose from in ClickUp. Here are some of the most commonly used ones, categorized by their function:

Task Reporting Widgets

These widgets pull data from your tasks:

- **Task List**: Displays tasks that meet specific filters (e.g., overdue, in progress, assigned to a user).

- **Pie Chart or Bar Chart**: Visualize tasks by status, assignee, priority, etc.

- **Line Chart**: Track changes in task counts over time.

- **Completed vs. Incomplete Tasks**: See how much has been done vs. what's remaining.

Time Tracking Widgets

Use these to monitor where time is going:

- **Time Tracked**: Total hours logged in a time period.

- **Time Tracked by Assignee**: See which team members are logging the most time.

- **Billable vs. Non-Billable**: Separate client-billable time from internal time.

Workload and Capacity Widgets

Perfect for managers to prevent burnout:

- **Workload by Assignee**: View how much work each team member has based on time estimates.

- **Tasks by Due Date**: Spot bottlenecks in upcoming days or weeks.

Goal and Portfolio Widgets

Track strategic progress:

- **Goal Tracking**: View progress toward ClickUp goals set at the workspace level.

- **Portfolio**: A snapshot of different projects' health, progress, and risks.

Custom Widgets

- **Embed**: Add Google Docs, websites, Loom videos, etc.

- **Text Blocks**: Add written notes, titles, or comments.

- **Image Blocks**: Embed graphics or charts.

Best Practices for Dashboard Layout

A great dashboard isn't just about adding widgets—it's about organizing them in a way that makes data easy to digest. Here are some best practices:

1. Start With the Big Picture

Put high-level metrics like goal progress, overall task completion, or total time tracked at the top.

2. Group Widgets by Theme

Group related widgets together—for example, all time tracking widgets in one row, task statuses in another.

3. Limit to One Screen If Possible

Try to keep your dashboard to a single scrollable screen for quick reviews. Use multiple dashboards for different purposes if needed.

4. Use Clear Labels and Titles

Every widget allows you to edit its title—make sure it's descriptive, like "Tasks Due This Week" or "Design Team Workload".

5. Regularly Review and Refine

As your projects evolve, your dashboards should too. Schedule monthly check-ins to remove outdated widgets and add new ones.

Use Case Examples

Let's explore a few real-world use cases to see dashboards in action:

1. Weekly Team Sync Dashboard

- Pie chart showing task status breakdown

- Task list for overdue items

- Time tracked by team members
- Goals progress widget
- Text block with weekly agenda

2. Executive Overview Dashboard

- Project portfolio widget
- Line graph of completed tasks over past month
- Milestone tracking
- Goal completion rate
- Time tracked by department

3. Personal Productivity Dashboard

- Task list of high-priority tasks
- Time tracked this week
- Completed vs. incomplete tasks widget
- Goals widget for personal OKRs
- Text block with a motivational quote or reminder

Collaborating With Dashboards

You can share dashboards with:

- **Individuals**
- **Teams**
- **Clients (via guest access)**

To share:

1. Click the **Share** button on the top right.
2. Choose users or groups.

3. Assign permissions: **View**, **Comment**, or **Edit**.

This makes dashboards an excellent tool for **status reporting**, **cross-functional visibility**, and **client transparency**.

Conclusion: Building Insightful Dashboards

Creating effective dashboards in ClickUp is part art, part science. When designed well, a dashboard becomes a command center for your work—giving you instant visibility into performance, priorities, and productivity.

Whether you need a simple task monitor or a comprehensive executive overview, ClickUp's dashboards give you the flexibility and power to make your data work for you. The key lies in thoughtful design, consistent usage, and ongoing refinement.

In the next section, we'll explore the powerful reporting capabilities beyond dashboards, such as **custom widgets** and **interactive reports** to take your productivity to the next level.

5.3.2 Widgets and Custom Reports

Tracking productivity in ClickUp doesn't end with completing tasks—it begins with understanding how work flows, identifying bottlenecks, and optimizing performance based on actionable insights. That's where **widgets** and **custom reports** come into play. ClickUp provides robust reporting capabilities through its **Dashboards** feature, allowing users and teams to visualize their workload, monitor KPIs, and tailor data displays using a variety of widgets.

This section will walk you through the different types of widgets available, how to use them effectively, and how to build powerful **custom reports** tailored to your unique workflows. Whether you're a solopreneur monitoring personal productivity or a team lead overseeing multiple departments, this section will help you turn raw data into meaningful insights.

What Are Widgets in ClickUp?

Widgets are the building blocks of Dashboards in ClickUp. Each widget is a visual or interactive module that displays specific data or functionality—ranging from task counts and time tracked, to charts, goals, and even embedded content. Think of them as mini-reports or interactive windows into your workspace's data.

Widgets are highly configurable, and ClickUp provides dozens of widget types to suit different purposes. Some provide real-time analytics, while others allow you to take action directly within the Dashboard.

Categories of Widgets

Widgets in ClickUp fall into several broad categories, each serving different purposes:

1. Task Widgets

These widgets help you track the number and status of tasks in your workspace.

- **Task List:** Displays a list of tasks based on filters like assignee, status, due date, etc.
- **Task Count:** Shows the total number of tasks fitting specific criteria.
- **Completed Tasks:** Tracks completed items over a time range.
- **Task Status Breakdown:** Pie or bar charts showing how tasks are distributed across statuses.

Use case example: A project manager might use a Task Status Breakdown to ensure no tasks are stuck in "In Review" or "Waiting on Client" for too long.

2. Time Tracking Widgets

Time is one of your most valuable assets. ClickUp's time widgets give a detailed view of how it's being spent.

- **Time Tracked:** Total time tracked by a person or team over a specific date range.
- **Time by Status or Task:** See where the most time is being invested.
- **Time Estimated vs. Actual:** Compares estimated time with logged hours.

Use case example: A team leader can use the "Time by Task" widget to identify which tasks are consistently taking longer than estimated, helping to improve time forecasts.

3. Workload Widgets

These widgets help balance team effort and avoid burnout.

- **Workload View:** Shows tasks assigned to team members over time.

- **Effort Summary:** Total task weight (using time estimates or custom fields) per team member.

- **Capacity Planning:** Compare available work hours vs. assigned tasks.

Use case example: A manager planning resource allocation for a sprint may use Workload View to prevent overallocation and balance team responsibilities.

4. Goal Widgets

If you're using ClickUp Goals (as covered in Section 5.2), you can integrate goal tracking directly into your Dashboard.

- **Goal Tracking:** Displays goal progress visually.

- **Target Metrics:** Tracks numeric goals such as revenue, leads generated, etc.

- **Goal Completion Rate:** Shows how many goals have been completed within a timeframe.

Use case example: A sales team might use goal widgets to track quarterly targets and visually monitor how close they are to reaching key milestones.

5. Chart Widgets

These are great for visual thinkers who want to analyze performance at a glance.

- **Pie Charts, Bar Graphs, and Line Graphs:** Represent task data based on custom filters.

- **Cumulative Flow Diagrams:** Shows task progression over time (ideal for agile teams).

- **Burndown/Burnup Charts:** Great for sprint and project management.

Use case example: Agile teams running sprints can use burndown charts to ensure that tasks are being completed in alignment with timelines.

6. Custom Widgets

Custom widgets allow you to craft your own reports based on formulas, advanced filters, or specific metrics.

- **Custom Task Table:** Display tasks with selected columns, filters, and sorting.

- **Formula Widgets:** Run calculations using custom fields.

- **Embedded Widgets:** Add external data, charts, or services via iframes.

Use case example: An operations lead may create a custom table showing overdue tasks by department, paired with a formula that calculates the average delay per team.

Building a Custom Report with Widgets

Here's a step-by-step guide to building your own custom report using widgets on a ClickUp Dashboard.

Step 1: Define the Purpose of Your Report

Before you create a Dashboard, clarify its purpose. Are you tracking overall productivity? Team member performance? Project timelines? Time usage?

Example goals:

- Visualize overdue tasks across departments.

- Compare estimated vs. actual time across multiple projects.

- Monitor open bugs and QA tasks in software development.

Step 2: Create a New Dashboard

1. Go to the Dashboards tab.

2. Click **+ New Dashboard**.

3. Name your Dashboard.

4. Choose sharing permissions (private, shared with workspace, or specific people).

Step 3: Add Widgets

1. Click **+ Add Widget**.

2. Choose a category: Task, Time, Goal, Chart, etc.

3. Select your widget and customize filters:

   o   Choose **Locations** (Spaces, Folders, Lists)

   o   Set **Assignees**, **Tags**, **Priorities**, or **Statuses**

   o   Choose **Date ranges**

4. Adjust visual format: table, chart, or summary.

5. Repeat this process to build a multi-widget layout.

Step 4: Arrange and Optimize Layout

- Drag-and-drop widgets to reorder them.

- Resize widgets for better viewing.

- Use **sections** to group related widgets (e.g., "Sprint Metrics," "Time Logs").

Pro tip: Keep your Dashboard clean. Too many widgets can cause clutter and reduce clarity.

Examples of Useful Custom Reports

1. Team Performance Dashboard

Widgets:

- Task Completion Rate (Pie Chart)

- Overdue Tasks by Assignee

- Time Logged This Week

- Goal Progress Tracker

2. Sprint Tracking Dashboard

Widgets:

- Burndown Chart

- Tasks by Status (Kanban)

- Bugs Remaining

- Time Estimated vs. Time Tracked

3. Personal Productivity Dashboard

Widgets:

- Daily Task List

- Time Tracked Today

- Completed Tasks by Week

- Time on Admin vs. Deep Work (custom field filter)

Tips for Effective Reporting

- **Be intentional with each widget**: Ask "What will this show me?" before adding it.

- **Don't duplicate information**: Choose complementary views instead.

- **Use filters smartly**: Refine data to avoid irrelevant clutter.

- **Update regularly**: Dashboards evolve as teams and priorities change.

- **Train your team**: Everyone should know how to read and use the reports.

Limitations to Be Aware Of

While ClickUp Dashboards are powerful, keep the following in mind:

- **Performance**: Loading can slow down with many complex widgets.

- **Permissions**: Users can only see data they have access to.

- **Data Freshness**: Some metrics are updated every few minutes, not live.

If you're working with large data sets or need frequent refreshes, plan your widget layout accordingly.

Conclusion: Turning Data Into Action

Reporting is not just about data—it's about driving decisions. ClickUp's Dashboard widgets and custom reports transform raw task lists into powerful visual narratives. Whether you're trying to balance workload, streamline execution, or hit performance benchmarks, the right Dashboard setup can serve as your mission control center.

Use this section as your launchpad to experiment, iterate, and build a reporting system that works for your needs—then share it with your team to elevate everyone's performance.

5.3.3 Visualizing Workload and Performance

In any productivity system, having the ability to **see** how your team is performing, where resources are allocated, and which tasks are piling up is crucial for smart decision-making. ClickUp offers a powerful set of tools to **visualize workload and performance** through its **Dashboards** and **Workload views**, enabling individuals and teams to track progress, identify bottlenecks, and optimize processes in real time.

This section will walk you through the essential concepts, tools, and best practices to use **ClickUp's workload and performance visualizations** effectively—whether you're managing a solo freelance workflow or leading a cross-functional team of dozens.

Understanding the Value of Visual Workload Management

Before we dive into the technical "how," let's start with the "why."

In many organizations, **overwork**, **task overlap**, and **missed deadlines** don't stem from a lack of effort—but from a **lack of visibility**. When managers and contributors don't have a clear picture of what's being worked on (and by whom), the team becomes vulnerable to poor planning and inefficiency.

ClickUp helps overcome this problem with visual dashboards that provide:

- **Instant visibility** into tasks, time, and effort

- **Workload balance**, avoiding burnout or underutilization

- **Performance analytics** that help managers coach, plan, and support their teams

---

Workload View: Who's Doing What (and How Much)?

The **Workload view** is one of ClickUp's most impactful tools for visualizing task distribution across team members. It's like a digital control center that shows you how busy each person is during a selected time period.

Setting Up the Workload View

To set up a Workload view:

1. Go to any **Space**, **Folder**, or **List**.

2. Click the **+ View** button at the top.

3. Select **Workload**.

4. Customize the view by selecting the **time period** (day, week, month), **grouping method**, and **resource type**.

You can view workload based on:

- **Task count**

- **Time estimates** (if you're using time tracking or estimations)

- **Sprint points** (if you're in Agile workflows)

Using Time Estimates to Power Workload

Workload view becomes most effective when **time estimates** are applied to tasks. By assigning estimated durations to each task, ClickUp can calculate how many hours each person is expected to work per day and highlight **overbooked** or **underutilized** team members.

To add time estimates:

- Open a task

- Click the **time estimate** field

- Enter the expected hours or minutes

Interpreting Workload Capacity

Each user in the Workload view has a **capacity bar** for the selected time period. If a person is over capacity, their bar will be red. If they're under capacity, it may be green or gray. This lets project managers reassign or redistribute tasks intelligently.

Performance Metrics in Dashboards

While Workload view focuses on task assignments and capacity, **Dashboards** are where ClickUp's performance metrics come to life.

A Dashboard in ClickUp is a **custom visual reporting hub** where you can track everything from project progress to sprint velocity to task completion rates.

Creating a Dashboard

To create a Dashboard:

1. Go to the left sidebar and click **Dashboards**.

2. Click **+ New Dashboard**.

3. Name your Dashboard and choose visibility (private or shared).

4. Add **Widgets** to track the data that matters most.

Key Widgets for Performance Visualization

Here are some essential widgets you should consider for performance reporting:

- **Task Completion Widget**: Shows tasks completed vs. overdue

- **Burnup/Burndown Charts**: Great for Agile teams to track scope and completion

- **Time Tracked Widget**: See time logged per task, list, user, or space

- **Workload by User Widget**: A visual way to monitor resource allocation

- **Pie or Bar Charts**: Visualize task statuses, assignees, priorities

- **Line Graphs**: Monitor task creation/completion trends over time

Each widget can be filtered by:

- Date range

- Specific users or teams

- Folders, lists, or tags

- Custom fields

Combining Widgets into Performance Dashboards

The real power comes when you combine multiple widgets into a **thematic dashboard**. Here are some examples:

- **Team Performance Dashboard**: Task completion, time tracked, workload, overdue tasks

- **Project Health Dashboard**: On-track vs. overdue, burnup chart, milestones

- **Executive Summary Dashboard**: Cross-team summaries, high-priority task breakdown, workload spikes

Best Practices for Using Dashboards Effectively

Dashboards are incredibly powerful, but like any tool, they require thoughtful design. Here are some best practices to maximize their value:

1. Tailor Dashboards to Your Audience

A dashboard for executives should look different from one for developers. Always ask:

- Who is this for?

- What do they need to know at a glance?

For example:

- **Executives** may want strategic overviews (KPIs, risks, milestones)

- **Team Leads** may want sprint performance, blockers, workloads

- **Individual Contributors** may want progress tracking or personal time logs

2. Use Consistent Metrics

Avoid confusion by using standardized:

- Task statuses (e.g., To Do, In Progress, Done)

- Time tracking units (hours vs. minutes)

- Project labels or tags

This consistency allows for accurate, apples-to-apples comparisons between teams or time periods.

3. Automate Where Possible

Use **ClickUp Automations** to update task statuses, assign priorities, or log time—so your dashboards reflect the most accurate, real-time data with minimal manual effort.

4. Revisit and Refine Your Dashboards Monthly

As your team's priorities evolve, your dashboards should, too. Schedule a regular review:

- Are the widgets still relevant?

- Are users engaging with the dashboard?

- Are key metrics easy to find and understand?

Visualizing Performance Over Time

Understanding daily performance is helpful—but what's more important is **identifying trends** over time. ClickUp lets you do this with:

Line and Bar Graphs

Track trends like:

- Tasks completed per week

- Average time to completion

- Volume of new tasks by category

This can help managers answer questions like:

- Are we improving our delivery times?

- Is scope increasing too fast?

- Which team is overloaded this quarter?

Goal Progress Charts

If you're using **ClickUp Goals**, you can create widgets that show progress toward those goals (e.g., 65% of quarterly tasks completed). These progress bars offer **motivational visual feedback** that keeps teams aligned and focused.

Real-World Use Case: Marketing Team Dashboard

Let's say you're running a **marketing team**. Your dashboard might include:

- **Task Completion by Campaign** (Pie Chart)

- **Content Calendar View** (Calendar Widget)

- **Workload by Team Member** (Workload Widget)

- **Time Tracked per Project** (Time Widget)

- **Blog Post Pipeline** (Table Widget with filters)

This single view allows the marketing lead to:

- See if deadlines are being met

- Reassign tasks if someone is overloaded

- Adjust planning based on past effort estimates

Common Pitfalls to Avoid

Even with the right tools, many teams struggle with data visibility. Watch out for these mistakes:

- **Inconsistent Task Statuses**: Makes reporting inaccurate

- **Neglecting Time Estimates**: Breaks workload calculation

- **Too Many Dashboards**: Creates confusion and fragmentation

- **Outdated Widgets**: Reduces trust in data

- **Using Dashboards for Micromanagement**: Dashboards should empower, not control

The Future of Work Visualization in ClickUp

ClickUp continues to evolve its analytics and visualization capabilities. In the near future, we can expect:

- **AI-powered insights**: Predictive task delays or bottlenecks

- **Deeper integrations with BI tools** like Tableau or Power BI

- **Customizable KPI dashboards** with smart suggestions

As work becomes increasingly complex and remote, the ability to quickly **see, interpret, and act on data** will define successful teams. And with ClickUp's visualization tools, you're well on your way.

Summary: Key Takeaways

- **Workload View** helps balance task distribution and prevent burnout.

- **Dashboards** are your custom reporting hub for performance insights.

- **Widgets** are modular, allowing tailored visualization for every role.

- Combine **consistency, automation, and thoughtful design** for maximum clarity.

- Regular reviews and refinement keep your reporting relevant and actionable.

Ready to build your first performance dashboard in ClickUp? In the next chapter, we'll explore **ClickApps and Integrations** to unlock even more functionality.

CHAPTER VI
Advanced Features and Integrations

6.1 ClickApps and Add-ons

6.1.1 Enabling and Managing ClickApps

ClickUp is designed to be highly adaptable to a wide variety of workflows—from simple personal task management to complex cross-functional team operations. One of the most powerful tools that enable this adaptability is the **ClickApp** system. ClickApps are modular feature enhancements that can be toggled on or off based on your workspace's specific needs. Whether you're a solopreneur looking to streamline repetitive work, or a project manager orchestrating a team of dozens, enabling the right ClickApps can transform the way you use ClickUp.

In this section, you'll learn:

- What ClickApps are and how they function

- How to enable or disable ClickApps

- Best practices for managing ClickApps across spaces

- Tips for aligning ClickApps with team needs and workflows

- How to audit ClickApps to prevent feature overload

What Are ClickApps?

ClickApps are optional features that add advanced functionality to your ClickUp workspace. Think of them as modular plugins or extensions that allow you to tailor the platform to match your project needs. Instead of cluttering the interface with unnecessary tools, ClickApps let you **opt in** to features you want and **ignore** the ones you don't.

Some examples of commonly used ClickApps include:

- **Time Tracking** – allows users to log and track the time spent on tasks

- **Custom Fields** – add customizable data fields to tasks

- **Dependencies** – create relationships between tasks (e.g., blocking, waiting on)

- **Automation** – build "if this, then that" logic to reduce repetitive work

- **Sprints** – use agile sprint management with velocity charts and burndown

- **Workload** – view team capacity and balance task assignments

Each ClickApp serves a specific purpose. Some are helpful for **individuals** managing personal projects, while others are critical for **teams** who need structured processes and performance insights.

How to Enable ClickApps

To enable ClickApps for your workspace or specific Spaces, follow these steps:

Step 1: Open Workspace Settings

1. Click your **profile avatar** or workspace name in the lower-left corner.

2. Select **"Workspace settings"** from the menu.

Step 2: Navigate to ClickApps

1. In the sidebar of your Workspace Settings page, locate and click **"ClickApps."**

2. You'll see a categorized list of available ClickApps with toggles next to each.

Step 3: Enable the Desired ClickApps

1. To **enable** a ClickApp, simply toggle it **on**.

2. Some ClickApps have additional configuration options. For example, if you enable **Custom Fields**, you may also define field types or default values later.

3. ClickApps often apply **globally** across all spaces but can be customized at the Space level depending on the feature.

Managing ClickApps Across Spaces

Once enabled, most ClickApps can be managed individually within each **Space**. This is especially useful if you work in a diverse organization with teams using different workflows.

Per-Space Customization

To adjust ClickApps per Space:

1. Click the **Space settings** (gear icon next to a space name).

2. Navigate to the **ClickApps tab** inside the Space settings.

3. Toggle individual ClickApps **on or off** for that specific space.

For instance, your **development team** may need the **Sprints and GitHub ClickApps**, while your **marketing team** may only require **Custom Fields** and **Time Tracking**. This flexibility prevents feature bloat and ensures team members only see what's relevant.

ClickApp Permissions and Roles

Only **Workspace owners and admins** can enable or disable ClickApps at the workspace level. However, depending on the ClickApp, some permissions can be assigned or restricted per **user role**.

For example:

- **Time Tracking** can be enabled for everyone, but only **managers** can view total hours logged.

- **Custom Fields** can be edited by **admins** only, while **members** can view and input data.

It's important to communicate with your team to determine which features are necessary and who should manage them.

ClickApps That Require Additional Setup

While most ClickApps can be toggled on and used immediately, some require **additional configuration**. Let's take a look at a few:

☑ **Automations**

- After enabling, you must define your own custom rules using the **"Automations"** tab in your task view or list view.

- Example: *When status changes to "Done," mark due date as complete.*

☑ **Time Tracking**

- Choose whether users can **manually enter time**, **use timers**, or **both**.

- Integrate with **Harvest**, **Everhour**, or ClickUp's native tracker.

☑ **Sprints**

- Create sprint cycles, define sprint durations, and set up sprint velocity tracking.

- Assign tasks to sprints and review progress in **sprint dashboards**.

☑ **Goals**

- After activation, you'll need to create **objectives**, **targets**, and link them to specific tasks.

Best Practices for Enabling ClickApps

To ensure your team benefits from the power of ClickApps without becoming overwhelmed:

☑ **Start Small**

Don't enable everything at once. Begin with the **core features** your team already needs (e.g., Custom Fields, Automations) and expand as your workflows mature.

☑ **Review Monthly**

Set a recurring task or automation to **review ClickApps** monthly. Check if any are underutilized, or if newer ClickApps would solve emerging needs.

✅ Educate Your Team

Before rolling out a new ClickApp, share:

- A **brief training** session

- **Internal documentation**

- Links to relevant ClickUp Help Center articles or Loom walkthroughs

✅ Use Templates with ClickApps

If your team uses recurring projects, create **Space templates** or **List templates** that come pre-loaded with the necessary ClickApps. This reduces the onboarding time for new teams or new projects.

Auditing and Maintaining ClickApp Use

ClickApps, while powerful, can clutter your interface if mismanaged. To maintain a clean and efficient workspace:

- Periodically **audit** which ClickApps are enabled.

- Ask teams: *Are we using this feature regularly? Does it add value to our workflow?*

- **Deactivate** ClickApps that are not in active use. Don't worry—data stored through ClickApps will be preserved in most cases even if the ClickApp is turned off.

You can also create a **ClickApp Usage Policy** for your workspace to document:

- Who is allowed to enable new ClickApps

- How new features are evaluated before use

- Feedback loops to evaluate ClickApp effectiveness

Troubleshooting Common ClickApp Issues

Here are some common problems users face with ClickApps and how to solve them:

Issue	Possible Cause	Solution
A ClickApp is enabled, but features aren't appearing in tasks	Not enabled in the specific Space	Check the Space settings under ClickApps
Users can't see data from Custom Fields	Permission restrictions	Check field-level permissions and user roles
Automation rules not working	Conditions not defined properly	Review your trigger/action combinations
Time tracking not recording time	Timer not started or app integration broken	Reauthorize integrations or train users on proper tracking steps

Conclusion: The Power of Modular Customization

ClickApps represent one of ClickUp's most defining advantages—**modular control**. They let you build a workspace that grows with you, adapting to your needs without overwhelming users from day one. Whether you want just a to-do list or a full agile development suite, the power is in your hands.

As you progress through using ClickUp, remember that the right combination of ClickApps can streamline your workflows, automate busywork, empower team visibility, and—most importantly—help you work smarter, not harder.

In the next section, we'll explore some of the most **popular and high-impact ClickApps** you should consider adding to your toolkit.

6.1.2 Popular ClickApps to Try

ClickUp's power doesn't just lie in its core task management capabilities—it's also in its incredible customizability. One of the key ways to extend ClickUp's functionality is through **ClickApps**.

ClickApps are modular features that you can enable or disable to match the needs of your workspace. Think of them as **feature toggles** that allow you to craft a lean and tailored project management experience. Whether you're managing a complex software development lifecycle or a simple content calendar, ClickApps let you add exactly what you need—and nothing more.

In this section, we'll take a deep dive into the **most popular and valuable ClickApps**, explain what they do, when to use them, and provide some real-world use cases. By the end of this chapter, you'll be equipped to selectively power up your workspace with the features that truly matter to your team.

⚒ 1. Custom Fields

What It Does: Custom Fields let you add personalized data columns to your tasks and views. They transform your lists into powerful databases tailored to your unique workflow.

Field types include:

- Text

- Number

- Dropdowns

- Date

- Checkbox

- Formula

- Progress bar

- Currency, and more.

When to Use It: Any time you need to capture more than the default task information (status, assignee, priority), custom fields are your best friend. They're crucial for sales pipelines, content calendars, inventory tracking, client onboarding, and more.

Use Case Example: A real estate agency can use custom fields for property address, price, number of rooms, availability date, and assigned agent—turning ClickUp into a client-friendly CRM.

⚲ 2. Time Tracking

What It Does: This ClickApp enables native time tracking within tasks, allowing users to start/stop timers or manually log time spent on each task.

When to Use It: For teams billing clients by the hour, freelancers, agencies, or any business that values time-based accountability.

Use Case Example: A design agency logs hours spent on client tasks and uses the time reports feature to generate invoices at the end of the month.

🔗 3. Relationships

What It Does: The Relationships ClickApp allows you to link tasks together across spaces and folders. You can create two-way references between related tasks, documents, or goals.

When to Use It: When managing dependencies between tasks, or when different parts of a project need to reference the same key assets or milestones.

Use Case Example: A product development team creates a feature task that links to a set of research tasks, test cases, and documentation tasks for comprehensive project visibility.

📄 4. Docs

What It Does: The Docs ClickApp integrates a full-featured document editor into ClickUp. Create internal wikis, SOPs, notes, meeting agendas, or project briefs—all within your workspace.

When to Use It: Whenever written documentation is needed to support projects or serve as long-term resources. Especially useful for team knowledge bases.

Use Case Example: An HR team stores onboarding checklists and policy documents in ClickUp Docs, linking each to the relevant HR process tasks.

🔄 5. Automations

What It Does: Automations allow users to create "if this, then that" workflows. Set up triggers and actions to automate repetitive steps—no code needed.

When to Use It: Ideal for reducing manual tasks like moving statuses, assigning team members, or sending reminders when due dates are approaching.

Use Case Example: A marketing team uses automations to assign tasks to specific designers when a blog post is marked as "Ready for Design."

6. Milestones

What It Does: Milestones transform regular tasks into key project checkpoints. In Gantt view, these are shown with diamond icons to indicate major goals or deliverables.

When to Use It: Whenever you're managing a project with defined phases or deliverables. Helps teams stay on track with major deadlines.

Use Case Example: In a product launch timeline, milestones can mark "MVP Complete," "User Testing Phase Start," and "Launch Day."

7. Dependencies

What It Does: This ClickApp allows you to define how tasks are related—what needs to be done before or after a particular task. ClickUp will even notify you if you try to start a task that's waiting on another.

When to Use It: Use dependencies to manage complex projects with sequential or interconnected tasks. Crucial for timeline accuracy in Gantt charts.

Use Case Example: In software development, a QA testing task is set to depend on the "Code Review Complete" task.

8. Task Remapping

What It Does: Task Remapping lets you automatically shift due dates for tasks, subtasks, and dependencies when you duplicate a list or apply a template.

When to Use It: Use this when creating repeating projects (e.g., monthly reports or campaigns) that need new due dates each time they're cloned.

Use Case Example: A content team clones their monthly editorial calendar and all associated due dates adjust to the current month.

9. Work in Progress Limits (WIP Limits)

What It Does: Set WIP limits on board columns to manage capacity and prevent team overload. You'll get visual cues when limits are exceeded.

When to Use It: Ideal for Agile or Kanban workflows, especially for dev teams, designers, or support teams who need to limit simultaneous work.

Use Case Example: A support team sets a 5-task limit for "In Progress" to ensure agents don't get overburdened.

---

10. AI ClickApp (ClickUp AI)

What It Does: ClickUp's AI tool offers suggestions, summarizes content, and helps generate task descriptions, documents, meeting notes, and more.

When to Use It: Perfect for accelerating content creation, brainstorming, or summarizing complex tasks and documents.

Use Case Example: A product manager uses ClickUp AI to generate user stories and acceptance criteria from a product brief in seconds.

---

11. Tags

What It Does: Enabling Tags allows you to apply keywords to tasks across your workspace for filtering and categorization.

When to Use It: Use tags to label tasks across projects—like "urgent," "client X," or "Q2 goals"—for easier sorting and searching.

Use Case Example: A marketing team uses tags like "social," "email," and "video" across all content projects to filter by campaign type.

---

12. Checklists

What It Does: Adds the ability to create simple to-do style checklists within tasks. Can be used for steps, processes, or recurring sub-actions.

When to Use It: Great for SOPs, QA steps, or when you don't need full subtasks.

Use Case Example: A QA tester uses a checklist within the task "Test Checkout Flow" for browser testing steps: Chrome, Firefox, Safari.

☀ Pro Tips for Using ClickApps

- **Start simple.** Don't enable everything at once. Start with just a few ClickApps that match your current workflow.

- **Review periodically.** As your team evolves, revisit your enabled ClickApps—some may no longer be needed, while others can now add value.

- **Combine ClickApps.** The true power lies in using ClickApps **together**. For example, combine Automations + Custom Fields + Milestones for a fully-automated product launch process.

- **Train your team.** When enabling new features, take time to onboard your team so they use the tools effectively, not just as a novelty.

By leveraging the right ClickApps, ClickUp becomes **much more than a task list**—it transforms into a **fully customizable work management ecosystem** tailored to your team's needs.

Up next, we'll dive into the world of **Integrations and Syncing**, where ClickUp truly shines as a **central hub for all your tools and data**.

6.1.3 Combining ClickApps for Efficiency

ClickUp is more than just a task management tool. One of its most powerful capabilities lies in its **modular and customizable features**, particularly **ClickApps**—small, optional add-ons that can be toggled on or off depending on your workspace needs. While each ClickApp provides value individually, combining multiple ClickApps into a cohesive system can **unlock new levels of productivity, visibility, and automation**.

In this section, we'll explore how to **strategically combine ClickApps** to create efficient workflows, collaborate better, and ultimately make ClickUp a system tailored exactly to your goals.

What Are ClickApps? A Quick Recap

Before diving into combinations, let's quickly recap what ClickApps are.

ClickApps are modular features in ClickUp that you can enable or disable at the **Workspace or Space** level. They allow you to **enhance and extend** your ClickUp environment with tools like:

- Time Tracking

- Dependencies

- Custom Fields

- Sprints

- Automation

- Milestones

- Tags

- Task Priorities

- Relationships

- Goals, and more

Each ClickApp solves a particular problem. But when combined with others thoughtfully, they become a **synergistic system**.

Principles for Combining ClickApps Effectively

Not all ClickApps need to be turned on at once. Combining them well requires:

1. **Understanding Your Workflow** – Map your real-life processes before recreating them in ClickUp.

2. **Prioritizing Clarity over Complexity** – Don't overwhelm users with too many options.

3. **Testing in Stages** – Gradually introduce new ClickApps into a workflow.

4. **Using ClickApps to Fill Gaps** – Choose ClickApps that address specific problems or bottlenecks.

Now let's explore practical combinations of ClickApps, categorized by different **use cases** and **workflow types**.

✅ Combination 1: Managing Projects with Deadlines and Dependencies

Ideal for: Project managers, product development teams, service providers

ClickApps to combine:

- Dependencies
- Milestones
- Time Estimates
- Custom Fields
- Automations

How they work together:

- **Dependencies** ensure that tasks are completed in the right sequence.
- **Milestones** help track key moments and deliverables.
- **Time Estimates** help with planning and capacity allocation.
- **Custom Fields** track additional project data (e.g., budget, owner, phase).
- **Automations** trigger status changes or reminders based on progress.

Example:
You can automatically mark a milestone as "Completed" when all its dependent tasks are done. Or, use automation to change a task's status to "Ready to Review" once its preceding task is completed.

💬 Combination 2: Agile Workflow for Development Teams

Ideal for: Software developers, IT teams, startups

ClickApps to combine:

- Sprints

- Priorities

- Time Tracking

- GitHub/GitLab Integration

- Goals

- Relationships

How they work together:

- **Sprints** organize work into 1–2-week cycles.

- **Priorities** help triage tasks.

- **Time Tracking** captures effort across tasks and sprints.

- **Relationships** link tasks, bugs, or epics for context.

- **Goals** measure sprint velocity or delivery objectives.

Example:
Use the **Sprints ClickApp** to assign tasks for a given cycle, track progress in the **Sprint widget**, and log time using **native or integrated time trackers**. Connect tasks with **GitHub PRs** for traceability.

Combination 3: CRM and Client Management System

Ideal for: Freelancers, agencies, sales teams

ClickApps to combine:

- Custom Fields

- Relationships

- Forms

- Automations

- Task Templates
- Email (ClickUp Business Plan+)

How they work together:

- **Custom Fields** track client details (name, email, status, service type).
- **Forms** feed data into tasks (e.g., intake form → new lead).
- **Relationships** connect clients to their projects, invoices, or team members.
- **Automations** send follow-up emails or change task statuses.
- **Email** allows you to send emails directly from tasks.

Example:
When a potential client fills out a **form**, a new task is created with all contact info, tagged as "Lead," and assigned to a salesperson. If the task isn't updated in 5 days, an **automation** notifies the team.

Combination 4: Content Calendar + Production Pipeline

Ideal for: Marketing teams, social media managers, content creators

ClickApps to combine:

- Calendar View
- Recurring Tasks
- Custom Fields (e.g., Platform, Status)
- Tags
- Checklists
- Automations

How they work together:

- **Calendar View** helps visualize the entire editorial calendar.
- **Recurring Tasks** auto-create new weekly or monthly content.

- **Tags** help filter by platform or type (video, blog, reel).

- **Checklists** break content into steps (draft, edit, schedule, post).

- **Automations** move content to "Scheduled" once the checklist is completed.

Example:
A recurring blog post task is created weekly, tagged "Blog," with a checklist of production steps. Once all steps are completed, an automation assigns it to the scheduling team and changes the status.

🔒 Combination 5: Managing Sensitive Work with Controlled Access

Ideal for: HR, legal teams, finance departments

ClickApps to combine:

- Permissions

- Custom Fields

- Automations

- Forms

- Task Relationships

How they work together:

- **Permissions** restrict access to certain folders or tasks.

- **Forms** allow external submission of sensitive info.

- **Automations** notify the right person based on the form's content.

- **Relationships** keep linked documentation (contracts, policies) in sync.

Example:
An employee submits a PTO request through a form. The task is created in a protected list, assigned to HR, and linked to the employee's record via **Relationships**. No one else can view it.

⚙ Best Practices for Combining ClickApps

1. **Start with the End in Mind**: Clearly define the outcome you want from combining ClickApps (e.g., better reporting, easier intake, quicker workflows).

2. **Test in Sandbox Mode**: Use a test Space to experiment with new combinations before rolling them out across your whole Workspace.

3. **Educate Your Team**: Provide clear documentation or mini-training on any new combinations to avoid confusion.

4. **Document Your System**: Keep a simple manual or ClickUp Doc that explains how your workflows use different ClickApps.

5. **Review and Iterate**: Set a monthly or quarterly check-in to review what's working and what needs tweaking.

💡 Pro Tip: Use Templates with ClickApps

Create **List or Task Templates** that come pre-loaded with the right ClickApp structure (e.g., checklists, custom fields, dependencies). This way, you ensure that every new project or campaign benefits from your setup without needing to rebuild it from scratch.

Conclusion: A Modular System for Scalable Success

Combining ClickApps is like building with LEGO: each piece has a unique role, but together, they form something much more powerful.

The beauty of ClickUp is its **modularity**—it can scale from simple to sophisticated without overwhelming users. When you thoughtfully combine ClickApps, you create a system that **automates repetitive tasks, improves team alignment, and brings clarity to your entire operation**.

Whether you're a solo user or managing a cross-functional team, leveraging ClickApp combinations allows you to **work smarter, not harder.**

6.2 Integrations and Syncing

6.2.1 Connecting Google Drive, Slack, and Calendar

In today's digital workspace, using multiple tools in harmony is essential for productivity. While ClickUp is powerful on its own, its true strength is amplified when it's seamlessly integrated with the tools your team already uses. Whether you're storing documents on **Google Drive**, communicating through **Slack**, or scheduling meetings on **Google Calendar or Outlook**, ClickUp enables robust integrations that bring your work together under one platform.

This section explores how to connect and use **Google Drive**, **Slack**, and **Calendar integrations** effectively in ClickUp. You'll learn step-by-step how to set them up, the benefits of each, common use cases, and best practices to keep your workflows smooth and centralized.

🔗 Overview: Why Integrations Matter

Before diving into the how-to, let's first understand **why** these integrations matter:

- **Eliminate Context Switching**: Integrations allow users to stay in ClickUp while accessing files, messages, and events from other platforms.

- **Centralized Workflow**: Your tasks, files, chats, and calendars all live in one place.

- **Automation and Sync**: When these tools talk to each other, you save time, reduce errors, and maintain better coordination across your team.

Integrating Google Drive with ClickUp

Benefits of Integrating Google Drive

- **Attach files directly from Drive to tasks or docs**

- **Quick preview of Docs, Sheets, Slides within ClickUp**

- **Eliminate duplicated uploads and version confusion**

Step-by-Step: Connecting Google Drive

1. **Navigate to Your Profile Settings**: Go to your Avatar > Apps > Integrations or search "Google Drive" in the ClickApps settings.

2. **Enable Google Drive Integration**: Toggle the switch on and select "Connect".

3. **Authenticate with Your Google Account**: A pop-up will appear. Choose the Google account you want to link, and grant ClickUp the necessary permissions.

4. **Start Using Google Drive in ClickUp** Once connected, you can:

   - Attach Google Drive files to any task using the attachment button.

   - Embed live documents inside ClickUp Docs.

   - Use the Google Drive widget inside Dashboards to view recent files.

Tips and Best Practices

- Use folders in Drive for each project or client, then reference them inside ClickUp tasks.

- Embed read-only or editable links based on your team's needs.

- When using Docs or Sheets for collaboration, set permissions within Google Drive itself to control access, rather than relying solely on ClickUp visibility.

Integrating Slack with ClickUp

Benefits of Slack Integration

- Instant updates in Slack for task activity

- Create and manage tasks from within Slack

- Streamline communication between chat and action

How to Connect Slack to ClickUp

1. **Go to ClickApps Settings**: Navigate to **Settings > ClickApps > Slack Integration**.

2. **Install the Slack App**: You'll be redirected to Slack to install the ClickUp app into your workspace. Confirm access and select the channels.

3. **Configure Notifications** Choose what activity to send to Slack:

   o   New task created

   o   Comments added

   o   Task status changes

   o   Reminders and due date alerts

4. **Use the /clickup Slash Command**: Inside any Slack channel, type /clickup new to create a new task without leaving Slack.

5. **Two-Way Sync** Comments or status changes made via Slack can update in ClickUp automatically.

Common Use Cases

- A manager receives real-time updates in a Slack project channel whenever a high-priority task changes status.

- A team lead creates tasks on the fly in Slack during meetings using /clickup new.

- Developers can link a bug report in ClickUp and tag QA teammates directly from Slack.

Tips and Best Practices

- Use **dedicated Slack channels** per ClickUp Space or Folder for better organization.

- Mute channels that get too noisy by customizing notification triggers.

- Encourage teams to use task links when discussing work in Slack—keeping context attached to the conversation.

Syncing Google Calendar or Outlook Calendar with ClickUp

Why Sync Calendars with ClickUp?

- Align your task deadlines with scheduled meetings

- Get a full view of your workload and time availability

- Avoid double-booking or missing due dates

Two-Way vs. One-Way Sync: What's the Difference?

- **Two-Way Sync**: Events and tasks are synced both ways. Editing on either side (ClickUp or Calendar) reflects in both platforms.

- **One-Way Sync**: Only ClickUp tasks appear in your calendar, but changes to the calendar don't affect ClickUp.

Setting Up Calendar Sync

Two-Way Sync with Google Calendar

1. **Go to Settings > Integrations > Calendar**

2. Choose **Connect Google Calendar**

3. Authenticate your account and select which ClickUp Spaces or Lists to sync.

4. Map ClickUp task dates to calendar events.

Two-Way Sync with Outlook Calendar

1. Similar process, but connect using **Microsoft Outlook account** credentials.

2. Choose specific Spaces or Lists to show up on your calendar.

3. Customize which fields show on your calendar (task title, assignee, due date).

One-Way Sync (Subscribe to a ClickUp Calendar Feed)

1. From any List or Folder view, click the **"..." menu > Calendar > Subscribe**.

2. Copy the iCal feed URL.

3. Paste into Google Calendar > Other Calendars > From URL.

4. The ClickUp task dates will now appear in your calendar.

Tips for Using Calendar Integration

- Set **start and due dates** for tasks if you want full event blocks to appear in your calendar.

- Use **time estimates** on tasks to block out time, especially in Time View or Calendar View.

- Color-code Lists or Spaces to visually segment your calendar by type of work.

- Turn on **reminders and time-based alerts** to avoid missing key deadlines.

Common Troubleshooting Tips

- **Issue**: Calendar sync doesn't show recent updates.
  Solution: Try re-authenticating the connection and refreshing the feed.

- **Issue**: Google Drive not attaching properly.
  Solution: Ensure you're logged into the correct Google account that has access to the file.

- **Issue**: Slack notifications overwhelming your channel.
  Solution: Customize which events trigger notifications or move ClickUp activity to a dedicated Slack channel.

Real-World Use Case: Marketing Team Example

A marketing agency uses ClickUp to manage content production. Here's how they integrate tools:

- **Google Drive**: Stores all blog post drafts and social media images. Linked directly in task descriptions.

- **Slack**: Used for internal communication; tasks are created from brainstorming sessions via /clickup new.

- **Calendar Sync**: Weekly content deadlines and campaign launches appear on both Google Calendar and ClickUp Timeline View.

By using all three integrations together, they reduced duplicated effort, improved visibility, and kept everyone aligned.

✅ Key Takeaways

- Google Drive helps keep file attachments live and collaborative.

- Slack makes communication around tasks quick and contextual.

- Calendar sync ensures your schedule and task list stay in harmony.

- Customizing your integrations allows your team to work smarter—not harder.

6.2.2 Zapier, Make (Integromat), and API Options

In today's interconnected digital landscape, managing your workflow in isolation is no longer practical. For ClickUp to become your ultimate productivity hub, it needs to interact fluidly with other tools you and your team use daily. This is where integration platforms like **Zapier**, **Make (formerly Integromat)**, and the **ClickUp API** come into play. These tools allow ClickUp to sync with hundreds, even thousands, of external apps—unlocking automation superpowers and bridging gaps between services.

In this section, we'll explore how these integration options work, what makes each unique, and how you can leverage them to **streamline workflows**, **eliminate repetitive tasks**, and **create a more connected digital workspace**.

🔄 Why Use Third-Party Integrations?

Before we dive into the tools themselves, let's clarify the *why*:

- **Save Time**: Automate recurring or manual tasks such as data entry, task creation, and notifications.

- **Improve Accuracy**: Reduce errors from manual copying/pasting or switching between platforms.

- **Centralize Workflows**: Make ClickUp the "command center" for your operations.

- **Scale Your Work**: Manage larger teams or projects without increasing manual labor.

Now, let's break down each integration option.

⚡ Zapier + ClickUp: Automate Without Coding

🔍 What is Zapier?

Zapier is one of the most popular "no-code" automation platforms, letting you create workflows (called **Zaps**) between ClickUp and 5,000+ other apps including Gmail, Slack, Trello, Asana, Google Sheets, Notion, and more.

🛠 How It Works

A **Zap** is a trigger-action pair:

- **Trigger**: An event in one app (e.g., "New task created in ClickUp").

- **Action**: What Zapier does in response (e.g., "Send a message in Slack").

These chains can get quite complex with multi-step workflows and filters, but even basic Zaps can make a huge difference in your efficiency.

🔗 Common Use Cases

1. **Gmail → ClickUp**: Automatically turn emails into tasks.

2. **Form tools (e.g., Typeform, Google Forms) → ClickUp**: Create tasks based on form submissions.

3. **ClickUp → Google Sheets**: Log task data into a spreadsheet in real-time.

4. **ClickUp → Slack**: Notify channels when tasks are assigned, completed, or overdue.

5. **CRM → ClickUp**: Create follow-up tasks when deals are closed in HubSpot or Salesforce.

✅ Getting Started with Zapier

1. **Sign up** at Zapier.com and connect your ClickUp account.

2. Choose a Trigger App (e.g., ClickUp, Gmail).

3. Define the specific event (e.g., "New Task Created").

4. Choose an Action App (e.g., Google Sheets).

5. Configure the Action (e.g., "Add Row with task name and due date").

6. Test your Zap.

7. Turn it on and let it run in the background.

💡 Pro Tips for Zapier

- Use **Filters** to narrow triggers (e.g., only tasks with a certain status).

- Add **Delays** if you want actions to occur after a specific time.

- Use **Paths** to create conditional workflows (Pro plans only).

- Set up error handling to avoid disruptions.

🧠 Make (Integromat) + ClickUp: Advanced Visual Automation

🔍 What is Make?

Make is a powerful visual automation platform that lets you design workflows between apps using a flowchart-like interface. It offers more granular control compared to Zapier, ideal for users with more technical experience or advanced needs.

Think of Make as a **logic-driven automation engine** where you can manipulate data, apply conditional logic, and build custom integrations at scale.

🛠 How It Works

Workflows in Make are called **Scenarios** and are built with a series of **Modules**:

- Triggers (start the flow)

- Actions (perform operations)

- Routers (branching logic)

- Tools (data transformers, aggregators)

You can connect dozens of apps in one scenario and process data from one step to another seamlessly.

🔗 Common Use Cases

1. **ClickUp → Email Parser → CRM**: Create leads based on parsed data from ClickUp tasks.

2. **ClickUp ↔ Airtable**: Keep task information synced in both systems.

3. **ClickUp → Notion**: Update your personal knowledge base when project milestones are achieved.

4. **ClickUp → PDF Generator → Email**: Send auto-generated reports when a project phase ends.

✅ Getting Started with Make

1. Create a free account at Make.com.

2. Connect your ClickUp account using an API token.

3. Start a new **Scenario**, and choose **ClickUp** as the trigger app.

4. Add subsequent steps (Modules) such as data processing, conditional logic, or multi-step branches.

5. Test the workflow, make adjustments, then **schedule** it.

💡 Pro Tips for Make

- Use **Routers** to split scenarios based on task conditions.

- Integrate **Webhooks** to receive real-time data from external apps.

- Apply **Data Stores** to hold and reuse information across multiple runs.

- Try using **Iterators** for looping through subtasks or comments.

⚡ ClickUp API: Full Flexibility for Developers

🔍 What is the ClickUp API?

The **ClickUp API** is a powerful RESTful interface that allows developers to programmatically interact with ClickUp's backend. With it, you can **create**, **read**, **update**, and **delete** data in ClickUp, as well as perform actions not yet available through the UI or integrations.

Perfect for development teams or advanced users building:

- Custom dashboards

- Enterprise-level integrations

- Internal tools and analytics systems

🔑 API Basics

- **Base URL**: https://api.clickup.com/api/v2/

- **Authentication**: Bearer token (you can generate this from your ClickUp profile settings)

- **Rate Limits**: 100 requests per minute per token

- **Formats**: JSON-based requests and responses

📦 Available Endpoints (Selected Examples)

- **Tasks**: Create, update, or delete tasks

- **Lists & Folders**: Manage hierarchy and structure

- **Users**: Get member info, assign users

- **Time Tracking**: Retrieve time entries and durations

- **Webhooks**: Get real-time updates pushed to your app

💼 Tools for Working with the API

- **Postman**: Use this for testing endpoints and building mockups.

- **Insomnia**: Another REST client for managing and documenting requests.
- **Custom apps**: Integrate the API into your own tools via JavaScript, Python, or any language that supports HTTP requests.

🛠 Sample Use Cases for the API

1. **Bulk task import** from legacy systems.
2. **Advanced analytics dashboard** with BI tools like Tableau or Power BI.
3. **Sync project data** with an ERP or inventory system.
4. **Trigger workflows** when a task changes status (via Webhooks).
5. **Auto-create tasks** when a condition in your proprietary system is met.

💡 Developer Best Practices

- Always **test in a sandbox** workspace before deploying to production.
- Use **retry logic** to handle temporary outages or API limits.
- Keep your API tokens **secure and never hardcoded**.
- Respect **rate limits** to prevent service disruptions.

❋ Choosing the Right Integration Path

Need	Use Zapier	Use Make	Use API
No-code, quick setup	✓	✓	✗
Complex logic & data handling	✗	✓	✓
Full customization	✗	⚠	✓
Real-time automation	⚠	✓	✓
Best for teams with no devs	✓	⚠	✗

Need	Use Zapier	Use Make	Use API
Best for developers	✗	☑	☑

🚀 Wrapping Up: Integration = Multiplication

The true power of ClickUp comes not just from what it can do internally—but what it can do when connected to your larger digital ecosystem. Whether you choose **Zapier for ease**, **Make for flexibility**, or **the API for full customization**, integrating ClickUp with your favorite tools supercharges your productivity and sets your workflows on autopilot.

Start small—automate one repetitive task this week. Then grow. Soon, you'll have a self-operating system that saves time, reduces friction, and lets you focus on what truly matters.

6.2.3 ClickUp with GitHub, Outlook, Zoom, and More

In the modern digital workspace, the tools we use often determine how well we can work — or how much time we lose switching between apps. That's why **ClickUp's integrations** are so powerful. They allow teams and individuals to connect ClickUp with the tools they're already using, reducing context switching and creating a centralized system of work.

This section explores how you can connect **GitHub, Outlook, Zoom**, and other powerful platforms with ClickUp to supercharge your productivity and streamline your daily operations.

🔧 Why Integrate with Other Tools?

Before diving into each integration, let's discuss **why integrations matter**:

- **Centralized Workflow:** Reduces the need to toggle between apps and platforms.
- **Improved Communication:** Keeps updates, code commits, calendar events, and meeting notes in one place.

- **Better Collaboration:** Enhances visibility across departments using different tools.

- **Time Savings:** Automates repetitive tasks, increases accuracy, and minimizes human error.

Let's break down how ClickUp connects with some of the most essential platforms used in software development, communication, and scheduling.

🏛 ClickUp + GitHub: Bridging Development and Project Management

If you're a software development team using **GitHub**, ClickUp's GitHub integration is a game-changer. It brings development activity directly into your project management dashboard.

◆ What You Can Do with the GitHub Integration:

- Link GitHub commits, branches, and pull requests to ClickUp tasks.

- See GitHub activity as comments in tasks.

- Automatically close ClickUp tasks when pull requests are merged.

◆ How to Set It Up:

1. **Navigate to:**

    o ClickUp Workspace Settings > Integrations > GitHub.

2. **Connect Your GitHub Account:**

    o Authorize access to your GitHub repositories.

3. **Link Repositories to Spaces or Folders:**

    o You can choose which repos should sync with specific workspaces or spaces.

◆ Best Practices:

- Use branch names with the ClickUp task ID (e.g., feature/CP-123-new-ui) to auto-link commits.

- Enable automatic status changes when pull requests are merged to streamline agile workflows.

- Use GitHub activity as a changelog within the task thread.

ClickUp + Outlook: Synchronizing Emails and Calendars

Microsoft Outlook is the go-to for emails and calendars in many corporate environments. With the ClickUp integration, you can bring **email-based communication** and **calendar events** into your workflow.

Email Integration:

With **ClickUp Email for Outlook**, you can send and receive emails directly from ClickUp tasks.

Key Features:

- Send email replies from within a task.

- Automatically convert an email into a ClickUp task.

- Keep communication threaded and linked to work items.

Setup:

1. Install the **ClickUp Add-in for Outlook** via Microsoft AppSource.

2. Authenticate your ClickUp account.

3. Link emails to specific tasks or create new ones from the message view.

Calendar Sync:

ClickUp allows two-way sync with Outlook Calendar.

Benefits:

- View scheduled ClickUp tasks in your Outlook calendar.

- Block off time for deep work by syncing deadlines and events.

- Stay aware of deadlines even when working primarily in Outlook.

Setup:

1. Go to your **ClickUp profile settings**.

2. Select **Calendar Sync > Outlook**.

3. Choose one-way or two-way syncing.

🎥 ClickUp + Zoom: Seamless Meeting Management

If Zoom is your virtual meeting room, ClickUp helps you make the most of it by embedding meeting planning directly into your workflow.

- **Meeting Integration Capabilities:**

  - Schedule Zoom meetings from within ClickUp.

  - Add Zoom links to tasks or calendar events.

  - Start a Zoom call from a task with one click.

- **Setup:**

  1. Go to **ClickApps > Zoom**.

  2. Enable the Zoom ClickApp.

  3. Authorize your Zoom account.

Once enabled, a Zoom icon will appear in your task toolbar, allowing you to:

- **Start** a meeting instantly with your team.

- **Attach** meeting recordings or links to relevant tasks.

- Keep a record of discussions tied to deliverables.

- **Use Case Examples:**

- Schedule daily stand-ups directly from a ClickUp task.

- Attach a Zoom meeting to a client deliverable for review.

- Record Zoom calls and link them to project documentation.

ClickUp with Other Tools and Platforms

Beyond GitHub, Outlook, and Zoom, ClickUp supports dozens of other tools — either natively or through third-party automation platforms like **Zapier**, **Make**, and its **public API**.

Here are a few additional tools that integrate seamlessly with ClickUp:

Google Drive, Dropbox, OneDrive

- Attach cloud-stored files directly to tasks.

- Preview documents without leaving ClickUp.

- Maintain version control on collaborative documents.

Pro Tip:

Use Custom Fields to track file versions and team comments for collaborative editing.

Slack

- Receive task updates, reminders, and notifications directly in Slack.

- Create new ClickUp tasks from Slack messages.

- Use slash commands to interact with ClickUp from within Slack.

Example Workflow:

- A teammate posts a bug report in Slack → You turn it into a task in ClickUp instantly.

Notion, Evernote, or Confluence (via API/Zapier)

- Push notes from Notion into ClickUp as tasks.

- Log meeting notes from Evernote directly into a project folder.

- Maintain a dynamic knowledge base with two-way syncing.

Time-Tracking and Finance Tools

- Integrate with tools like **Harvest**, **Toggl**, and **QuickBooks**.

- Track billable hours from within tasks.

- Sync time logs with invoices and payroll systems.

CRM Platforms (HubSpot, Salesforce, Pipedrive)

- Create ClickUp tasks from CRM events (e.g., leads, deals).

- Track the client journey with automated follow-ups.

- Connect pre-sales and post-sales workflows in one place.

Best Practices for Using Integrations in ClickUp

To make the most of these integrations, keep the following tips in mind:

1. **Start Small:** Focus on 1–2 critical integrations that will reduce the most friction in your workflow.

2. **Maintain Clean Structures:** Integrations work best with a well-structured ClickUp hierarchy. Avoid clutter.

3. **Document Automation Rules:** Keep a document or page where your team can refer to what automations/integrations are active.

4. **Educate the Team:** Make sure everyone understands how and why integrations are used, especially if they impact task flow.

5. **Review Regularly:** Tools evolve — check periodically for new integration features or better configuration methods.

🌐 ClickUp Public API and Developer Tools

If your organization has in-house developers or uses custom-built tools, ClickUp's **public API** opens the door to endless automation possibilities.

API Use Cases:

- Build custom dashboards.

- Sync ClickUp with legacy systems.

- Push or pull data for advanced analytics.

Developer Resources:

- ClickUp API Docs (https://developer.clickup.com/)

- SDKs and Postman Collections available

- Webhook and OAuth2 support for secure connections

✅ Summary: Bringing It All Together

ClickUp becomes exponentially more powerful when integrated with the tools you already use. Whether you're automating code workflows with GitHub, coordinating meetings via Zoom, syncing your calendar through Outlook, or tying in documents from Google Drive — **ClickUp helps bring it all under one roof**.

Done right, integrations eliminate data silos, improve team collaboration, and give you a 360° view of your work — all in one intuitive workspace.

Next Step: Try integrating one of your most-used tools today. Start with GitHub, Outlook, or Zoom, and experience firsthand how streamlined your workflow can become with ClickUp.

6.3 Using ClickUp Mobile and Desktop Appss

6.3.1 Mobile App Interface

In today's fast-paced and mobile-driven world, the ability to manage tasks, collaborate with teammates, and monitor project progress on the go is crucial. ClickUp recognizes this need and delivers a powerful mobile experience through its dedicated apps for both **iOS** and **Android**. Whether you're commuting, attending meetings, or simply away from your desk, the **ClickUp mobile app interface** keeps your productivity at your fingertips.

This section will walk you through the ClickUp mobile app interface, explain its core features, and provide actionable tips to get the most out of working from your phone or tablet.

⚙ Overview of the ClickUp Mobile App

The ClickUp mobile app is not just a miniaturized version of the desktop platform. It is a thoughtfully designed interface that prioritizes **ease of use, speed, and flexibility**. While some advanced functions are better suited to the desktop, the mobile app offers an excellent balance of features that support on-the-go task and team management.

Key Highlights:

- Compatible with iOS (iPhone/iPad) and Android devices.

- Syncs in real-time with your ClickUp workspace.

- Offers offline mode with automatic syncing when back online.

- Supports native system notifications and widgets (especially helpful for reminders and quick task creation).

- Streamlined navigation adapted for touch-based interaction.

▦ Getting Started with the Mobile App

Before diving into the interface, let's ensure everything is properly set up.

Download and Login:

1. **Download the App** from the Apple App Store or Google Play Store.

2. Open the app and **log in** with your ClickUp credentials.

3. You can choose to stay logged in, and biometric security (Face ID, fingerprint) is supported on most devices.

Syncing:

- ClickUp automatically syncs your mobile and desktop data in real time.

- Any changes you make on mobile—creating a task, changing status, leaving a comment—are instantly reflected across devices.

Understanding the Mobile Interface

The ClickUp mobile app uses a simplified, icon-based design to keep navigation intuitive. Let's explore the major components:

1. Home Screen

Your starting point in the mobile app, the Home screen gives you an overview of what's important right now.

Main elements include:

- **Inbox:** View updates and notifications for tasks assigned to you or followed by you.

- **Today View:** See tasks due today or scheduled events.

- **Next & Overdue:** Easily access tasks that are coming up or overdue, helping you stay on top of priorities.

Tip: You can customize your Home layout in the settings to show or hide specific modules.

📋 2. Task View and Management

Clicking on any task from your home screen or list brings up the task detail view.

Here, you can:

- **Edit task titles and descriptions**
- **Add comments, attachments, or subtasks**
- **Change priority, status, assignees, and due dates**
- **Log time** directly within the task (if time tracking is enabled)

The task view is one of the most powerful areas in the mobile app. You can swipe between sections, tap icons to quickly access features like:

- Checklists
- Assigned comments
- Custom fields

☑ *Tip: Tap the "..." icon for advanced options like duplicating, moving, or archiving a task.*

❄ 3. Navigation Bar

At the bottom of the screen, you'll find the **main navigation bar**:

- **Home:** Your personal dashboard
- **Tasks:** A broader view across Spaces, Folders, and Lists
- **Notifications:** Real-time alerts and updates
- **Quick Add (+):** Create new tasks, Docs, Goals, or Time entries
- **More:** Access Docs, Goals, Dashboards, and Settings

☑ *Tip: Use the Quick Add button as your go-to for capturing ideas, even on the fly.*

Navigating Spaces, Folders, and Lists

Unlike the desktop version where the left sidebar dominates navigation, the mobile app keeps things more compact.

To navigate your workspace:

- Tap on the **Tasks** icon in the bottom navigation bar

- Use the **hierarchical dropdowns** to select your Space > Folder > List

- You can **favorite** important Lists or Spaces to keep them accessible with one tap

Tip: Use the search icon to instantly locate tasks by name, tag, or keyword.

Editing and Creating Tasks on Mobile

Task creation on mobile is fast, yet customizable.

When you tap the "+" button:

1. Choose "Task"

2. Select the List where it will live

3. Add a title (required)

4. Optional fields:

   o   Description

   o   Assignees

   o   Priority

   o   Tags

   o   Start and Due Dates

   o   Subtasks

   o   Attachments

The **task editor** supports **voice dictation** and **attachments from your device's camera or storage**, perfect for capturing real-world context.

Managing Notifications

The mobile app keeps you up to date with:

- **Push notifications** (customizable per workspace)
- **Inbox updates**
- **Activity feeds** for task-level monitoring

You can control notifications in:

- **Profile > Settings > Notifications**
- Mute notifications temporarily with **Do Not Disturb mode**

Tip: Enable smart notifications only for assigned tasks and comments to avoid overload.

What Can't You Do on Mobile (Yet)?

While ClickUp mobile is incredibly capable, a few advanced features are currently desktop-only or limited in mobile:

- Creating complex **Automations**
- Detailed **Dashboard configuration**
- Full **Mind Maps** and **Whiteboards**
- Advanced **Goal planning and reporting**

However, ClickUp continuously updates the mobile app, and new features are frequently rolled out.

Productivity Tips for Using ClickUp Mobile

1. **Use Widgets** (iOS & Android):

   o   Add "Tasks Today" or "Quick Add" widgets for instant access.

2. **Voice-to-Task**:

   o   Use your phone's voice assistant (like Siri or Google Assistant) to create tasks via ClickUp integrations.

3. **Offline Mode**:

   o   Work offline and sync when you reconnect. Great for flights, commutes, or remote areas.

4. **Dark Mode**:

   o   Enable it from Settings for nighttime use or energy saving.

5. **Split Screen Mode** (for tablets):

   o   Use ClickUp side-by-side with email, notes, or a browser.

Who Should Use the Mobile App Most?

The ClickUp mobile app is especially beneficial for:

- **Remote workers** who need access on the go

- **Field teams** (e.g., contractors, salespeople)

- **Managers** who need to stay updated during travel

- **Freelancers** juggling multiple projects from anywhere

- **Students** managing assignments and schedules from class

Mobile and Desktop Harmony

One of the strengths of ClickUp is its seamless sync between mobile and desktop platforms. This harmony allows you to:

- Create tasks on mobile, elaborate on desktop

- View detailed reports on desktop, mark them complete on mobile

- Share a comment or file from your phone while in a meeting, and continue collaboration from your computer later

☑ *Work doesn't have to stop when you leave your desk. With ClickUp's mobile app, it continues—efficiently and intelligently.*

6.3.2 Offline Mode and Syncing

In today's increasingly mobile and remote work environments, staying connected to your tasks and projects—no matter where you are or whether you have internet access—is crucial. ClickUp addresses this need with a growing suite of **offline features and intelligent syncing capabilities**, allowing users to continue working even when disconnected. In this section, we'll explore **how offline mode works in ClickUp**, what its current limitations are, and how data is synchronized once you're back online.

Understanding ClickUp's Offline Functionality

ClickUp's mobile and desktop apps are designed to allow limited interaction with your workspaces while offline. Although full offline functionality is still being gradually rolled out and expanded, users can already **view, edit, and create certain task types and lists** without an internet connection. Once a connection is re-established, your changes will be synced to your account automatically.

Here's a breakdown of what you can expect:

☑ **What You *Can* Do Offline:**

- View previously loaded tasks, subtasks, and lists

- Create new tasks (limited fields)

- Add comments to tasks

- Edit task descriptions and checklists

- Mark tasks as complete

- Use time tracking (mobile)

- Add attachments (synced later)

- Create reminders or notifications (mobile-specific)

✕ **What You *Cannot* Do Offline (Currently):**

- Access new/unloaded workspaces, folders, or views

- Sync changes between team members

- Access Dashboards or Gantt view

- Use Automations or integrations

- Enable/disable ClickApps

- Create or apply templates

- View real-time updates or user activities

Note: Offline access works best on the mobile app (iOS/Android) as of now. The desktop app offers minimal offline features but is gradually being enhanced.

Preparing to Work Offline: Best Practices

To ensure a smooth experience when working offline, it's important to prepare your environment beforehand. Here are some proactive steps to take:

1. Load Your Tasks Before Disconnecting

ClickUp's offline mode depends on **cached data**—meaning, the tasks and lists you've recently accessed online will be available offline. To make sure you can work effectively without a connection:

- Open important Lists, Folders, and Tasks while you're online

- Navigate to key views like "My Work" or Favorites to preload content

- Download necessary attachments beforehand (ClickUp does not download them offline by default)

2. Use Favorites to Prioritize Offline Access

ClickUp lets you star key tasks, lists, and dashboards. Favoriting a task ensures it stays easy to access and more likely to be cached for offline work. Before going offline:

- Favorite tasks you know you'll need

- Add them to your Home or My Work page

- Open and briefly interact with them to cache the data

3. Download the Latest Mobile App Updates

ClickUp frequently updates the mobile app to expand offline functionality. Always ensure your app is updated to the latest version from the App Store or Google Play before going into offline mode.

How Syncing Works in ClickUp

When you reconnect to the internet, ClickUp automatically attempts to **sync all offline changes** with the cloud. This includes any:

- Newly created tasks

- Edits to existing tasks

- Comments

- Attachments

- Task completions or checklist changes

- Time logs (mobile)

This syncing process is automatic and typically seamless, but there are a few technical considerations to keep in mind:

🔄 Sync Prioritization

ClickUp prioritizes syncing actions in the order they were made. For example, if you create a new task and later add a checklist to it offline, the task will first be uploaded, followed by the checklist.

⚠ Conflict Resolution

If two users make changes to the same task—one offline and one online—ClickUp handles it as follows:

- **User-specific changes** (like comments or time logs) are merged

- **Field-based conflicts** (like two people editing a task description) may prompt one version to override the other, usually based on timestamps

- In some cases, ClickUp may flag the conflict and allow you to choose which version to keep

Tip: Avoid simultaneous editing of the same tasks while offline to reduce risk of conflicts.

Use Case Scenarios

Understanding offline functionality can be especially helpful in these common scenarios:

☑ Use Case 1: Traveling Professionals

You're on a long flight with no Wi-Fi. Before boarding, you open the mobile app and review your priority list. During the flight, you update several task descriptions, mark tasks as complete, and add notes. When you land and reconnect to the internet, all changes sync automatically.

☑ Use Case 2: Field Workers

Construction supervisors, sales reps, or engineers working in remote locations without reliable connectivity can continue updating project notes, task progress, and checklists in ClickUp mobile. Once they return to an area with service, everything uploads without needing to manually sync.

☑ Use Case 3: Emergency Brainstorms

Imagine a flash of inspiration strikes when you're hiking with no signal. Open ClickUp mobile, create a new task for the idea, and jot down notes. When you're back online, it syncs and is instantly accessible across all devices.

Limitations and Upcoming Features

ClickUp is constantly developing its offline features. Some known limitations include:

- **View Limitations**: Not all views (like Gantt or Timeline) are available offline
- **Attachments**: Large file uploads may delay or fail if the reconnection is unstable
- **Real-time Collaboration**: You cannot see real-time edits made by team members while offline

According to the ClickUp product roadmap, future offline updates may include:

- Offline templates
- Full offline task creation with custom fields
- Local storage of larger workspaces and dashboards
- Offline dashboard interaction

Stay tuned to ClickUp's changelog and blog for official announcements on these updates.

Tips for Smooth Offline Use

Here are some general recommendations to enhance your offline ClickUp experience:

- **Use Checklists Frequently** – They're lightweight and sync easily
- **Minimize Dependencies Offline** – Avoid creating new task relationships
- **Take Advantage of Reminders** – These work even offline on mobile
- **Label Offline-Edited Tasks** – Consider using a tag like "OfflineEdit" to track what you modified without internet access

- **Test Before Going Fully Offline** – Try working in airplane mode for 5–10 minutes to see what functionality you can access

Troubleshooting Offline Sync Issues

If you experience issues with syncing after reconnecting:

1. **Check Your Connection Quality** – Weak Wi-Fi or mobile data may delay sync

2. **Force a Sync (Mobile)** – Swipe down on your workspace screen

3. **Restart the App** – Especially after long periods offline

4. **Reinstall If Needed** – If sync fails repeatedly, reinstalling the app can refresh your local data cache

5. **Contact Support** – ClickUp's Help Center and Live Chat are available if issues persist

Summary: Work Without Limits

Offline mode and syncing in ClickUp empower users to stay productive anytime, anywhere. Whether you're traveling, working in low-connectivity areas, or just want the peace of mind of having your work accessible anytime, ClickUp's offline tools provide a safety net that keeps your momentum going.

While the feature set is still evolving, even the current capabilities allow you to:

- Stay focused and organized during travel or internet downtime

- Keep ideas flowing by quickly capturing them offline

- Contribute to your projects without waiting on connectivity

As ClickUp continues to expand its offline feature set, the gap between connected and disconnected productivity will grow smaller—ensuring your work never skips a beat.

6.3.3 Best Use Cases on Mobile

As mobile work becomes the norm and teams increasingly operate across time zones and geographies, the ability to manage your tasks and collaborate with your team from your mobile device is no longer a luxury—it's a necessity. While the ClickUp desktop and web apps provide the full suite of features and power, the **ClickUp mobile app** offers targeted functionality that makes managing your work on-the-go both practical and productive.

This section explores **best use cases for using ClickUp on mobile**, helping you leverage the app's unique strengths to stay organized, responsive, and connected—whether you're commuting, in a meeting, at a client site, or simply away from your desk.

1. Quick Task Capture and Inbox Management

One of the most valuable mobile use cases is **quickly capturing tasks, ideas, or to-dos** as they arise. Ideas often strike when we're not in front of a computer, and ClickUp's mobile app makes it easy to log them instantly.

✅ **Best for:**

- Capturing tasks while commuting or walking

- Voice-to-text input for quick idea recording

- Managing your **Inbox** during idle time (e.g., standing in line, waiting for a meeting to start)

✖ **Pro Tips:**

- Use the **+ Task** button on the home screen for instant task creation.

- Dictate task details using your device's voice input feature.

- Quickly add attachments, checklists, priorities, or due dates before saving.

2. Updating Task Statuses On-the-Go

Project management doesn't pause just because you're not at your desk. With the mobile app, you can **update task statuses, add comments, or assign tasks in real time**, which is ideal when you're managing teams or coordinating logistics.

☑ **Best for:**

- Fieldwork or event management

- Sales or client-facing roles

- Supervisors managing teams in multiple locations

⚒ **Pro Tips:**

- Use **Swipe Actions** on your task list to quickly mark a task as "In Progress" or "Done."

- Filter tasks by "Due Today" or "Assigned to Me" to prioritize what needs immediate attention.

3. Checking Notifications and Assigned Comments

The **Notification Center** and **Inbox** features in the ClickUp mobile app are optimized for mobile use, making it easy to **stay in the loop without being overwhelmed**.

☑ **Best for:**

- Reviewing feedback or approval requests

- Responding to @mentions and assigned comments quickly

- Staying updated during travel or off-site meetings

⚒ **Pro Tips:**

- Use the "Mentions" and "Assigned Comments" filters to zero in on critical items.

- Long-press notifications to preview without fully opening the task.

4. Reviewing and Annotating Docs

ClickUp Docs are accessible from the mobile app, allowing you to **read, comment on, and annotate documentation** anytime, anywhere. While editing might be easier on a larger screen, review tasks are well-suited for mobile.

✅ **Best for:**

- Reviewing project briefs or meeting notes

- Adding comments to marketing or product drafts

- Checking SOPs while on-site

🛠 **Pro Tips:**

- Use the **comment mode** in Docs to leave contextual feedback.

- Bookmark frequently used Docs for easy mobile access.

---

5. Managing Calendar and Schedule

With built-in integration between **ClickUp tasks and calendars**, the mobile app can function like a portable planner. You can review your **daily, weekly, or monthly schedule**, view meetings, and adjust deadlines on the fly.

✅ **Best for:**

- Checking your schedule while traveling

- Rescheduling or adjusting priorities quickly

- Getting a snapshot of your workload before starting the day

🛠 **Pro Tips:**

- Use **Calendar View** or sync with your device's native calendar for even quicker access.

- Use the Today Widget (on iOS) or Android Home Widgets for real-time summaries.

---

6. Offline Task Management

ClickUp's mobile app supports **offline task viewing and editing**, which is crucial for those who often find themselves without internet access—on flights, in remote locations, or during outages.

☑ **Best for:**

- Updating field data or reports in remote areas

- Drafting project plans while commuting

- Preparing notes or checklists during offline meetings

⚒ **Pro Tips:**

- Sync your most-used Spaces, Lists, and Docs for offline availability.

- All changes made offline will auto-sync once you're reconnected.

---

7. Using ClickUp Chat for Team Communication

ClickUp includes a **Chat View**, allowing you to message team members directly in the platform. The mobile experience is streamlined for chat, offering a quick way to reach out without switching between apps.

☑ **Best for:**

- Quick check-ins with team members

- Sharing updates or links

- Asking for task clarification

⚒ **Pro Tips:**

- Pin important chat threads to the top for easy access.

- Use slash commands (e.g., /task) to reference or create tasks within a chat.

---

8. Field Team and Operations Work

ClickUp mobile is a perfect fit for **field teams**, operations managers, or anyone who performs work away from a desk. Whether you're **checking off inspection checklists**, updating **delivery statuses**, or **recording site issues**, the mobile app can streamline your processes.

☑ **Best for:**

- Construction, facilities, or logistics industries

- Field audits or site inspections

- Coordinating service teams

🛠 **Pro Tips:**

- Create reusable checklist templates for consistent reporting.

- Attach location-tagged photos and notes directly to tasks.

---

9. Keeping Leadership Informed

For managers or executives, ClickUp mobile can serve as a **dashboard for team performance**. Rather than waiting for reports, leaders can open the app to quickly check progress and key metrics.

☑ **Best for:**

- Reviewing dashboard widgets on the fly

- Checking high-priority project statuses

- Approving pending tasks or goals

🛠 **Pro Tips:**

- Customize your Home screen with important Dashboards or task filters.

- Set up Notifications for specific projects to be instantly alerted.

---

10. Emergency Problem-Solving and Crisis Response

When something goes wrong—whether it's a failed deployment, a missed deadline, or a team emergency—ClickUp mobile lets you **respond immediately** and start assigning tasks, logging issues, or launching recovery plans, even if you're off-site.

☑ **Best for:**

- Incident management and escalation

- Team coordination in urgent scenarios

- Delegating tasks while away from the computer

🛠 **Pro Tips:**

- Use **Task Comments** and **Mentions** to rally your team quickly.

- Create an **Emergency Template List** you can duplicate instantly in case of crises.

Final Thoughts: Mobile-First Mindset

ClickUp's mobile app isn't meant to replace the desktop version—but it excels as a **complementary tool for agility, responsiveness, and accessibility**. Whether you're leading a project, supporting a client, or juggling tasks throughout your day, learning to use ClickUp effectively on mobile can dramatically increase your **flexibility and productivity**.

Adopting a **mobile-first mindset** allows you to:

- Stay aligned with your team

- Capture ideas and action items at any time

- Keep momentum going—even when you're on the move

Ultimately, mastering mobile workflows ensures that **ClickUp works for you—wherever work happens.**

Conclusion

Key Takeaways and Best Practices

As you reach the end of this guide, it's clear that ClickUp isn't just another productivity tool—it's an ecosystem that, when used effectively, can transform the way individuals and teams work. Whether you're managing your own freelance projects or leading a team across continents, the right ClickUp setup can make your day clearer, more focused, and far more productive.

This concluding section summarizes the essential lessons from the book and shares a set of **best practices** to ensure your ClickUp workspace continues to support your long-term goals.

1. Embrace the ClickUp Mindset

ClickUp's power lies in its flexibility. Unlike rigid project management tools that force you into one structure, ClickUp adapts to how you think, plan, and act. This is both a strength and a challenge.

Key Takeaways:

- ClickUp is designed to serve multiple workflows. You can use it as a simple to-do list or as a comprehensive company-wide operations platform.

- There's no "one right way" to use ClickUp—only what works for you and your team.

- Take time to experiment. Start small, then scale your setup.

Best Practice:

Begin with the basics. Avoid building a complex workspace from day one. Instead, grow your ClickUp usage as your needs expand and your confidence increases.

2. Structure Drives Efficiency

One of the earliest hurdles users face is understanding ClickUp's hierarchy: **Workspaces → Spaces → Folders → Lists → Tasks → Subtasks**.

Key Takeaways:

- A well-structured workspace reduces cognitive overload.
- Keep your hierarchy as flat as possible without losing clarity.
- Use folders only when absolutely necessary; over-categorizing leads to clutter.

Best Practices:

- Use **Spaces** to separate broad areas (e.g., Marketing, Operations, Personal Projects).
- Use **Lists** to represent workflows or repeatable processes.
- Name items clearly and consistently. Establish naming conventions for tasks, docs, and folders.

---

3. Master the Art of Task Design

A task in ClickUp is more than a checkbox—it's a container of responsibility, context, and action.

Key Takeaways:

- Every task should have a clear purpose, owner, due date, and relevant context.
- Use **Custom Fields** to add clarity without clutter.
- Break down larger objectives into **subtasks**, and track progress logically.

Best Practices:

- Assign only one **primary assignee** per task when possible.
- Use **checklists** for repeating steps inside a task.
- Apply **priorities** (urgent, high, normal, low) to guide daily focus.

---

4. Visualize Work with the Right Views

ClickUp offers multiple ways to view your work: **List, Board, Calendar, Gantt, Timeline**, and more.

Key Takeaways:

- No single view fits all workflows. Switch views depending on the stage of work and the audience.

- Use **Board View** for agile workflows or creative brainstorming.

- Use **Gantt View** and **Timeline** for project planning and team visibility.

Best Practices:

- Save **custom views** for common routines (e.g., "Weekly Sprint Review," "Today's Priorities").

- Apply **filters** to cut through information overload.

- Share filtered views with team members to create role-specific dashboards.

5. Make Collaboration Seamless

ClickUp thrives in team environments when communication is centralized and purposeful.

Key Takeaways:

- Avoid using email or external chat for task-related discussions. Use **comments** directly within tasks.

- **Mentions** and **assigned comments** help nudge teammates without micromanaging.

- Track updates through the **Inbox** and **Activity Feed**.

Best Practices:

- Set team expectations for communication norms: Where to comment, when to tag, and how often to check ClickUp.

- Use **Docs** for meeting notes, knowledge bases, and project plans.

- Collaborate on docs in real time and link them directly to related tasks.

6. Use Templates and Automations to Save Time

Efficiency in ClickUp isn't just about organization—it's about reducing repetitive work.

Key Takeaways:

- **Templates** make recurring workflows faster and more reliable.
- **Automations** can assign tasks, move statuses, notify team members, and more—automatically.
- Consistency improves predictability and reduces decision fatigue.

Best Practices:

- Build templates for tasks, lists, and docs you use frequently.
- Start with simple automations like: "When task is moved to 'In Progress', assign to John."
- Regularly review automations to ensure they still align with your workflow.

7. Track Progress and Reflect Often

ClickUp isn't just about planning—it's about progress and performance.

Key Takeaways:

- Use **Time Tracking** to understand how long tasks really take.
- Use **Goals** to stay aligned on deliverables and progress markers.
- Build **Dashboards** to visualize performance in real time.

Best Practices:

- Set personal or team goals and update them weekly.
- Review task completion patterns to identify bottlenecks.
- Create a **Monthly Reflection Dashboard** with widgets like task completion rate, overdue tasks, and time logged.

8. Customize Without Overcomplicating

Customization in ClickUp is powerful—but too much complexity can become a trap.

Key Takeaways:

- Use only the **Custom Fields** and **ClickApps** you need.
- Avoid overwhelming your team with too many workflows or views.
- Focus on clarity, not control.

Best Practices:

- Review your workspace monthly. Ask: Is this still working?
- Archive or delete unused lists and templates.
- Keep your workspace clean and intuitive for new team members.

9. Integrate, Don't Duplicate

ClickUp doesn't exist in a vacuum. It plays well with other tools you already use.

Key Takeaways:

- Integrate with **Google Calendar, Slack, Zoom, GitHub**, and more to streamline context switching.
- Use **Zapier** or **Make (Integromat)** to connect ClickUp with non-native integrations.
- Syncing prevents data silos and duplicative effort.

Best Practices:

- Identify which external tools your team uses daily and look for automation points.
- Create a "Central Hub" in ClickUp that links to key resources from all tools.
- Use the **Email in ClickUp** feature to turn messages into actionable tasks.

10. Stay Curious and Keep Evolving

ClickUp is constantly improving. New features, integrations, and use cases appear regularly.

Key Takeaways:

- Learning ClickUp is not a one-time event—it's an ongoing skill.

- Be willing to experiment with new features (especially on test Spaces).

- Evolve your workspace as your work evolves.

Best Practices:

- Follow ClickUp's **release notes** and **YouTube tutorials**.

- Join the **ClickUp Community** and follow user stories and templates.

- Run quarterly reviews of your workspace and iterate based on team feedback.

Final Thoughts: Your Productivity, Your Way

There's no universal blueprint for productivity. The most successful teams and individuals are those who adapt tools like ClickUp to fit their needs—not the other way around.

Whether you're a solo creator managing deadlines, a team lead aligning global efforts, or an executive trying to bring visibility to fast-moving projects—**ClickUp can be your central nervous system**.

But remember: The best system is the one you use consistently.

So take the knowledge from this book and make it yours. Build your ideal workflow, communicate more clearly, track your time mindfully, and automate the boring stuff—**all with ClickUp.**

Let this be the beginning of your smarter work life.

Troubleshooting and Support Resources

No matter how powerful or intuitive a productivity platform is, there will always be moments when things don't go as planned. Whether you're running into bugs, dealing with configuration confusion, or simply unsure of how to best use a feature, ClickUp offers a wide range of troubleshooting tools and support resources to help you get back on track quickly. In this section, we'll walk you through everything you need to know to solve problems effectively and make the most of ClickUp's ecosystem of support.

1. Understanding Common Issues

Before diving into where to get help, it's important to recognize the types of issues users commonly encounter on ClickUp. Identifying the problem category can drastically speed up resolution.

1.1 Technical Issues

- Page not loading or displaying incorrectly
- Time tracking tool freezing or misreporting hours
- Dashboards not updating in real time
- Performance slowdowns when working with large spaces or multiple views

1.2 Workflow and Configuration Confusion

- Automations not triggering as expected
- Templates not applying properly
- Difficulty understanding hierarchy (e.g., why a task isn't showing in a list)
- Problems using dependencies or assigning statuses

1.3 Permissions and Access Issues

- Team members unable to view or edit content
- Inability to share files or links outside of the workspace

- Mistaken role assignments or access restrictions

1.4 Data Loss Concerns

- Accidentally deleted tasks or lists

- Incomplete import/export operations

- Sync errors between devices or integrations

1.5 Integration Breakdowns

- Google Calendar sync not updating

- Slack or email notifications not being received

- Errors connecting to third-party tools like GitHub or Zoom

2. Built-In Tools to Troubleshoot Yourself

Before reaching out to external support, you can often identify and resolve problems using ClickUp's built-in tools and logs.

2.1 Activity Log

The activity log, accessible from the sidebar or within tasks, shows a history of changes. Use it to:

- Trace who changed a task status or deleted something

- Recover lost data by identifying when it was changed or removed

- Understand task flow in collaborative projects

2.2 Undo and Archive Features

- Recently deleted tasks can often be found in the **Trash** under the Workspace settings.

- Archived items are not lost; they are hidden. Use filters or View Settings to restore archived content.

- The **Undo** button in many areas (like task movement, status change) helps with quick error recovery.

2.3 Notifications & Inbox

Sometimes it may seem like ClickUp isn't updating, but changes are simply not being displayed in the current view. Use the **Inbox** or Notifications Panel to review updates to tasks across your entire workspace.

3. Using the ClickUp Help Center

ClickUp's Help Center is a rich repository of documentation, tutorials, and troubleshooting guides.
Available at: https://help.clickup.com

3.1 Search Functionality

- Use specific keywords like "task automations not working" or "restore deleted task"

- Results include both written documentation and video walkthroughs

3.2 Article Categories

- **Getting Started:** Perfect for onboarding and setting up workspaces

- **Tasks & Projects:** Tips on creating and managing tasks, subtasks, views

- **Automation & Integrations:** Advanced usage and connectivity troubleshooting

- **Billing & Accounts:** Help with subscriptions, invoices, access control

4. Support Channels Provided by ClickUp

ClickUp offers several support options, depending on your account type and urgency level.

4.1 In-App Live Chat

- Available on paid plans

- Look for the chat icon in the lower-right corner of the screen
- Typically responds within a few minutes to an hour during business hours

4.2 Submitting a Ticket

- Visit https://help.clickup.com/hc/en-us/requests/new
- Fill out the form with detailed information, including workspace ID, screenshots, and a step-by-step breakdown of the issue
- Expect a response in 24–48 hours for most issues

4.3 ClickUp Status Page

- Check https://status.clickup.com/ for real-time information on system uptime and outages
- Useful if you're experiencing global issues (e.g., app not loading for all users)

4.4 Email Support

- Available to all users at help@clickup.com
- Great for detailed questions or account-specific concerns

---

5. Community-Based Resources

Sometimes, the fastest way to find a solution is to ask another user who has faced the same problem. ClickUp has a strong and growing community across platforms.

5.1 ClickUp Community Forum

- Found at: https://community.clickup.com
- Browse by topic or use search
- Ask questions, share solutions, and get best practices from other users

5.2 Facebook Groups and Reddit

- **Facebook Group**: "ClickUp User Group – Official"

- **Reddit**: r/ClickUp

- These platforms are useful for workflow discussions, user feedback, or creative solutions that aren't covered in documentation

5.3 YouTube Channel and Tutorials

- ClickUp's official YouTube channel contains tutorials, walkthroughs, and live streams

- Look for video guides especially for automations, dashboards, and integrations

- Great visual support when you're stuck on configuration or interface navigation

---

6. Premium and Enterprise Support (for Advanced Users)

If you're using ClickUp on a Business Plus or Enterprise plan, your support experience is elevated with:

6.1 Dedicated Success Managers

- Assigned to larger teams and enterprises

- Helps you create scalable solutions using ClickUp's full capabilities

- Personalized onboarding and implementation

6.2 SLA-Driven Support

- Guaranteed response times

- Faster escalation and bug fixes

- Access to exclusive beta features and roadmap previews

---

7. Best Practices for Reporting Issues

To ensure that support can assist you quickly and efficiently, keep the following in mind when reporting an issue:

7.1 Be Specific

- Describe the exact steps that led to the issue
- Include the names of lists, spaces, or automations involved

7.2 Provide Screenshots or Videos

- A screenshot is worth a thousand words
- Use tools like Loom or built-in screen recorders to provide visual context

7.3 Include System and Browser Info

- Note your device (Windows, macOS), browser (Chrome, Safari), and app version if applicable
- Mention any third-party tools or integrations involved in the error

8. Staying Updated on New Fixes and Features

ClickUp is updated frequently with new features, bug fixes, and UI improvements. Staying informed helps prevent confusion when features change.

8.1 Release Notes

- Check out: https://clickup.com/releases
- Weekly updates highlight fixes, enhancements, and upcoming beta features

8.2 Beta Programs

- Join beta testing for upcoming features by adjusting your user settings
- Early access gives insight into what's coming and lets you shape the future of the tool

8.3 Webinars and Feature Announcements

- ClickUp hosts regular **product webinars**, often introducing new features
- Great for team-wide learning or keeping up with the platform's evolution

Conclusion: Empowering Yourself with Support

ClickUp offers a wealth of support resources designed to keep you productive. Whether you prefer to search for answers independently, consult detailed documentation, or connect directly with customer support, the tools are there for you. The key to troubleshooting efficiently is to combine self-service tools with smart escalation when needed.

As you continue to evolve your workflow and scale your use of ClickUp, remember that support is not just about solving problems—it's also about discovering new ways to use the platform effectively.

Whether you're a team of one or a team of one hundred, the ability to troubleshoot and grow with confidence is what will make your ClickUp journey a long-term success.

Continuing Your ClickUp Journey

As you reach the end of *Work Smarter with ClickUp: Manage Tasks, Teams, and Time with Ease*, it's important to recognize that mastering a tool like ClickUp doesn't come from just reading about it—but from continuous exploration, application, and adaptation. The real power of ClickUp unfolds as you make it your own, tailoring it to your team's rhythm, your business goals, and your personal workflow preferences.

In this final section, let's walk through how you can **continue growing as a ClickUp power user**, **stay ahead of new features**, and **build a long-term productivity system** that evolves with your work and life.

1. Stay Curious, Stay Updated

ClickUp is a rapidly evolving platform. New features are rolled out frequently, user feedback is constantly integrated, and performance upgrades are regularly made. To continue your journey with ClickUp effectively:

1.1 Follow ClickUp's Official Updates

ClickUp has an active presence across several communication channels:

- ClickUp Blog: Regularly features new use cases, productivity tips, and feature launches.

- What's New page: Shows up-to-date release notes.

- **In-App Notifications**: When ClickUp releases a new feature or update, you'll often see an in-app notification with a short demo.

1.2 Join the ClickUp Community

The ClickUp user community is filled with productivity enthusiasts, workflow designers, business leaders, and creative professionals. Participating in discussions not only gives you practical insights but also shows how others are solving similar challenges.

Places to engage:

- **ClickUp Community (Facebook Group)**

- **ClickUp subreddit** (r/ClickUp)

- **LinkedIn groups for productivity and project management tools**
- **ClickUp Discord or Slack channels** (if applicable)

2. Experiment with Your Workflows

ClickUp's flexibility is one of its greatest strengths—and it's easy to miss opportunities for optimization if you just stick with default setups. Continuing your journey means embracing a mindset of experimentation.

2.1 Evolve Your Templates

Don't just set and forget your templates. As your team grows, as your project types evolve, and as your processes get more sophisticated:

- Revisit your **task templates** monthly or quarterly.
- Optimize **folder or list templates** for client onboarding, sprints, editorial calendars, etc.
- Explore **template versioning** to track evolution and performance.

2.2 Test New Views

Your default view may not always be the most effective one for every project.

- Try **Timeline view** for deadline-sensitive projects.
- Use **Table view** for data-heavy tasks with multiple custom fields.
- Explore **Mind Map view** for brainstorming or outlining strategy.

2.3 Play with ClickApps

ClickApps are mini add-ons that can radically change how you manage tasks and data.

- Try **Sprint ClickApp** for Agile workflows.
- Enable **Custom Task IDs** for clients or compliance.
- Use **Relationships** and **Linked Docs** for knowledge management.

3. Train Your Team and Stakeholders

ClickUp is only as effective as the people using it. Your journey will be a lonely one if you're the only power user in the room. Make ClickUp adoption part of your team culture.

3.1 Onboard New Users Properly

- Create or record a **welcome video** to explain your team's ClickUp setup.

- Use **ClickUp Docs** as internal wikis for SOPs, workflows, and FAQs.

- Walk new users through **notifications, assigned comments, and the importance of task updates**.

3.2 Provide Continuous Training

- Host **monthly ClickUp clinics** or "office hours" where team members can ask questions.

- Share **what's new in ClickUp** emails internally.

- Encourage experimentation with **personal dashboards or automations**.

3.3 Set Expectations Around Usage

If you want ClickUp to replace email, chat, or spreadsheets, you must enforce that behavior consistently.

- Use **task statuses** and **comment threads** as your team's official communication channel.

- Discourage updates being made via chat or external notes.

- Make it a team standard to check ClickUp **first** every morning.

---

4. Build Systems That Scale

As your team grows, and as your operations become more complex, your ClickUp setup will need to scale with it. Don't let it become the Wild West—plan ahead.

4.1 Establish Governance Guidelines

Create internal policies such as:

- Naming conventions for tasks, spaces, and lists.

- Rules around custom fields (e.g., when to create new ones).

- Guidelines for archiving vs. deleting.

4.2 Use Goals and Dashboards to Track Success

Don't let ClickUp be just a to-do list.

- Use **Goals** to tie project outcomes to KPIs or OKRs.

- Create **executive dashboards** for leadership to see progress at a glance.

- Link **goal targets to task completion**, time tracking, or sprint points.

4.3 Conduct Regular Audits

Every 6–12 months, conduct a full ClickUp audit:

- Are there outdated lists, templates, or workflows?

- Are automations still working?

- Is everyone using the platform consistently?

5. Leverage ClickUp Beyond Work

One of the most exciting opportunities with ClickUp is its flexibility to organize life—not just business.

5.1 Personal Productivity

ClickUp can manage your personal goals, errands, reading lists, and even journaling.

- Create a **Personal Space** with lists like:
    - Health & Wellness
    - Finance Tracker
    - Travel Planning
    - Books to Read

- Use **reminders**, **checklists**, and **automations** to build daily routines.

5.2 Family and Home Projects

Involve your family in:

- Moving checklists

- Home renovation timelines

- Vacation planning

- Weekly meal prep

5.3 Creative Projects and Side Hustles

Use ClickUp for:

- Content creation (blogs, videos, podcasts)

- Freelance project tracking

- Etsy or Shopify product management

- Podcast or YouTube editorial calendars

---

6. Expand Your Skills as a Workflow Architect

Once you understand how to mold ClickUp to your needs, you may find yourself taking on more than task management—you'll be thinking in **systems**.

6.1 Learn the Language of Systems Thinking

- Understand workflows as a series of **inputs, outputs, triggers, and feedback loops**.

- Use ClickUp to model real-world processes.

- Leverage **dependencies** and **automations** to mimic human decision trees.

6.2 Explore Advanced API and Automation Tools

If you want to go beyond what's possible in the UI:

- Explore **ClickUp's public API**

- Use **Zapier**, **Make**, or **Pabbly** for integrations

- Automate cross-platform processes (e.g., form submissions → ClickUp tasks → email notifications)

6.3 Build for Others

Consider helping others with:

- Freelance ClickUp setup and training

- Building and selling templates

- Teaching courses or webinars

7. Final Thoughts: The Tool is Only the Beginning

ClickUp is not just another app. When used well, it's a thinking system—one that reflects your goals, your habits, your structure, and your team's identity. But it's also just that: a **tool**. The impact comes not from ClickUp alone, but from **how you use it**.

By continuing your journey with curiosity, intentionality, and a willingness to improve over time, you turn ClickUp into more than just a digital workspace. You transform it into a **living system**—a second brain that helps you think clearly, move faster, and focus on what truly matters.

So go forward, explore boldly, and build your workflows to reflect your best self.

Acknowledgments

First and foremost, **thank you** for choosing to read *Work Smarter with ClickUp: Manage Tasks, Teams, and Time with Ease*. Whether you're a seasoned productivity enthusiast or just starting your journey with ClickUp, I'm incredibly grateful that you placed your trust in this guide.

Writing this book has been a labor of love—fueled by countless hours of research, experimentation, and real-world use. But it would all be meaningless without you, the reader. Your desire to learn, grow, and work more intentionally is what gives purpose to every page of this book.

To every professional, team leader, freelancer, student, and dreamer who picked up this book: thank you for believing in the power of better workflows. I hope this guide empowers you to reclaim your time, bring structure to your chaos, and find clarity in your work.

If this book has helped you in any way, inspired you to try something new, or simply made your daily tasks a bit easier—**that's the greatest reward I could ask for**.

Stay curious. Keep building. And above all—work smarter, not harder.

With deep gratitude,

www.ingramcontent.com/pod-product-compliance
Lightning Source LLC
LaVergne TN
LVHW081330050326
832903LV00024B/1092